CW00661622

Series FM1 no.29

Birth statistics

Review of the Registrar General on births and patterns of family building in England and Wales, 2000

Laid before Parliament pursuant to Section 19
Registration Service Act 1953

London: Office for National Statistics

ISBN 0 11 705584 0
ISSN 0140-2587

Contact points
For enquiries about this publication, contact
Vital Statistics Outputs Branch
Tel: 01329 813758
e-mail: **vsob@ons.gov.uk**

Single paper copies of this electronic publication can be
obtained through NS Direct. A charge will be made to cover
costs. Call NS Direct on 01633 812078 for further details.
Letters: NS Direct, Room 1015, Government Buildings,
Cardiff Road, Newport, NP10 8XG.
E-mail: **nsdirect@statistics.gov.uk**

For general enquiries, contact the National Statistics
Public Enquiry Service on 0845 601 3034
(minicom: 01633 812399)
e-mail: **info@statistics.gov.uk**
fax: 01633 652747
Letters: Room DG/18, 1 Drummond Gate,
London SW1V 2QQ

You can also find National Statistics on the Internet
at **www.statistics.gov.uk**

About the Office for National Statistics
The Office for National Statistics (ONS) is the government
agency responsible for compiling, analysing and disseminating
many of the United Kingdom's economic, social and
demographic statistics, including the retail prices index, trade
figures and labour market data, as well as the periodic census
of the population and health statistics. The Director of ONS is
also the National Statistician and the Registrar General for
England and Wales, and the agency that administers the
registration of births, marriages and deaths there.

A National Statistics Publication
National Statistics are produced to high professional standards
set out in the National Statistics Code of Practice. They undergo
regular quality assurance reviews to ensure that they meet
customer needs. They are produced free from any political
interference.

Series FM1 no.29

Birth
statistics

Contents

List of main tables and appendices

3 Age of parents

4 Previous liveborn children

8 Place of confinement

9 Birthplace of parents

10 Cohort analysis

Appendix: base population

Annexes

1 Introduction

Birth statistics 2000 presents statistics on births occurring annually in England and Wales between 1990 and 2000, and on conceptions between 1989 and 1999.

The 2000 annual commentary on fertility trends will be published in *Population Trends 106* in December 2001. Provisional data for the complete year are first published as Reports in *Population Trends* as soon as they become available.

This volume is produced by the Office for National Statistics (ONS). It is the second volume in this series to be published under the National Statistics logo, a new designation applied to statistical outputs which guarantees that those outputs have been produced to high professional standards set out in a code of practice, and have been produced free from political interference.

The registration of life events - that is births, deaths and marriages - is a service carried out by the Local Registration Service in partnership with the General Register Office (GRO) in Southport, which is part of ONS. ONS was formed on 1 April 1996, bringing together the Office of Population Censuses and Surveys (OPCS) and the Central Statistical Office (CSO). OPCS is referred to in this volume for historic events and publications.

1.1 Tables in this volume

The tables presented in this volume are set out in 12 sections, covering various fertility topics including characteristics of births and of the parents. Section 10 analyses trends in cohort fertility, while Section 12 gives statistics on conceptions; otherwise, the tables use period fertility measures.

For brevity, the time series shown here have been limited to a run of 11 years at most. Figures for earlier years are shown in earlier volumes of *Birth statistics*. This series includes a volume of historical fertility statistics[1] containing some time series back to 1838, the year following the introduction of compulsory birth registration. More detailed time series are also included for years from 1938, the year in which the first Population Statistics Act came into force - see Section 2.20.

1.2 Data analysed in this volume

The information used in tables in this volume is based largely on the details collected when births are registered.

Most of the information, for both live births and stillbirths, is supplied to registrars by one or other, or both of the parents. For live births, details of **birthweight** are notified to the local health authority by the hospital where the birth took place, or by the midwife or doctor in attendance at the birth. These details are then supplied to the registrar. For stillbirths, details of **cause of death, duration of pregnancy and weight of foetus** are supplied on a certificate or notification by the doctor or midwife either present at the birth, or who examined the body. The certificate or notification is then taken by the informant to a registrar. The registrar will use all this information to complete a draft entry *Form 309* (**Annex A**) for a live birth or *Form 308* (**Annex B**) for a stillbirth.

Information on abortions is derived from notifications supplied under the Abortions Act 1967. These are sent by registered practitioners to the Chief Medical Officer of the Department of Health, or to the Chief Medical Officer of the National Assembly for Wales. The details supplied include woman's **date of birth, marital status,** and **usual residence.** These are analysed in **Tables 12.1 to 12.8** with the data on conceptions. Further details may be found in the ONS annual volume of *Abortion statistics*[2].

The data used in this volume are summarised below. The items covered are collected for both live births and stillbirths.

The **date of birth** is supplied in a conventional way, except that where more than one child is liveborn at a confinement, then time is also recorded. **Place of birth** is entered as the usual name and the address of a hospital, maternity home or other communal establishment, or the address of a private dwelling. Using the appropriate postcode, ONS then codes place of birth to one of the groups of places in **Table 8.1.** The **sex** of the child is also recorded.

Although the **birthplace of the parents** may be recorded in detail if this was in the United Kingdom, the main interest in this volume is with parents born outside the United Kingdom - see **Tables 9.1 to 9.5**. The **mother's usual address** is entered, as is that of the informant where appropriate. This information is used for tables showing usual residence of mother **7.1 to 7.4**, as well as **Table 3.10,** which analyses jointly registered births outside marriage and whether the parents resided at the same address.

Occupation is recorded for both father if his name is entered in the register and mother. The informant is asked whether the father/mother was in gainful employment at any time before the child's birth, and a description of the

Table number	Year(s)	Area	Numbers/ rates/ percent-ages (N/R/P)	Live births/ stillbirths (LB/SB)	Mater-nities/ pater-nities (M/P)	Age of mother (Year of birth)	Age of father	Period of occur-ence	Period of regist-ration	Sole/ joint registra-tion (S/J)	Within/ outside marriage (W/O)
	Summary tables										
1.1	1990-00	E&W	NR	LB							WO
1.2	1990-00	E&W	NR	SB							WO
1.3	1990-00	E&W	NR	LB							
1.4	1990-00	E&W	R	LB							
1.5	1989-99	E&W	NR								
1.6	1990-00	E&W	Mean	LB		*					WO
1.7	1990-00	E&W	Mean	LB/SB		*					
1.8	1989-99	E&W	P	LB/SB		*					W
1.9	1990-00	E&W	R	LB		*					WO
	Seasonality										
2.1	1990-00	E&W	NR	LB					*		
2.2	1990-00	E&W	N	SB					*		
2.3	1990-00	E&W	NR	LB					*		
2.4	2000	E&W	N	LB/SB	M				*		WO
2.5	2000	E&W	N	LB					*	*	
	Age of parents										
3.1	1990-00	E&W	NR	LB		*					WO
3.2	2000	E&W	N	LB/SB	M	*					WO
3.3	1990-00	E&W	NR	LB			*				W
3.4	2000	E&W	N	LB/SB	P	*				J	WO
3.5	2000	E&W	R	LB/SB	P	*					W
3.6	2000	E&W	N	LB		*	*				W
3.7	2000	E&W	N	SB		*	*				W
3.8	2000	E&W	N	LB		*	*			SJ	O
3.9	1990-00	E&W	NP	LB		*				SJ	O
3.10	1990-00	E&W	NP	LB		*				J	O
	Previous liveborn children										
4.1	1990-00	E&W	N	LB		*					W
4.2	2000	E&W	N	LB		*					W
4.3	2000	E&W	NR	LB/SB		*					W
	Duration of marriage										
5.1	1990-00	E&W	N	LB		*					W
5.2	1990-00	E&W	N	LB		*					W
5.3	2000	E&W	N	LB		*					W
	Multiple births										
6.1	1990-00	E&W	NR		M	*					WO
6.2	2000	E&W	N	LB/SB	M	*					
6.3	2000	E&W	NR		M	*					W
6.4	2000	E&W	N	LB/SB	M	*					
	Area of usual residence										
7.1	2000	E&W+	NR	LB/SB							WO
7.2	2000	E&W+	NR	LB		*					
7.3	2000	E&W+	NP	LB							
7.4	2000	E&W+	NP	SB							

Sex	Previous liveborn children	Birth-weight	Place of confine-ment	Country of birth mother/father (M/F)	Social class of father/husband	Usual residence/place of occurence (R/O)	Marriage order	Out-come of preg-nancy	Year(s)	Table number
									Summary tables	
*									1990-00	1.1
*									1990-00	1.2
									1990-00	1.3
									1990-00	1.4
									1989-99	1.5
	*								1990-00	1.6
	*								1990-00	1.7
						*			1989-99	1.8
	*								1990-00	1.9
									Seasonality	
									1990-00	2.1
									1990-00	2.2
									1990-00	2.3
*									2000	2.4
									2000	2.5
									Age of parents	
									1990-00	3.1
*									2000	3.2
									1990-00	3.3
*									2000	3.4
*									2000	3.5
									2000	3.6
									2000	3.7
									2000	3.8
									1990-00	3.9
									1990-00	3.10
									Previous liveborn children	
	*								1990-00	4.1
	*								2000	4.2
*	*								2000	4.3
									Duration of marriage	
									1990-00	5.1
						*			1990-00	5.2
						*			2000	5.3
									Multiple births	
									1990-00	6.1
*									2000	6.2
	*								2000	6.3
*									2000	6.4
									Area of usual residence	
						R			2000	7.1
						R			2000	7.2
		*				R			2000	7.3
		*				R			2000	7.4

Table number	Year(s)	Area	Numbers/ rates/ percent-ages (N/R/P)	Live births/ stillbirths (LB/SB)	Mater-nities/ pater-nities (M/P)	Age of mother (Year of birth)	Age of father	Period of occur-ence	Period of regist-ration	Sole/ joint registra-tion (S/J)	Within/ outside marriage (W/O)
	Place of confinement										
8.1	2000	E&W	N		M	*					WO
8.2	2000	E&W+	N		M						
8.3	2000	E&W+	NR	LB/SB	M						
	Birthplace of parents										
9.1	1990, 1995-00	E&W	NP	LB							
9.2	2000	E&W+	NP	LB							
9.3	2000	E&W	N	LB							
9.4	2000	E&W	N	LB		*					
9.5	1990, 1998-00	E&W	NP	LB							WO
	Cohort analysis										
10.1	1920-85	E&W	R			*					
10.2	1920-85	E&W	Mean			*					
10.3	1920-85	E&W	Mean			*					
10.4	1920-81	E&W	Mean	LB		*		*			WO
10.5	1920-80	E&W	P	LB		*					
	Social class										
11.1	1990-00	E&W	N	LB		*					W
11.2	1990-00	E&W	NP	LB		*					W
11.3	1990-00	GB and E&W	Median	LB							W
11.4	1990-00	E&W	Mean	LB		*		*			W
11.5	1990-00	E&W	N	LB		*				J	O
	Conceptions										
12.1	1989-99	E&W	NRP			*					WO
12.2	1989-99	E&W	NR			*					
12.3	1989-99	E&W	NP			*					W
12.4	1989-99	E&W	N			*				SJ	O
12.5	1989-99	E&W	NR			*					W
12.6	1989-99	E&W	NR			*					O
12.7	1999	E&W+	NP			*				SJ	WO
12.8	1999	E&W+	NR			*					

occupation may be recorded. The informant may not wish to have details of the father/mother's occupation entered in the register, but it may still be recorded for use in statistical analyses. If the father is unemployed, his last full-time occupation will be recorded. As discussed in Section 3.10, this information is used for analyses of social class as defined by occupation, in **Tables 11.1** to **11.5.**

Informants are also required to provide further information, treated as confidential, under the provisions of the Population Statistics Acts, as below.

(i) the **father's date of birth,** if his name is entered in the register - i.e. the registration is joint;
(ii) the **mother's date of birth;**

If the child's parents were married to each other at the time of the birth:

(iii) the **date of the parents' marriage;**
(iv) **whether the mother has been married more than once;**
(v) **number of previous children** by her present husband and any former husband, (a) **born alive,** and (b) **stillborn.**

These confidential details are used extensively in this volume, in particular for analyses of **age of mother and father,** of **marriage duration,** and of **birth order.** See Section 1.3 below for details of issues affecting the quality of these variables in 2000.

Sex	Previous liveborn children	Birth-weight	Place of confine-ment	Country of birth mother/ father (M/F)	Social class of father/ husband	Usual residence/ place of occurence (R/O)	Marriage order	Out-come of preg-nancy	Year(s)	Table number
									Place of confinement	
	*		*						2000	8.1
			*			RO			2000	8.2
						O			2000	8.3
									Birthplace of parents	
				M					1990, 1995-00	9.1
				M		R			2000	9.2
				MF					2000	9.3
				M					2000	9.4
	*			M					1990, 1998-00	9.5
									Cohort analysis	
									1920-85	10.1
									1920-85	10.2
									1920-85	10.3
	*								1920-81	10.4
	*								1920-80	10.5
									Social class	
	*				*				1990-00	11.1
					*				1990-00	11.2
					*				1990-00	11.3
	*				*				1990-00	11.4
					*				1990-00	11.5
									Conceptions	
								*	1989-99	12.1
								*	1989-99	12.2
						*		*	1989-99	12.3
								*	1989-99	12.4
								*	1989-99	12.5
								*	1989-99	12.6
						R		*	1999	12.7
						R		*	1999	12.8

Other statistical information collected at registration includes the economic activity of the parents, i.e. **industry** and **employment status,** and whether the confinement resulted in a **multiple birth.**

1.3   Issues affecting the quality of the data in this volume

After the publication of the 1997 volume in this series, an error was discovered in the births database that resulted in 1,002 live births being excluded from the published 1997 statistics. Details of the error were included in Section D.1 of the 1998 volume[3]. All time series tables in this volume reflect the corrected data for 1997, as did those in the 1998 and 1999 volumes.

Conception figures in **Tables 12.1** to **12.8** reflect a change to the methodology for calculating mother's age at conception which ONS introduced in 1999. This change brought about an improvement in the estimation of age of mother for those live births where conception occurs in the same calendar month as the woman's birthday - see Section 2.13 for summary information. Full details together with an assessment of the impact of the change of methodology were included in Section D.2 of the 1998 volume[3].

As noted above, some statistical information is collected under the Population Statistics Acts at the registration of a birth. In 1999 the proportion of live birth registrations without this information received from one Register Office was higher than usual due to a combination of circumstances. The missing data on those records were imputed using a random sample of data from the particular area from the previous three years. This was a change from the usual method, but was used to improve the quality of the imputations. Procedures were put in place which mean that such a problem is unlikely to recur. For further information about this see Section C.2 of the 1999 volume[4].

A total of 34 live births which occurred before 1999 were removed from the 2000 database for this volume. These very late registrations were having an adverse effect on the quality of infant mortality data, which was linked to the live birth record. In view of this it was decided to include only those births registered in 2000 which occurred in either 1999 or 2000.

1.4 Associated publications

Historic data, and figures for UK countries

Comparable statistics for earlier years, and separate statistics for Scotland and Northern Ireland are published as follows:

England and Wales: from 1974-1999 in *Birth statistics;* for earlier years in the *Registrar General's Statistical Review of England and Wales.* Data for the years 1837-1983 are summarised in an earlier volume in the FM1 series[1].

Scotland: in the *Annual Report of the Registrar General for Scotland.*

Northern Ireland: in the *Annual Report of the Registrar General for Northern Ireland.*

A summary of fertility statistics for the United Kingdom and constituent countries appears in the *Annual Abstract of Statistics,* issued by ONS. Similar data also appear in the ONS quarterly journals *Population Trends and Health Statistics Quarterly.* Data for Europe are published in the Council of Europe annual volume *Recent demographic developments in Europe,* and the Eurostat publication *Demographic Statistics.* Statistics for United Nations member countries appear in the annual *UN Demographic Yearbook.*

Other related annual reference volumes published by ONS include:

- **DH3** *(Mortality statistics: childhood, infant and perinatal),* containing data on stillbirths, infant deaths, and childhood deaths. This includes figures for infant deaths linked to their corresponding birth records, as well as birthweight data for health regions analysed separately by age, social class and parity.

- **FM2** *(Marriage, divorce and adoption statistics),* providing data on marriages by age of bride and bridegroom, on divorces by ages of children involved, and on adoptions by age of child at adoption.

- **AB** *(Abortion statistics),* with statistics on legal abortions by age, marital status and usual residence of woman, as well as number of previous liveborn children. Also shown are numbers by statutory grounds for abortion, by gestation period, and by type of service purchaser.

Fertility data are also published annually in the ONS volume *Key population and vital statistics*[5] This volume provides data on population, births, deaths, and migration, for administrative areas in the United Kingdom, including local and health authorities.

Unpublished tables

Unpublished tables of annual vital statistics (the VS series) have been produced by ONS since 1981 for local and health authorities. At present, the series comprises six tables - VS1, VS2, VS3, VS4, VS4D and VS5 - of which three include birth statistics:

- **VS1** Vital statistics summary, giving population, numbers of births and deaths, fertility and mortality and comparisons with the region and with England and Wales.

- **VS2** Birth statistics, showing numbers of births by age of mother, number of previous children, type of communal establishment in which the birth occurred, birthweight, and whether the birth was within or outside marriage.

- **VS4** Vital statistics for wards, showing numbers of live births and stillbirths, and deaths by age, for males and females.

Specimen copies of the VS tables may be seen in a recent issue of *Key population and vital statistics*[5]. More information on these tables, and on their availability, may be obtained from ONS - see Section 2.22.

Quarterly publications and StatBase®

Up to 1998 ONS published annual data in monitors, known as the FM1 Series for conceptions and live births This contained basic information on annual conceptions and live birth registrations, issued soon after the data became available. However, these publications have been discontinued and from 1999 these data have appeared in Reports issued in the quarterly journal *Population Trends.* Since the beginning of 1999, ONS has published two quarterly journals: *Population Trends* which now has an emphasis on population and demography, covering most fertility topics: and *Health Statistics Quarterly,* covering mortality and health topics, including abortions, and some other fertility data In future the annual report on conceptions will be published in the February issue of *Health Statistics Quarterly*, and on live births by local and health authority areas in the June issue of *Population Trends.*

Population Trends and Health Statistics Quarterly both contain regular quarterly reference tables on a variety of population and health topics; for fertility these include analyses of births and conceptions (number and rates) by age of mother. These quarterly tables are now available on StatBase®, the National Statistics database set up to provide customers with a comprehensive set of key statistics drawn from a range of official statistics

Some of the data in this electronic publication can be obtained from a number of other sources. These include StatBase®, which can be found on the National Statistics website.

StatBase® (http://www.statistics.gov.uk/statbase/ mainmenu.asp) gives users access to two linked information systems. One system, called **StatSearch (http://www.statistics.gov.uk/statbase/ss.asp)** provides a wealth of information (called 'metadata') about all of the Government Statistical Services's (GSS's) statistical resources, i.e. all of its censuses, surveys, publications, periodicals, enquiry services, etc. The other system called **StatStore (http://www/statistics.gov.uk/statbase/ datasets2.asp)** contains a wide range of GSS data.

A product summary for this volumne of FM1 can be found on **http://www.statistics.gov.uk/products/p5768.asp**.

For more details about these services, contact On-Line Services, Zone B1/05, National Statistics, 1 Drummond Gate, London SW1V 2QQ. Telephone 020 7533 5675, fax 020 7533 5688 or go to the National Statistics website **www.statistics.gov.uk**.

1.5   Other publications

Some other recent background information on fertility data and other relevant articles and publications are listed below. Most are from the journal *Population Trends*, but copies of any not easily available may be obtained from ONS - see Section 2.22.

Trends in fertility

- Craig J. (1992). 'Fertility trends within the United Kingdom'. *Population Trends* 67, pp 17-21.
- Craig J. (1992). 'Recent fertility trends in Europe'. *Population Trends* 68, pp 20-23.
- Armitage R and Babb P. (1996). 'Population Review (4): Trends in fertility'. *Population Trends* 84, pp 7-13.
- Botting B and Dunnell K. (2000). 'Trends in fertility and contraception in the last quarter of the 20th century'. *Population Trends* 100, pp 32-40.
- ONS. (2001). 'Annual update: conceptions in 1999 and births in 2000, England and Wales'. *Population Trends 106*.

Age patterns

- Jones C. (1992). 'Fertility of the over thirties'. *Population Trends* 67, pp 10-16.
- Babb P. (1993). 'Teenage conceptions and fertility in England and Wales, 1971-91'. *Population Trends* 74, pp 12-17.
- Babb P. (1995). 'Fertility of the over forties'. *Population Trends* 79, pp 34-36.

Social class

- Cooper J and Botting B. (1992). 'Analysing fertility and infant mortality by mother's social class as defined by occupation'. *Population Trends* 70, pp 15-21.
- Botting B and Cooper J. (1993). 'Analysing fertility and infant mortality by mother's social class as defined by occupation - part II'. *Population Trends* 74, pp 27-33.

Birth order

- Cooper J and Jones C. (1992). 'Estimates of the numbers of first, second, third, and higher order births'. *Population Trends* 70, pp 8-14.
- Wood R. (1997). 'Trends in multiple births 1938-1995'. *Population Trends* 87, pp 29-35.

Conceptions

- Babb P. (1993). 'Teenage conceptions and fertility in England and Wales, 1971-91'. *Population Trends* 74, pp 12-17.
- Wood R. (1996). 'Subnational variations in conceptions'. *Population Trends* 84, pp 21-27.
- Wood R, Botting B and Dunnell K. (1997). 'Trends in conceptions before and after the 1995 pill scare'. *Population Trends* 89, pp 5-12.
- Botting B and Dunnell K. (2000). 'Trends in fertility and contraception in the last quarter of the 20th century'. *Population Trends* 100, pp 32-40.
- Griffiths C. and Kirby, L. (2000). 'Geographic variations in conceptions to women aged under 18 in Great Britain during the 1990s'. *Population Trends* 102, pp 13-23.

Future levels of fertility

- Shaw C. (1998). '1996-based national population projections for the United Kingdom and constituent countries'. *Population Trends 91,* pp 43-49.
- GAD. *1998-based national population projections (Series PP2 no 22)*. Fertility, Chapter 7, pp 23-26, The Stationery Office (2000).
- Craig J. (1994). 'Replacement level fertility and future population growth'. *Population Trends* 78, pp 20-22.
- Shaw, C. (2001). 'Assumptions for the 2000-based National Population Projections'. *Population Trends 105,* pp 45-47.

Other

- LS Medical Analysis Section. (1992). 'Fertility and infant mortality on the OPCS Longitudinal Study'. *Population Trends* 68, pp 24-29.
- Babb P and Bethune A. (1995). 'Trends in births outside marriage'. *Population Trends* 81, pp 17-22.
- Armitage R. (1997). 'Variation in fertility between different types of local area'. *Population Trends* 87, pp 20-28.
- Filakti H. (1997). 'Trends in abortion 1990-1995'. *Population Trends* 87, pp 11-19.
- Botting B, Rosato M and Wood R. (1998). 'Teenage mothers and the health of their children'. *Population Trends* 93, pp 19-28.
- Haskey J. (1999). 'Having a birth outside marriage: the proportion of lone mothers and cohabiting mothers who subsequently marry'. *Population Trends* 97, pp 6-18.
- Berthoud, R. (2001). 'Teenage births to ethnic minority women'. *Population Trends 104*, pp 12-18.
- Ghee, C. (2001). 'Population review of 2000, England and Wales' . *Population Trends 106*.

2 Notes and definitions

2.1 Base populations

The population figures shown in **Appendix Tables 1** and **2,** used to calculate various fertility rates in this volume, are mid-year estimates of the resident population of England and Wales, based on the 1991 Census of Population. These estimates include members of HM and non-UK armed forces stationed in England and Wales, but exclude those stationed outside. The estimates are updated annually by allowing for births, deaths and migration.

Estimates of the population by marital status, used in **Tables 1.1, 1.5, 3.5, 12.5** and **12.6,** are based upon proportions from Census figures, with due allowance for marriages, divorces, deaths and migration.

2.2 Occurrences and registrations

In this volume the total number of births for 2000 includes:

(a) births occurring in 2000 which were registered by 11 February 2001, and
(b) births occurring before 2000 which were registered between 12 February 2000 and 11 February 2001, that is births in the previous year which had not been tabulated previously.

Total annual births for 1994 to 1999 were derived in a similar way, except that births for earlier years were included in the annual totals, not just births in the previous year – see Section 1.3 for more details. Up to 1993 the cut off date was 31 January of the following year, but from 1994 this was then extended to the legal time limit by which a birth should be registered (42 days).

The number of 'residual' births in (b) was about 1,500 to 3,000 per year from 1987 to 1993, but from 1994 it fell to about 500 to 600 annually. In 2000 there were 517.

2.3 Areal coverage

The births recorded in this volume are those occurring (and then registered) in England and Wales. No distinction is made between births to civilians and births to non-civilians.

The birth to a mother whose usual residence is outside England and Wales is assigned to the country of residence. These births are included in total figures for England and Wales, but excluded from any sub-division of England and Wales. They are identified as a separate group in **Tables 7.1** to **7.4.**

2.4 Areal definitions

Government Office Regions

The composition of Government Office Regions in 2000 in terms of metropolitan and non-metropolitan counties and unitary authorities (UAs), is set out below:

North East
Darlington UA; Hartlepool UA; Middlesbrough UA; Redcar and Cleveland UA; Stockton-on-Tees UA; Durham; Northumberland; Tyne and Wear Metropolitan County.

North West
Blackburn with Darwen UA; Blackpool UA; Halton UA; Warrington UA; Cheshire; Cumbria; Greater Manchester Metropolitan County; Lancashire; Merseyside Metropolitan County.

Yorkshire and the Humber
East Riding of Yorkshire UA; City of Kingston upon Hull UA; North East Lincolnshire UA; North Lincolnshire UA; York UA; North Yorkshire; South Yorkshire Metropolitan County; West Yorkshire Metropolitan County.

East Midlands
Derby UA; Leicester UA; Nottingham UA; Rutland UA; Derbyshire; Leicestershire; Lincolnshire; Northamptonshire; Nottinghamshire.

West Midlands
County of Herefordshire UA; Stoke-on-Trent UA; Telford and Wrekin UA; Shropshire; Staffordshire; Warwickshire; West Midlands Metropolitan County; Worcestershire.

East
Luton UA; Peterborough UA; Southend-on-Sea UA; Thurrock UA; Bedfordshire; Cambridgeshire; Essex; Hertfordshire; Norfolk; Suffolk.

London
Inner London; Outer London.

South East
Bracknell Forest UA; Brighton and Hove UA; Isle of Wight UA; Medway UA; Milton Keynes UA; Portsmouth UA; Reading UA; Slough UA; Southampton UA; West Berkshire UA; Windsor and Maidenhead UA; Buckinghamshire; East Sussex; Hampshire; Kent; Oxfordshire; Surrey; West Sussex.

South West

Bath and North East Somerset UA; Bournemouth UA; City of Bristol UA; North Somerset UA; Plymouth UA; Poole UA; South Gloucestershire UA; Swindon UA; Torbay UA; Cornwall and Isles of Scilly; Devon; Dorset; Gloucestershire; Somerset; Wiltshire.

Wales

The Welsh administrative authorities are shown below.

Blaenau Gwent; Bridgend; Caerphilly; Cardiff; Carmarthenshire; Ceredigion; Conwy; Cynon; Denbighshire; Flintshire; Gwynedd; Isle of Anglesey; Merthyr Tydfil; Monmouthshire; Neath Port Talbot; Newport; Pembrokeshire; Powys; Rhondda; Swansea; Taff; Torfaen; The Vale of Glamorgan; Wrexham.

Health Regional Office Areas and Health Authorities

Health Authorities and Health Regional Office Areas in England were reorganised in April 1999. The composition of Health Regional Office Areas in 1999 in terms of Health Authorities is set out below.

Northern and Yorkshire

Bradford; Calderdale and Kirklees; County Durham; East Riding; Gateshead and South Tyneside; Leeds; Newcastle and North Tyneside; North Cumbria; Northumberland; North Yorkshire; Sunderland; Tees; Wakefield.

Trent

Barnsley; Doncaster; Leicestershire; Lincolnshire; North Derbyshire; North Nottinghamshire; Nottingham; Rotherham; Sheffield; Southern Derbyshire; South Humber.

Eastern

Bedfordshire; Cambridgeshire; East and North Hertfordshire; Norfolk; North Essex; South Essex; Suffolk; West Hertfordshire.

London

Barking and Havering; Barnet; Bexley and Greenwich; Brent and Harrow; Bromley; Camden and Islington; Croydon; Ealing, Hammersmith and Hounslow; East London and The City; Enfield and Haringey; Hillingdon; Kensington & Chelsea and Westminster; Kingston and Richmond; Lambeth, Southwark and Lewisham; Merton, Sutton and Wandsworth; Redbridge and Waltham Forest.

South East

Berkshire; Buckinghamshire; East Kent; East Surrey; East Sussex, Brighton and Hove; Isle of Wight; Northamptonshire; North and Mid Hampshire; Oxfordshire; Portsmouth and South East Hampshire; Southampton and South West Hampshire; West Kent; West Surrey; West Sussex.

South West

Avon; Cornwall and Isles of Scilly; Dorset; Gloucestershire; North and East Devon; Somerset; South and West Devon; Wiltshire.

West Midlands

Birmingham; Coventry; Dudley; Herefordshire; North Staffordshire; Sandwell; Shropshire; Solihull; South Staffordshire; Walsall; Warwickshire; Wolverhampton; Worcestershire.

North West

Bury and Rochdale; East Lancashire; Liverpool; Manchester; Morecambe Bay; North Cheshire; North West Lancashire; St Helens and Knowsley; Salford and Trafford; Sefton; South Cheshire; South Lancashire; Stockport; West Pennine; Wigan and Bolton; Wirral.

Wales

North Wales; Dyfed Powys; Morgannwg; Bro Taf; Gwent.

2.5   Registration of births

Every registrar of births and deaths is required to secure the prompt registration of births occurring within the sub-district covered. Registration of a birth is legally required within 42 days of its occurrence, and the registrar will, if necessary, send a requisition to the person whose duty it is to register the birth.

Under the National Health Service Act 1977, births must also be notified, within 36 hours, to the Director of Public Health in the health authority where the birth occurred. This is carried out by the hospital where the birth took place, or by the midwife or doctor in attendance at the birth. Each month, a list of the births which have occurred in the sub-district is supplied to the registrar, who will then check whether every birth has been registered.

The following people are qualified to give information to the registrar concerning a birth:

a. the mother of the child, and the father if the child was born within marriage;
b. the occupier of the house in which the child was, to the knowledge of that occupier, born;
c. any person present at the birth;
d. any person having charge of the child.

The duty of giving information is placed primarily upon the parents of the child but, in the case of death or inability of the parents, the duty falls on one of the other qualified informants.

The particulars to be registered concerning a birth are prescribed by the Births and Deaths Registration Act 1953 and are covered in Section 1.2. Certain other particulars are collected for statistical purposes under the Population

Statistics Acts 1938 and 1960, and are not entered in the register. All details are entered on a draft entry *Form 309* (**Annex A**) for a live birth, or *Form 308* (**Annex B**) for a stillbirth. These are checked by the informant before being entered in the register.

The procedures and information required for stillbirths are similar to those for live births. The main difference is the recording of the cause of death of the stillborn child, on evidence given by the doctor or midwife present at the birth, or who examined the body.

Usually, information for the registration of a birth must be given personally by the informant to the registrar for the sub-district in which the birth occurred. However, since April 1997 an informant may supply this information to any registrar by making a declaration of these particulars. The declaration is sent to the registrar of the sub-district where the birth occurred, and that registrar will enter the particulars in the register.

2.6 Visitors and overseas registrations

As mentioned above, the coverage of this volume is of births occurring, and then registered, in England and Wales. Births to residents of England and Wales which are registered elsewhere are thus excluded, while births registered in England and Wales to mothers whose usual residence is elsewhere, are included. In 2000, there were 311 live births in England and Wales to visitors whose usual residence was elsewhere.

In 2000, 9,351 births occurring outside the United Kingdom to British nationals were voluntarily registered with British Consulates, British High Commissioners, or HM Armed Forces registration centres. Most of these, however, were births to women who had emigrated from the United Kingdom - that is, had lived outside the UK for at least one year - and were thus not residents of England and Wales. Such persons are not included in population estimates for England and Wales.

ONS estimates that at any time on average about 100 thousand women of childbearing age (defined as 15-44), usually resident in England and Wales, are temporarily absent overseas. But most of these women are absent for only a short period, and it is unlikely that more than a few hundred per year give birth while overseas. Also, the number of births during 2000 to residents of England and Wales which were registered in Scotland and Northern Ireland were 177 and 42 respectively.

Thus, the number of births to residents of England and Wales occurring outside the country is likely to be of the same order as the number of births occurring in England and Wales to visitors resident elsewhere. The effect on fertility rates of the difference between the definitions used for birth event numerators and population denominators is assumed to be negligible.

2.7 Foundlings

From their nature, few if any details are known about abandoned children, and they are thus not included in the statistics given in this volume. However, these infants are included in the 'Abandoned children register' maintained at the GRO in Southport, and three such entries were made in 2000.

2.8 Country of birth of parents

The country of birth of parents for children born in England and Wales has been recorded at birth registration since April 1969.

Country of birth groupings represent the Commonwealth and European Union as constituted in 1997. The details for country of birth groupings are shown in **Table A**.

Table A Country groupings for birthplace of parents

United Kingdom	England, Wales, Scotland, Northern Ireland
Elsewhere in United Kingdom	Channel Islands, Isle of Man, UK (part not stated)
Outside United Kingdom	
Irish Republic	Irish Republic, Ireland (part not stated)
Other European Union countries	Austria, Belgium, Denmark, Finland, France, Germany, Greece, Italy, Luxembourg, Netherlands, Portugal, Spain, Sweden
Rest of Europe	All other European countries, including Turkey, Russia and former Soviet republics
Commonwealth	
Australia, Canada and New Zealand	
New Commonwealth	
Asia	Bangladesh, India, Pakistan
East Africa	Kenya, Malawi, Tanzania, Uganda, Zambia
Southern Africa	Botswana, Lesotho, Namibia, South Africa, Swaziland
Rest of Africa	Cameroon, The Gambia, Ghana, Mauritius, Mozambique, Nigeria, Seychelles, Sierra Leone, Zimbabwe
Far East	Brunei, Malaysia, Singapore
Mediterranean	Cyprus, Gibraltar, Malta
Caribbean	Anguilla, Antigua and Barbuda, Bahamas, Barbados, Belize, Bermuda, British Virgin Islands, Cayman Islands, Dominica, Grenada, Guyana, Jamaica,

xxi

	Montserrat, St Christopher and Nevis, St Lucia, St Vincent, Trinidad and Tobago, Turks and Caicos Islands
Rest of the New Commonwealth	Cook Islands, Falkland Islands, Fiji, Kiribati, Maldives, Nauru, Papua New Guinea, St Helena, Solomon Islands, Sri Lanka, Tonga, Tuvalu, Vanauta, Western Samoa, British Indian Ocean Territory
Rest of the World	

These differ from those used in volumes prior to 1998; major changes from the listing between 1994 and 1997 by year are:

From 1994 - Namibia and South Africa moved from the *Rest of the World* to *New Commonwealth - Southern Africa.*

From 1995 - Cameroon and Mozambique moved from the *Rest of the World* to *New Commonwealth Rest of Africa*; Austria, Finland and Sweden moved from *Rest of Europe* to *Other European Union countries.*

From 1997 - Hong Kong moved from *New Commonwealth - Far East* to the *Rest of the World*; Fiji moved from the *Rest of the World* to the *Rest of the New Commonwealth.*

2.9 Maternities and paternities

The term *maternity* denotes a confinement resulting in the birth of one or more liveborn or stillborn children.

As a result, the number of maternities or paternities is less than the total number of live births and stillbirths.

2.10 Stillbirths

In Section 41 of the Births and Deaths Registration Act 1953, a stillbirth is defined as 'a child which has issued forth from its mother after the twenty-eighth week of pregnancy and which did not at any time after being completely expelled from its mother breathe or show other signs of life'. This definition was used up to 30 September 1992.

On 1 October 1992 the Stillbirth (Definition) Act 1992 came into force, altering the above definition of a stillbirth to 24 or more weeks completed gestation. Figures for stillbirths from 1993 are thus not fully comparable with those for previous years. The effect of this change on figures for 1992 is analysed in the annual volume for that year[6].

2.11 Conceptions

Conception statistics bring together records of birth registrations and of abortions under the 1967 Act. They include all the pregnancies of women usually resident in England and Wales which lead to one of the following outcomes:

(i)   a maternity at which one or more live births or stillbirths occur, which is registered in England and Wales;

(ii)   a termination of a pregnancy by abortion under the 1967 Act, in England and Wales.

Pregnancies which lead to spontaneous abortions (ie miscarriages) are not included. Maternities which result in one or more live births or stillbirths are counted once only.

2.12 Estimating the date of conception

Information on the exact date of conception cannot be obtained from the registration details for either births or abortions. The date is estimated as follows:

Maternities (one or more live births)

The date of conception is estimated as 38 weeks before the date of birth. The average duration of pregnancy, or gestation period, measured between the first day of the last menstrual period and the date of birth, is 40 weeks; conception occurs on average 14 days after the first day of the last menstrual period.

Maternities (all stillbirths)

Date of birth less the stated gestation period.

Abortions under the 1967 Act

For conceptions in 1980 and earlier years, the date of conception is taken as the date of the start of the last menstrual period, plus 14 days. For conceptions in 1981 and subsequent years, it is taken as the date of termination less the stated gestation period, plus 14 days. Here, the gestation period is estimated from the first day of the last menstrual period.

2.13 Estimating a woman's age at conception

A woman's age at conception is estimated from her date of birth, as stated on the birth registration or abortion notification, together with the estimated date of conception. In the small number of cases for which the woman's date of birth was not stated, an age is imputed, using the date of birth stated on a previous comparable record.

There are two stages in estimating the age at conception. First, the date of conception is estimated by subtracting the gestation period from the date of birth or abortion. In the case of live births, the gestation period is assumed to be 38 weeks, while the recorded gestation period is used for abortions and stillbirths - see Section 2.12 for details. Second, the woman's age at conception is calculated as the interval in complete years between her date of birth and the date she conceived. However, where conception occurs in the same calendar month as the woman's birthday, this can result in the estimated age of mother at conception being either a year too low – if the baby is born live after less than 38 weeks – or a year too high – if the baby is born live at over 38 weeks. The method for estimating a woman's age at conception in such cases was revised in 1999 to take into account the mother's *day* of birth and *day* of conception in addition to the month and year as used previously. This resulted in a revision to figures published before 1999. All figures in this volume are based on this revised methodology. A full explanation can be found in the 1998 volume[3].

2.14 Conceptions outside marriage

Conceptions outside marriage which lead to maternities within marriage are restricted here to those where birth occurred within 8 months (35 weeks) of marriage. This maintains consistency with tables elsewhere in this volume, and avoids erroneous classification of maternities with gestation periods below the average of 38 weeks. However, the date of conception and age of woman at conception are estimated from a date 38 weeks before birth, as in the case of all other conceptions leading to live births.

2.15 True birth order

When a birth is within marriage, information is obtained on the number of the mother's previous children, both live births and stillbirths. This allows determination of the *marital birth order* of the mother - that is, the number of previous live births plus the birth which has just occurred, all within marriage. However, this measure is deficient in two respects:

a.   at registration, the question on previous live births and stillbirths is not asked where the birth occurred outside marriage, and

b.   at the registration of births and stillbirths occurring within marriage, previous live births occurring outside marriage are not counted. However, because of the ambiguous nature of the question asked at registration (see **Annex A**) it is likely that births that took place outside marriage where the father was a man that the woman had subsequently married are included.

As an example, a woman's first live birth may be in a cohabiting relationship. If she then marries another partner

and subsequently has another live birth, her marital birth order will be 1 and her true birth order 2. If she then divorces, cohabits again, and then has another live birth, her true birth order will be 3. Her marital birth order, not actually determined at registration, will remain at 1. Finally, if she marries for a second time (this time to her current partner) and has another live birth, her marital birth order becomes 3, while her true birth order is now 4.

The proportion of births occurring outside marriage has risen steadily in recent years. To allow for this, the information collected on birth order has been supplemented to give estimates of overall or *true birth order* - that is, a measure which includes births both within and outside marriage. These estimates are obtained from details provided by the General Household Survey (GHS).

In volumes of *Birth statistics* prior to 1991, data from the GHS for 1979 to 1982 were[7] used to estimate true birth order. *Birth statistics* 1991 gave true birth order estimates updated with information from the GHS for 1986 to 1989. In this volume, three tables are based on these updated estimates: **Table 1.7** (mean age at childbirth), **Table 10.3** (average number of first births by age of mother), and **Table 10.5** (distribution of women by number of previous liveborn children). A description of how these estimates were made may be found in an earlier volume of *Birth statistics* (FM1 Series)[8]. The figures in these tables should be treated with caution as the factors now require updating. Revised tables with new factors will be made available in the next FM1 volume.

2.16 Births within marriage, and sole and joint registration

In general, a birth within marriage is that of a child born to parents who were lawfully married to each other either:

a.   at the date of the child's birth, or

b.   when the child was conceived, even if they later divorced or the father died before the child's birth.

Only for a birth within marriage will the registrar enter on the draft entry in the register (*Form 309* - **Annex A** or *Form 308* - **Annex B**) confidential particulars relating to the date of the parents' marriage, whether the mother has been married more than once, and the number of the mother's previous liveborn and stillborn children - see Section 1.2.

Births occurring outside marriage may be registered either jointly or solely. A *joint registration* records details of both parents, and requires them both to be present. A *sole registration* records only the mother's details. In a few cases a joint registration is made in the absence of the father if an affiliation order or statutory declaration is provided.

Information from draft birth entries is used to determine whether the mother and father jointly registering a birth outside marriage were usually resident at the same address at the time of registration - see **Table 3.10.** Births with both parents at the same address are identified by a single entry for the informant's usual address, while different addresses are identified by two entries.

2.17 Rates

In this volume, fertility rates have been calculated using the most appropriate estimates of the female population see Section 2.1 and **Appendix Tables 1** and **2.**

The most commonly used rates are described below[9]:

Crude birth rate

This is the simplest overall measure of fertility in the population, given by the number of live births in a year per 1,000 mid-year population. It is unsophisticated, since it takes no account of the composition of the population, in particular the age and sex distribution.

It is given by $(B/P) \times 1,000$
where B = total live births in the year, and
    P = mid-year population.

In this volume it is used in **Tables 1.1b** and **1.3.**

General fertility rate (GFR)

This is an easily calculated measure of current fertility levels, and denotes the number of children born alive per women aged 15-44. However, it makes no allowance for different sized cohorts of women at childbearing ages.

It is given by $(B/P^f_{15-44}) \times 1,000$
where B – total live births in the year, and
    P^f_{15-44} = female population aged 15-44.

In this volume it is used in **Tables 1.1b** and **7.1.**

Age-specific fertility rates (ASFRs)

ASFRs are a measure of fertility specific to the age of the mother, and are useful for comparing the reproductive behaviour of women at different ages. They are calculated by dividing the number of live births to mothers of each age group by the number of females in the population of that age and then expressed per 1,000 women in the age group. They can be calculated for single ages, but are usually calculated for five-year age groups in the reproductive age range, from under 20 up to 45 and over. They provide the basis for a detailed analysis of fertility levels by age of mother when giving birth.

The ASFR based on fife-year age groups is given by
$$F_a = (B_a/P^f_a) \times 1,000$$
where F_a = age-specific birth rate for age-group a,
    B_a = live births to women in age-group a,
    P^f_a = females population in age-group a, and
    a = age-group under 20, ... , 45 and over.

For the groups under 20 and 45 and over, the female populations used are women aged 15-19, and women aged 45-49 respectively.

Age-specific fertility rates are used in **Tables 3.1b, 7.2** and **10.1** of this volume.

Total fertility rate (TFR)

In this volume, for most tables the TFR is derived by summing single-year age-specific fertility rates over all ages within the childbearing lifespan. It is a measure independent of variations in the age distribution of women of childbearing age. It may be interpreted as representing the completed fertility of a synthetic cohort of women - that is, the average number of children which a woman would bear, if the female population experienced the age-specific fertility rates of the calendar year in question throughout their childbearing lifespan.

From the above the $\text{TFR} = \sum\limits_{a=\text{under } 16}^{a=44 \text{ and over}} f_a$

where $f_a = B_a/P^f_a$
and B_a = live births to women in age-group a,
    P^f_a = female population in age-group a, and
    a = ages under 16, 16, 17, ... , 42, 43, 44 and over.

For the groups under 16 and 44 and over, the female populations used are women aged 15, and women aged 44 respectively.

The TFR is used in **Tables 1.4, 1.9, 2.1, 2.3** and **7.1.**

Gross reproduction rate (GRR)

The GRR is the sum of age-specific fertility rates for female births only, calculated in the same way as the TFR. It represents the average number of *daughters* that a woman would bear alive in her life, if the female population experienced current ASFRs based on female births throughout their childbearing period.

The GRR is shown in **Table 1.4.**

Net reproduction rate (NRR)

The NRR is similar to the GRR, but allows for the effect of mortality to women of childbearing age. Not all women survive to the end of the possible reproductive period. It represents the average number of daughters that a woman would bear alive, if the female population experienced current ASFRs and female survival rates throughout their childbearing period.

The NRR is used in **Table 1.4.**

Average family size

Average family size is presented in this volume for women by year of birth and age, in tables on cohort fertility. For each cohort (ie women born in a particular year) it represents the number of births per woman, and is shown by birth order for births within marriage. Thus in **Table 10.4** the cohort born in 1951 had between ages 20 and 24 borne on average 0.65 children per woman. Of these, 0.59 were within marriage, of which 0.31 were first births per woman, 0.21 second births, and so on.

Stillbirth rate

The stillbirth rate is defined as the number of stillbirths per 1,000 live births and stillbirths, and is used in **Tables 1.2, 7.1** and **8.3.**

Sex ratio

Expressed as males per 1,000 females, most often for live births, but also for stillbirths. It is used here in **Tables 1.1b, 1.2** and **4.3.**

Other rates used in this volume include:

Live births within marriage per 1,000 married women, by age - **Tables 1.1b** and **3.1b.**

Live births within marriage per 1,000 married men, by age - **Tables 3.3** and **3.5.**

Live births outside marriage per 1,000 single, widowed and divorced women, by age - **Tables 1.1b** and **3.1b.**

Live births outside marriage per 1,000 live births - **Tables 1.1b** and **7.1.**

Paternities within marriage per 1,000 married men, by age - **Table 3.5.**

Stillbirths within marriage per 1,000 married men, by age - **Table 3.5.**

Maternities with multiple births per 1,000 total maternities, by age - **Table 6.1b.**

Maternities within marriage with multiple births, per 1,000 maternities within marriage, by age - **Tables 6.1b** and **6.3.**

Maternities outside marriage with multiple births, per 1,000 maternities outside marriage, by age - **Table 6.1b.**

Conceptions per 1,000 women, by age and outcome - **Tables 12.1, 12.2** and **12.8.**

Conceptions within marriage per 1,000 married women, by age and outcome - **Table 12.5.**

Conceptions outside marriage per 1,000 single, widowed and divorced women, by age and outcome - **Table 12.6.**

2.18 Accuracy of information

The accuracy of information contained in the draft birth entry (*Form 309* for a live birth or *Form 308* for a stillbirth - **Annex A** and **B** respectively) is the responsibility of the informant(s) - usually the mother, or the mother and father where the registration is a joint one outside marriage. Wilfully supplying false information may render the informant(s) liable to prosecution for perjury.

It is believed that in general the information supplied by the informant(s) is correct. Computerised internal consistency checks are applied to each record to eliminate, as far as possible, errors made in the supply and recording of information on births.

There are a few, very small, known errors in the database each year which it is not possible to correct. Their effects on the statistics are explained in relevant sections of these notes - for instance, duration of marriage in Section 3.4.

2.19 Historical information

The formal registration of live births commenced on 1 July 1837, while stillbirths have been registered only since 1 July 1927. Confidential particulars for statistical purposes have been ascertained since 1 July 1938, under the Population Statistics Act of that year. From the later date, it has also been possible to routinely distinguish multiple births.

The Population Statistics Act 1960, effective from 1 January 1961, added a question on father's date of birth to the confidential particulars requested in the case of births within marriage. This applied also to births outside marriage where the father's name is entered in the register. Questions on father's and mother's place of birth were introduced on 1 April 1969 by the Registration of Births, Deaths and Marriages Regulations 1968.

As noted in Section 2.9, the Stillbirth (Definition) Act of 1992 altered the definition of the gestation period for a stillbirth from 28 to 24 completed weeks.

2.20 Legislation

The main statutes concerning birth registration and provision of information on births are given below:

- **Census Act 1920,** which in Section 5 provides for the collection and publication of statistical information on the population by the Registrar General.

- **Population Statistics Act 1938,** which deals with the statistical information collected at registration.

- **Births and Deaths Registration Act 1953,** which covers all aspects of the registration of births and deaths.

- **Registration Service Act 1953,** which in Section 19 requires the Registrar General to provide annual abstracts of live births and stillbirths.

- **Population Statistics Act 1960,** which makes further provision for collecting statistical detail at registration.

- **Abortions Act 1967,** which permits termination of pregnancy by a registered practitioner, subject to certain conditions.

- **Registration of Births, Deaths and Marriages Regulations 1968,** which added questions on father's and mother's place of birth to the details requested at registration.

- **National Health Service Act 1977,** which requires notification of a birth to the health authority in whose area the birth occurred.

- **Stillbirth (Definition) Act 1992,** which altered the definition of a stillbirth to 24 or more weeks completed gestation, instead of the previous definition of 28 or more weeks completed gestation.

- **Health Act 1999,** a section of which includes specific provision for the supply of information on individual births to the National Health Service.

2.21 Symbols and conventions

In this volume:

    :   denotes 'not appropriate'
    0   denotes less than 0.5
    -    denotes nil.

Where data are not yet available, cells in tables are left blank. Rates calculated from fewer than 20 events (for example Table 3.5) are distinguished by italic type as a warning to users that their reliability as a measure may be affected by the small number of events.

2.22 Further information

Requests for conceptions data and births data, as well as background information on this volume, on unpublished VS tables, and on data quality, should be made to:

Vital Statistics Outputs Branch
Office for National Statistics
Segensworth Road
Titchfield
Fareham
Hants PO15 5RR
Telephone: 01329 813758; Fax:01329 813548
email: vsob@ons.gov.uk

Requests for secondary analyses of fertility data, and for other unpublished tables, should be made to:

Family Demography Unit
Population and D   emography
Office for National Statistics
1 Drummond Gate
London SW1V 2QQ
Telephone 0207533 5207
Email: fertility@ons.gov.uk

Requests for secondary analyses of conceptions data only, and for other unpublished tables, should be made to:

Child Health Branch
Health and Care
Office for National Statistics
1 Drummond Gate
London SW1V 2QQ
Telephone 0207533 5113
email: CIM@ons.gov.uk fax: 0207533 5635

Enquiries on StatBase® and its use may be made to:
OnLine Services StatBase Support
Office for National Statistics
Segensworth Road
Titchfield
Fareham
Hants PO15 5RR
Telephone 01329 813521; Fax: 01329 813230
email: idb.dataunit@ons.gov.uk

3   Notes on tables

3.1   Seasonality *(Tables 2.1 to 2.5)*

Seasonally adjusted numbers of live births are obtained using the X-11 ARIMA adjustment package developed by Statistics Canada. This package adjusts the monthly totals to allow for different number of days in each month; other seasonal factors are adjusted by modelling the data on the latest 12 years data, ensuring that the seasonally adjusted figures sum to the actual annual total. Seasonally adjusted TFRs are calculated using these numbers. For further information see contacts given in Section 2.22.

3.2   Age of parents *(Tables 3.1 to 3.10)*

The mother's or father's date of birth is recorded and translated into the age at the birthday **preceding** the date of the child's birth. This age is often termed *age last birthday*. Special checks are carried out on those dates of birth which imply that the age of the mother is over 50 years. While most dates of birth are confirmed, these extreme values tend to occur more often among women born outside England and Wales - see **Tables 9.1** to **9.5** - and may result from age misreporting.

If either the mother's date of birth or the father's date of birth (when applicable) is not given, an age is imputed from the last processed record with completely stated and otherwise matching particulars. In 2000, the mother's date of birth was not stated for 0.51 per cent of all live births, and the father's date of birth was not stated for 0.33 per cent of all live births where father's details were present.

3.3   Previous liveborn children *(Tables 4.1 to 4.3)*

Information on previous liveborn children is available only for women having a birth within marriage. It denotes the number of previous liveborn children by the present and any former husband, as stated at registration. This information is also used to determine *marital birth order* - see Section 2.15.

If the number of previous liveborn children is not given, a value is imputed from the last processed record with completely stated and otherwise matching particulars. In 2000, the number of previous liveborn children was not stated for 0.09 per cent of all live births to women having a birth within marriage.

3.4   Duration of marriage *(Tables 5.1 to 5.3)*

Pre-maritally conceived live births are, by convention, taken to be those where the calculated duration of marriage is less than eight months - that is, 0-7 completed months. At registration only the month and year of marriage are recorded, so the calculation relates to the interval in completed months between the middle of the month of marriage and the date of the child's birth. Other durations of marriage are calculated in a similar way.

If the date of marriage is not given, a value for the date of marriage is imputed from the last processed record with completely stated and otherwise matching particulars. In 2000, the year of marriage was not stated for 0.44 per cent of all live births within marriage. For women who have been married more than once, duration refers to the length of the current marriage.

In **Table 1.8**, the percentages shown are based on live births where the mother married in the year shown, and the birth was within eight months of marriage, and on first marriages in the same year. Thus the percentages (by age) for year of marriage 1999 would be based on (a) the number of live births in 1999 or 2000 where the mother conceived in 1999 and gave birth within eight months of marriage, and (b) the number of first marriages occurring in 1999.

3.5   Multiple births *(Tables 6.1 to 6.4)*

Multiple births arising from a single pregnancy are counted as one maternity or paternity, although each child born is reckoned separately in analyses of birth statistics. In tables analysing births by the number of previous liveborn children, multiple births are counted as if they had occurred separately - in the case of twins for instance, as one first and one second birth.

3.6   Birthweight *(Tables 7.1 to 7.4)*

Birthweight is measured in grams, and is notified to the local health authority by the hospital where the birth took place, or by the midwife or doctor in attendance at the birth. These details are then supplied to the registrar. For stillbirths, details of the weight of the foetus are supplied on a certificate or notification by a doctor or midwife. The certificate or notification is then taken by an informant to the registrar.

In cases where no birthweight is recorded, the birth is included in the total 'all weights' but not distributed amongst the individual categories. (These categories may thus not add to the total in **Tables 7.3** and **7.4.**). In 2000, birthweight was not stated for 0.20 per cent of all live births, and for 7.58 per cent of stillbirths.

3.7 Place of confinement and area of occurrence
(Tables 8.1 to 8.3)

Place of confinement describes the type of building in which a birth occurs; in this volume it is categorised as follows:

NHS Establishments - generally hospitals, maternity units and maternity wings;

Non-NHS Establishments - including private maternity units, military hospitals, and private hospitals;

At home - denoting the usual place of residence of the mother;

Elsewhere - including all locations not covered above: most of these are at a private residence not that of the mother, or are on the way to a hospital.

A birth is usually assigned to an area according to the usual residence of the mother at the time of birth, as stated at registration. However, a birth may take place in an area other than that of the mother's usual residence. **Table 8.2** shows whether a confinement takes place in the same area as the mother's usual area of residence, or if it occurred in a different area. **Table 8.3** shows the numbers of maternities, live births and stillbirths occurring in NHS and non-NHS establishments, by area of occurrence.

3.8 Country of birth of mother *(Tables 9.1 to 9.5)*

For children born in England and Wales, the country of birth of parents has been recorded at birth registration since April 1969. However, it should be noted that birthplace does not necessarily equate with ethnic group. A fuller discussion of this subject may be found elsewhere[10].

Country of birth groupings represent the Commonwealth and European Union as constituted in 1997 - see Section 2.8. Data in **Tables 9.1** and **9.5** have been revised back to 1994.

3.9 Birth cohorts *(Tables 10.1 to 10.5)*

Birth statistics analysed by year of occurrence and by age of mother have been available since 1938. Tables in Section 10 show these statistics in cohort form - that is, by the year of birth of the mother rather than the year of birth of the child. The years of birth shown are by necessity

approximate, since data are available only by calendar year of occurrence and age of mother at childbirth. For instance, women aged 32 giving birth to children in 2000 could have been born in either 1967 or 1968; for convenience however, such women are here regarded as belonging to the 1968 cohort. In some earlier volumes of *Birth statistics* (FM1 nos. 11 to 16) it was incorrectly stated that such births were attributed to the earlier year cohort - in the example, to 1967.

Tables 10.1 to **10.5** all refer to age in completed years. **Table 10.2** gives for a particular cohort (women born in a given year) the average number of liveborn children after n completed years of age. When data become available for a given cohort from 15 to 45 completed years, then the figure shown after 45 completed years of age measures the average completed family size for women born in that cohort. This is calculated by summing the age-specific birth rates for that cohort shown in **Table 10.1** up to and including age n. For example, **Table 10.2** shows that women born in 1970 had given birth to 0.22 children on average after 20 completed years of age. This was calculated by adding the age-specific birth rates for the 1970 cohort in **Table 10.1** up to and including age 20 - that is, $(3+12+28+48+61+72)/1,000 = 0.22$.

3.10 Social class as defined by occupation *(Tables 11.1 to 11.5)*

The information on occupation is coded for only a sample of one in ten births, and by combining this with the employment status, a code for social class (as defined by occupation) may be derived. From 1982 to 1990 the occupation of the father shown on the selected birth record was coded using the *Classification of occupations* 1980[11]. This classification was updated in 1990, and since 1991 the father's occupation from births has been coded using the *Standard Occupational Classification*[12].

Occupation codes have been allocated as far as possible to the Registrar General's social classes, as used up to now by the Census. This is approximate, since the questions asked at the time of birth registration are less detailed than those in the Census. These social class categories are outlined below.

Non-manual

I	Professional
II	Managerial and technical
IIIN	Skilled occupations (non-manual)

Manual

IIIM	Skilled occupations (manual)
IV	Partly skilled occupations
V	Unskilled occupations

Other

Residential groups including the unemployed, armed forces and students, and those whose occupation was inadequately described.

The sample figures in **Tables 11.1** to **11.5** have been grossed-up to agree with known totals derived from the 100 per cent processing of birth registrations by mother's age and previous liveborn children in **Table 4.1 (a).** This ensures consistency with sub-totals, and improves the quality of sample estimates. **Appendix Tables 3** and **4** show *standard errors* for selected numbers of births and percentages. The standard error is a conventional measure of the sampling variation occurring by chance when only part of the total population - in this case, one in ten live births - has been selected. Thus, if the estimated grossed-up number in a particular category was 50.0 thousand, then from **Appendix Table 3** the standard error of that estimate would be approximately 0.64 thousand. Based on statistical theory, this means that for the type of distribution being considered there is about a 95 per cent chance that the 'true' number in the population lies within two standard errors of the estimates. This true number is that which would have been obtained had all the information been collected, rather than a one in ten sample.

In this example, the 95 per cent confidence interval would be:

50.0 ± 1.3 thousand, or 48.7 to 51.3 thousand.

In other words, we could say that we are 95 per cent confident that the true value, if we had collected all the information instead of a 10 per cent sample, lies somewhere between 48.7 and 51.3 thousand.

3.11 Birth intervals *(Table 11.3)*

The median intervals between marriage and first birth shown in **Table 11.3** are derived from birth registration data, and refer to the interval between marriage and the first birth within marriage. In this table the latter is defined as the first birth within any marriage. Thus if a woman marries and subsequently divorces without having borne any children, then remarries and gives birth in the second marriage, the interval used would be that between the date of the second marriage and the birth. If she had borne a child in the first marriage the interval used here would be that between the date of that marriage and the first birth in it.

This is consistent with the use of information on number of previous liveborn children, in Section 3.3. The details collected at registration are for liveborn children by the present and any former husband. **Table 11.3** gives the median interval from marriage to first birth for women married once only, and for remarried women, for England and Wales.

Registration data does not provide information about the time interval between the present birth being registered and previous births. Before 1998 the median intervals between subsequent births (first to second etc.), for Great Britain were calculated based on a 1 per cent sample of new claims for child benefit payments from the then Department of Social Security[13]. These benefit data included all births - whether they occurred within or outside marriage - and were thus not strictly comparable with those from birth registration data. Since 1998 a new system has been in use in the Department of Social Security, now the Department for Work and Pensions, and these data are no longer available on the same basis. This part of **Table 11.3** therefore shows data to 1997 only.

The *median* is the value for which half the data is below and half is above; it is a measure often used as an alternative to the mean. For example in **Table 11.3** the median interval between first and second birth to women in Great Britain in 1997 is 36 months. This means that exactly half the women had a gap of 36 months or less between their first and second birth; the remaining half had a gap of more than 36 months.

References

1. OPCS (1987). *Birth statistics 1837-1983,* series FM1 no 13.
2. ONS (2001). *Abortion statistics 2000,* series AB no 26.
3. ONS (1999). *Births statistics* 1998, series FM1 no 27
4. ONS (2000). *Birth Statistics* 1999, series FM1, no 28
5. ONS (2000). *Key population and vital statistics - local and health authority areas 1999,* series VS no 26, PP1 no 22.
6. OPCS (1994). *Birth statistics* 1992, series FM1 no 21.
7. OPCS (1993). *Birth statistics* 1991, series FM1 no 20.
8. OPCS (1987). *Period and cohort birth order statistics,* series FM1 no 14.
9. Shryock, HS. and Siegel, JS. (1973). *The methods and materials of demography,* chapter 16. (US Government Printing Office, Washington DC, 1973).
10. Shaw C. (1988). 'Components of growth in the ethnic minority population'. *Population Trends* 52, pp 26-30.
11. OPCS (1980). *Classification of occupations* 1980.
12. OPCS (1990). *Standard Occupational Classification,* volumes 1-3.
13. DSS (1998). *Child Benefit and One Parent Benefit.*

Table 1.1 Live births: occurrence within/outside marriage and sex, 1990-2000 **England and Wales**
  a. numbers

Year	All			Within marriage			Outside marriage		
	Total	Males	Females	Total	Males	Females	Total	Males	Females
1990	**706,140**	361,412	344,728	506,141	259,050	247,091	199,999	102,362	97,637
1991	**699,217**	358,407	340,810	487,923	250,094	237,829	211,294	108,313	102,981
1992	**689,656**	353,694	335,962	474,431	243,266	231,165	215,225	110,428	104,797
1993	**673,467**	345,835	327,632	456,919	234,935	221,984	216,548	110,900	105,648
1994	**664,726**	341,321	323,405	449,190	230,733	218,457	215,536	110,588	104,948
1995	**648,138**	332,188	315,950	428,189	219,475	208,714	219,949	112,713	107,236
1996	**649,485**	333,490	315,995	416,822	214,542	202,280	232,663	118,948	113,715
1997	**643,095**	329,577	313,518	404,873	207,199	197,674	238,222	122,378	115,844
1998	**635,901**	325,903	309,998	395,290	202,762	192,528	240,611	123,141	117,470
1999	**621,872**	319,255	302,617	379,983	194,935	185,048	241,889	124,320	117,569
2000	**604,441**	309,625	294,816	365,836	187,367	178,469	238,605	122,258	116,347

Table 1.1 Live births: occurrence within/outside marriage and sex, 1990-2000 **England and Wales**
  b. rates and sex ratios

Year	Crude birth rate: all births per 1,000 population of all ages	General fertility rate: all births per 1,000 women aged 15-44	Births within marriage per 1,000 married women aged 15-44*	Births outside marriage per 1,000 single, widowed and divorced women aged 15-44*	Births outside marriage per 1,000 total births	Sex ratio: male births per 1,000 female births		
						All	Within marriage	Outside marriage
1990	13.9	64.2	86.7	38.9	283.2	1,048	1,048	1,048
1991	13.7	63.6	84.6	40.5	302.2	1,052	1,052	1,052
1992	13.4	63.5	85.1	40.8	312.1	1,053	1,052	1,054
1993	13.1	62.6	84.4	40.5	321.5	1,056	1,058	1,050
1994	12.9	61.9	85.0	39.5	324.2	1,055	1,056	1,054
1995	12.5	60.4	83.3	39.4	339.4	1,051	1,052	1,051
1996	12.5	60.5	82.9	40.7	358.2	1,055	1,061	1,046
1997	12.3	59.8	82.4	40.8	370.4	1,051	1,048	1,056
1998	12.1	59.0	82.3	40.3	378.4	1,051	1,053	1,048
1999	11.8	57.6	80.8	39.7	389.0	1,055	1,053	1,057
2000	11.4	55.7	79.3	38.3	394.8	1,050	1,050	1,051

* See Section 2.1

Table 1.2 Stillbirths (numbers, rates and sex ratios): occurrence within/outside marriage and sex, 1990-2000 **England and Wales**

Year	Numbers									Rates			
	All			Within marriage			Outside marriage			Stillbirths per 1,000 live births and stillbirths	Sex ratio: male births per 1,000 female births		
	Total	Males	Females	Total	Males	Females	Total	Males	Females		All	Within marriage	Outside marriage
1990	**3,256**	1,753	1,503	**2,176**	1,153	1,023	**1,080**	600	480	4.6	1,166	1,127	1,250
1991	**3,254**	1,725	1,529	**2,100**	1,123	977	**1,154**	602	552	4.6	1,128	1,149	1,091
1992	**2,944**	1,592	1,352	**1,898**	1,017	881	**1,046**	575	471	4.3	1,178	1,154	1,221
1993	**3,855**	2,076	1,779	**2,431**	1,317	1,114	**1,424**	759	665	5.7	1,167	1,182	1,141
1994	**3,813**	2,034	1,779	**2,361**	1,287	1,074	**1,452**	747	705	5.7	1,143	1,198	1,060
1995	**3,600**	1,912	1,688	**2,224**	1,197	1,027	**1,376**	715	661	5.5	1,133	1,166	1,082
1996	**3,539**	1,808	1,731	**2,114**	1,057	1,057	**1,425**	751	674	5.4	1,044	1,000	1,114
1997	**3,439**	1,801	1,638	**2,010**	1,070	940	**1,429**	731	698	5.3	1,100	1,138	1,047
1998	**3,417**	1,822	1,595	**1,966**	1,054	912	**1,451**	768	683	5.3	1,142	1,156	1,124
1999	**3,305**	1,727	1,578	**1,875**	973	902	**1,430**	754	676	5.3	1,094	1,079	1,115
2000	**3,203**	1,731	1,472	**1,830**	979	851	**1,373**	752	621	5.3	1,176	1,150	1,211

Table 1.3 Natural change in population **England and Wales**
(numbers and rates), 1990-2000

Year	Numbers			Rates per 1,000 population of all ages		
	Live births	Deaths	Natural change: live births minus deaths	Live births (crude birth rate)	Deaths (crude death rate)	Natural change
1990	706,140	564,846	141,294	13.9	11.1	2.8
1991	699,217	570,044	129,173	13.7	11.2	2.5
1992	689,656	558,313	131,343	13.4	10.9	2.5
1993	673,467	578,799	94,668	13.1	11.3	1.8
1994	664,726	553,194	111,532	12.9	10.7	2.2
1995	648,138	569,683	78,455	12.5	11.0	1.5
1996	649,485	560,135	89,350	12.5	10.8	1.7
1997	643,095	555,281	87,814	12.3	10.6	1.7
1998	635,901	555,015	80,886	12.1	10.6	1.5
1999	621,872	556,118	65,754	11.8	10.6	1.2
2000	604,441	535,664	68,777	11.4	10.1	1.3

Note: Numbers of deaths for years prior to 1993 are registrations in those years. From1993 these numbers represent actual occurrences.

Table 1.4 Total fertility, gross and net **England and Wales**
reproduction rates, 1990-2000

Year	Total fertility rate (TFR)	Gross reproduction rate (GRR)	Net reproduction rate (NRR)
1990	1.84	0.91	0.90
1991	1.82	0.89	0.89
1992	1.80	0.88	0.88
1993	1.76	0.86	0.86
1994	1.75	0.86	0.85
1995	1.72	0.84	0.84
1996	1.73	0.85	0.84
1997	1.73	0.85	0.84
1998	1.72	0.84	0.84
1999	1.70	0.83	0.82
2000	1.66	0.81	0.81

Table 1.5 Marriages (numbers and rates): sex, 1989-1999 **England and Wal**

Year	Number of marriages			Marriage rates*				
	All	Bachelors	Spinsters	Crude marriage rate - all persons marrying per 1,000 population of all ages	Males marrying per 1,000 single, widowed and divorced males aged 16 and over	Females marrying per 1,000 single, widowed and divorced females aged 16 and over	Bachelors marrying per 1,000 single males aged 16 and over	Spinsters marrying per 1,000 single females aged 16 and over
1989	346,697	252,230	254,763	13.7	45.0	38.3	42.6	53.5
1990	331,150	241,274	243,825	13.1	42.4	36.4	40.4	51.0
1991	306,756	222,823	224,812	12.0	38.6	33.1	37.0	46.6
1992	311,564	224,152	225,608	12.2	38.5	33.3	36.8	46.3
1993	299,197	213,476	214,987	11.6	36.4	31.6	34.7	43.8
1994	291,069	206,077	206,332	11.3	34.8	30.4	33.1	41.6
1995	283,012	198,208	198,603	10.9	33.1	29.1	31.2	39.3
1996	278,975	193,306	192,707	10.7	31.9	28.3	29.8	37.3
1997	272,536	188,268	188,457	10.4	30.4	27.2	28.4	35.6
1998	267,303	186,329	187,391	10.2	29.2	26.3	27.5	34.6
1999	263,515	184,266	185,328	10.0	28.1	25.6	26.6	33.5

* See Section 2.1
Note: These figures relate only to marriages solemnised in England and Wales.

Table 1.6 Mean age of all women at marriage and **England and Wales**
of mothers at live birth, 1990-2000

Year	Mean age at marriage		Mean ages at live birth						
	All brides	Spinsters	All births	Births outside marriage	Births within marriage				
					All birth orders	First birth	Second birth	Third birth	Fourth birth
1990	28.8	25.2	**27.5**	24.6	28.6	27.2	28.7	30.3	31.4
1991	29.1	25.5	**27.7**	24.8	28.9	27.5	28.9	30.4	31.6
1992	29.5	25.9	**27.9**	25.2	29.1	27.8	29.2	30.5	31.6
1993	29.9	26.2	**28.1**	25.5	29.3	28.0	29.4	30.7	31.8
1994	30.3	26.5	**28.4**	25.8	29.6	28.3	29.7	30.9	32.0
1995	28.1	26.0	**28.5**	26.0	29.8	28.5	30.0	31.1	32.0
1996	31.1	27.2	**28.6**	26.1	30.1	28.8	30.3	31.3	32.2
1997	31.4	27.5	**28.8**	26.2	30.3	29.0	30.5	31.5	32.4
1998	31.6	27.7	**28.9**	26.3	30.5	29.2	30.7	31.8	32.6
1999	31.8	28.0	**29.0**	26.4	30.6	29.3	30.9	32.0	32.7
2000			**29.1**	26.5	30.8	29.6	31.1	32.1	32.8

Note: The mean ages presented in this table do not take account of the changing population distribution of women

Table 1.7 Mean ages of mothers by birth order*, 1990-2000 **England and Wales**

Year	All births	All births			
		First	Second	Third	Fourth
1990	**27.5**	25.5	27.7	29.7	30.9
1991	**27.7**	25.7	27.9	29.8	31.0
1992	**27.9**	26.0	28.1	30.0	30.9
1993	**28.1**	26.2	28.3	30.1	31.0
1994	**28.4**	26.5	28.6	30.3	31.2
1995	**28.5**	26.7	28.8	30.5	31.2
1996	**28.6**	26.7	29.0	30.6	31.4
1997	**28.8**	26.8	29.2	30.8	31.6
1998	**28.9**	26.9	29.4	31.0	31.7
1999	**29.0**	27.0	29.5	31.1	31.8
2000	**29.1**	27.1	29.7	31.2	31.9

* See Section 2.15
Note: The mean ages presented in this table do not take account of the changing population distribution of women.

Table 1.8 Percentage of first marriages with a birth within 8 months **England and Wales**
of marriage: age of mother at marriage, 1989-1999

Year of marriage	Woman's age at marriage				
	Under 20	20-24	25-29	30-44	Under 45
1989	24.9	10.7	10.0	11.9	12.1
1990	24.0	10.4	9.5	11.7	11.5
1991	23.8	10.5	9.5	11.9	11.4
1992	20.1	9.3	8.8	11.3	10.1
1993	22.8	9.9	8.9	11.2	10.6
1994	22.5	9.9	8.3	11.1	10.2
1995	20.6	10.3	8.3	10.8	10.1
1996	23.1	11.0	8.5	10.5	10.5
1997	21.9	11.1	8.6	10.8	10.5
1998	22.7	11.4	8.3	10.4	10.4
1999	22.7	11.1	8.0	10.0	10.0

Note: Percentages are based on first marriages in each year, and live births to women within eight months of marriage, when the latter was in in the same year - see Section 3.4.

Table 1.9 Components of total fertility rates*: occurrence within/outside marriage, birth order and age of mother, 1990-2000   **England and Wales**

Year	All live births	Live births outside marriage	Live births within marriage All	First	Second	Third	Fourth	Fifth and later	Year	All live births	Live births outside marriage	Live births within marriage All	First	Second	Third	Fourth	Fifth and later
	All ages of mother at birth								**25-29**								
1990	**1.84**	0.53	1.31	0.51	0.48	0.21	0.07	0.04	1990	**0.61**	0.12	0.50	0.21	0.19	0.07	0.02	0.01
1991	**1.82**	0.56	1.26	0.49	0.46	0.20	0.07	0.04	1991	**0.60**	0.13	0.47	0.20	0.18	0.06	0.02	0.01
1992	**1.80**	0.58	1.22	0.48	0.44	0.19	0.06	0.04	1992	**0.59**	0.13	0.45	0.20	0.17	0.06	0.02	0.01
1993	**1.76**	0.59	1.17	0.46	0.43	0.18	0.06	0.04	1993	**0.57**	0.14	0.43	0.19	0.16	0.06	0.02	0.01
1994	**1.75**	0.60	1.15	0.45	0.42	0.18	0.06	0.04	1994	**0.56**	0.14	0.42	0.19	0.15	0.06	0.02	0.01
1995	**1.72**	0.62	1.10	0.44	0.40	0.17	0.06	0.03	1995	**0.54**	0.15	0.39	0.18	0.14	0.05	0.02	0.01
1996	**1.73**	0.66	1.07	0.43	0.39	0.17	0.06	0.03	1996	**0.53**	0.16	0.38	0.17	0.13	0.05	0.02	0.01
1997	**1.73**	0.68	1.05	0.41	0.39	0.16	0.05	0.03	1997	**0.52**	0.16	0.36	0.16	0.13	0.05	0.01	0.01
1998	**1.72**	0.69	1.03	0.41	0.38	0.15	0.05	0.03	1998	**0.51**	0.16	0.34	0.16	0.12	0.04	0.01	0.01
1999	**1.70**	0.70	1.00	0.41	0.36	0.15	0.05	0.03	1999	**0.49**	0.17	0.33	0.16	0.11	0.04	0.01	0.01
2000	**1.66**	0.69	0.97	0.40	0.35	0.14	0.05	0.03	2000	**0.47**	0.17	0.31	0.15	0.11	0.04	0.01	0.01
	Under 20								**30-34**								
1990	**0.16**	0.13	0.03	0.02	0.01	0.00	0.00	0.00	1990	**0.43**	0.06	0.37	0.11	0.15	0.08	0.03	0.02
1991	**0.16**	0.13	0.03	0.02	0.01	0.00	0.00	0.00	1991	**0.43**	0.07	0.36	0.11	0.14	0.07	0.03	0.02
1992	**0.15**	0.13	0.02	0.02	0.01	0.00	0.00	0.00	1992	**0.43**	0.08	0.36	0.11	0.14	0.07	0.02	0.01
1993	**0.15**	0.13	0.02	0.02	0.01	0.00	0.00	0.00	1993	**0.43**	0.08	0.35	0.11	0.14	0.07	0.02	0.01
1994	**0.15**	0.12	0.02	0.02	0.00	0.00	0.00	0.00	1994	**0.44**	0.08	0.36	0.11	0.14	0.07	0.02	0.01
1995	**0.15**	0.13	0.02	0.02	0.00	0.00	0.00	0.00	1995	**0.44**	0.09	0.35	0.11	0.14	0.06	0.02	0.01
1996	**0.15**	0.13	0.02	0.01	0.00	0.00	0.00	0.00	1996	**0.44**	0.10	0.35	0.11	0.14	0.06	0.02	0.01
1997	**0.15**	0.13	0.02	0.01	0.00	0.00	0.00	0.00	1997	**0.44**	0.10	0.34	0.11	0.14	0.06	0.02	0.01
1998	**0.15**	0.14	0.02	0.01	0.00	0.00	0.00	0.00	1998	**0.45**	0.10	0.34	0.12	0.14	0.06	0.02	0.01
1999	**0.15**	0.14	0.02	0.01	0.00	0.00	0.00	0.00	1999	**0.45**	0.11	0.34	0.12	0.14	0.05	0.02	0.01
2000	**0.15**	0.13	0.02	0.01	0.00	0.00	0.00	0.00	2000	**0.44**	0.11	0.33	0.12	0.13	0.05	0.02	0.01
	20-24								**35 and over**								
1990	**0.45**	0.19	0.27	0.14	0.09	0.03	0.01	0.00	1990	**0.18**	0.03	0.15	0.03	0.05	0.04	0.02	0.02
1991	**0.45**	0.20	0.24	0.13	0.08	0.02	0.01	0.00	1991	**0.19**	0.04	0.15	0.03	0.05	0.04	0.02	0.02
1992	**0.43**	0.20	0.23	0.12	0.08	0.02	0.01	0.00	1992	**0.20**	0.04	0.16	0.04	0.05	0.04	0.02	0.02
1993	**0.41**	0.21	0.21	0.11	0.07	0.02	0.00	0.00	1993	**0.20**	0.04	0.16	0.04	0.05	0.04	0.02	0.02
1994	**0.39**	0.20	0.19	0.10	0.07	0.02	0.00	0.00	1994	**0.21**	0.05	0.16	0.04	0.06	0.04	0.02	0.02
1995	**0.38**	0.21	0.17	0.09	0.06	0.02	0.00	0.00	1995	**0.21**	0.05	0.16	0.04	0.06	0.04	0.02	0.02
1996	**0.39**	0.22	0.17	0.09	0.06	0.02	0.00	0.00	1996	**0.22**	0.05	0.17	0.04	0.06	0.04	0.02	0.0
1997	**0.38**	0.22	0.16	0.08	0.05	0.02	0.00	0.00	1997	**0.23**	0.06	0.17	0.04	0.06	0.04	0.02	0.0
1998	**0.38**	0.22	0.15	0.08	0.05	0.02	0.00	0.00	1998	**0.24**	0.06	0.18	0.04	0.06	0.04	0.02	0.0
1999	**0.37**	0.23	0.14	0.08	0.05	0.01	0.00	0.00	1999	**0.24**	0.06	0.17	0.05	0.06	0.04	0.02	0.0
2000	**0.35**	0.22	0.13	0.07	0.05	0.01	0.00	0.00	2000	**0.24**	0.07	0.18	0.05	0.07	0.04	0.02	0.0

* See Sections 2.15 and 2.17

Table 2.1 **Live births (actual and seasonally adjusted numbers and rates):** **England and Wales**
quarter of occurrence, 1990-2000

Year	Total	Quarter ended				Total	Quarter ended			
		31 March	30 June	30 September	31 December		31 March	30 June	30 September	31 December
	Number (thousands)					**Total fertility rate (TFR)**				
	Live births					**Actual TFR**				
1990	**706.1**	168.3	179.3	184.0	174.5	**1.84**	1.76	1.87	1.92	1.82
1991	**699.2**	171.5	175.8	181.8	170.2	**1.82**	1.78	1.83	1.89	1.77
1992	**689.7**	172.7	175.6	178.1	163.3	**1.80**	1.80	1.83	1.86	1.70
1993	**673.5**	162.3	170.1	175.9	165.2	**1.76**	1.70	1.78	1.84	1.73
1994	**664.7**	164.3	170.7	168.9	160.9	**1.75**	1.72	1.79	1.78	1.69
1995	**648.1**	158.5	164.7	167.4	157.5	**1.72**	1.66	1.73	1.76	1.66
1996	**649.5**	157.3	158.1	169.9	164.2	**1.73**	1.67	1.68	1.82	1.77
1997	**643.1**	158.1	163.3	164.9	156.8	**1.73**	1.70	1.75	1.78	1.70
1998	**635.9**	155.8	158.6	166.1	155.4	**1.72**	1.68	1.71	1.81	1.70
1999	**621.9**	152.1	157.3	160.1	152.4	**1.70**	1.66	1.71	1.75	1.67
2000	**604.4**	148.7	150.7	155.0	150.1	**1.66**	1.63	1.65	1.70	1.65
	Seasonally adjusted live births*					**Seasonally adjusted TFR***				
1990		172.7	176.4	177.8	179.7		1.80	1.84	1.85	1.87
1991		176.2	173.2	175.5	175.0		1.83	1.80	1.83	1.82
1992		175.6	173.1	171.8	166.8		1.83	1.80	1.79	1.74
1993		167.1	167.6	169.9	169.1		1.74	1.75	1.78	1.77
1994		169.0	168.1	163.4	164.5		1.77	1.77	1.72	1.74
1995		163.1	162.1	162.5	160.9		1.72	1.73	1.71	1.69
1996		160.4	157.6	164.9	166.5		1.71	1.68	1.76	1.79
1997		163.3	162.4	158.7	158.6		1.75	1.74	1.71	1.72
1998		159.9	158.1	160.3	157.6		1.73	1.71	1.74	1.72
1999		156.4	156.2	154.4	154.9		1.70	1.70	1.69	1.70
2000		151.5	150.3	150.1	152.6		1.66	1.64	1.65	1.68

* See Section 3.1

Table 2.2 **Stillbirths: quarter of occurrence, 1990-2000** **England and Wales**

Year	Total	Quarter ended			
		31 March	30 June	30 September	31 December
1990	**3,256**	814	820	833	789
1991	**3,254**	844	797	831	782
1992	**2,944**	760	715	777	692
1993	**3,855**	941	944	981	989
1994	**3,813**	986	926	952	949
1995	**3,600**	958	865	904	873
1996	**3,539**	875	886	917	861
1997	**3,439**	867	870	839	863
1998	**3,417**	865	849	824	879
1999	**3,305**	867	834	818	786
2000	**3,203**	808	776	797	822

Table 2.3 Live births (actual and seasonally adjusted numbers and rates):   **England and Wales**
month of occurrence, 1990-2000

Year	Total	January	February	March	April	May	June	July	August	September	October	November	December
Numbers (thousands)													
Live births													
1990	**706.1**	56.5	52.9	58.9	57.2	61.4	60.7	62.5	61.2	60.3	59.9	57.6	57.1
1991	**699.2**	58.8	54.1	58.5	56.7	60.1	59.0	62.0	60.4	59.4	58.7	55.3	56.2
1992	**689.7**	58.3	55.6	58.8	57.6	59.4	58.6	61.0	58.8	58.3	56.4	53.3	53.5
1993	**673.5**	55.4	50.7	56.3	54.8	57.6	57.7	59.0	57.8	59.0	56.8	52.6	55.8
1994	**664.7**	55.4	51.0	57.9	55.4	58.1	57.1	57.3	55.5	56.1	55.5	52.2	53.1
1995	**648.1**	53.5	49.7	55.4	52.2	56.7	55.8	56.5	55.6	55.3	54.9	51.4	51.2
1996	**649.5**	53.5	50.4	53.4	50.5	53.8	53.7	57.6	56.0	56.4	56.2	53.8	54.2
1997	**643.1**	54.5	49.5	54.1	54.0	55.4	53.9	56.4	54.8	53.7	53.0	50.7	53.1
1998	**635.9**	53.4	48.8	53.6	52.4	53.0	53.1	56.4	54.4	55.3	53.6	50.1	51.6
1999	**621.9**	51.2	47.6	53.3	50.8	53.5	53.0	54.5	52.9	52.7	51.0	49.8	51.6
2000	**604.4**	50.5	47.0	51.1	49.0	51.8	49.9	52.6	51.9	50.4	50.9	49.8	49.5
Seasonally adjusted live births*													
1990		57.2	57.7	57.8	58.2	58.7	59.5	59.5	59.0	59.3	59.7	60.5	59.5
1991		59.2	59.0	57.9	57.6	57.4	58.1	58.6	58.5	58.4	58.3	58.1	58.6
1992		58.5	58.8	58.3	58.4	57.5	57.3	57.5	57.6	56.8	55.9	56.2	55.2
1993		56.2	55.4	55.4	55.5	55.9	56.2	56.0	56.6	57.4	56.4	55.3	57.4
1994		56.4	55.9	56.7	56.5	56.1	55.5	54.8	54.0	54.6	55.0	54.6	54.9
1995		54.4	54.6	54.1	53.5	54.3	54.2	54.4	54.1	54.1	54.1	53.6	53.2
1996		53.8	53.5	53.1	51.9	52.1	53.6	55.0	54.7	55.3	55.0	55.8	55.7
1997		54.8	54.3	54.2	54.7	54.1	53.6	53.2	53.5	52.1	52.2	52.8	53.6
1998		53.4	53.4	53.2	53.3	52.0	52.7	53.3	53.4	53.6	53.0	52.4	52.3
1999		51.7	52.1	52.5	51.6	52.4	52.3	51.6	51.5	51.3	51.0	51.8	52.0
2000		51.3	49.8	50.5	50.3	50.5	49.5	50.4	50.4	49.3	50.7	51.5	50.4
Total fertility rates (TFR)													
Actual TFR													
1990	**1.84**	1.77	1.66	1.84	1.79	1.92	1.90	1.95	1.91	1.88	1.87	1.80	1.78
1991	**1.82**	1.84	1.69	1.83	1.77	1.87	1.84	1.93	1.88	1.85	1.83	1.73	1.76
1992	**1.80**	1.82	1.74	1.84	1.80	1.86	1.83	1.91	1.84	1.82	1.77	1.67	1.68
1993	**1.76**	1.74	1.59	1.76	1.72	1.81	1.81	1.85	1.82	1.85	1.79	1.66	1.75
1994	**1.75**	1.74	1.61	1.82	1.75	1.83	1.80	1.81	1.75	1.77	1.75	1.65	1.68
1995	**1.72**	1.69	1.57	1.75	1.65	1.79	1.76	1.78	1.76	1.75	1.74	1.63	1.63
1996	**1.73**	1.71	1.61	1.70	1.61	1.72	1.72	1.84	1.80	1.81	1.81	1.73	1.75
1997	**1.73**	1.76	1.60	1.74	1.74	1.78	1.74	1.82	1.77	1.73	1.72	1.65	1.72
1998	**1.72**	1.73	1.58	1.74	1.70	1.72	1.72	1.83	1.77	1.81	1.75	1.64	1.69
1999	**1.70**	1.68	1.56	1.74	1.66	1.75	1.73	1.79	1.74	1.73	1.67	1.64	1.70
2000	**1.66**	1.66	1.54	1.68	1.61	1.70	1.64	1.73	1.71	1.67	1.68	1.64	1.64
Seasonally adjusted TFR*													
1990		1.79	1.81	1.81	1.82	1.83	1.86	1.86	1.84	1.85	1.87	1.89	1.86
1991		1.85	1.84	1.81	1.80	1.79	1.81	1.83	1.82	1.83	1.82	1.81	1.83
1992		1.83	1.84	1.82	1.82	1.80	1.79	1.80	1.80	1.78	1.75	1.76	1.73
1993		1.76	1.73	1.74	1.75	1.76	1.77	1.76	1.77	1.80	1.77	1.74	1.80
1994		1.77	1.76	1.79	1.79	1.78	1.76	1.73	1.70	1.72	1.73	1.75	1.73
1995		1.72	1.72	1.72	1.72	1.73	1.73	1.73	1.71	1.70	1.71	1.69	1.67
1996		1.72	1.71	1.69	1.66	1.66	1.72	1.76	1.75	1.78	1.77	1.80	1.80
1997		1.77	1.75	1.75	1.76	1.74	1.73	1.72	1.73	1.68	1.69	1.71	1.74
1998		1.73	1.73	1.72	1.73	1.69	1.71	1.73	1.74	1.75	1.73	1.72	1.72
1999		1.69	1.70	1.72	1.68	1.71	1.71	1.69	1.69	1.68	1.67	1.70	1.71
2000		1.69	1.63	1.65	1.65	1.66	1.63	1.66	1.66	1.63	1.67	1.70	1.67

* See Section 3.1

Table 2.4 Maternities, live births and stillbirths: quarter and month of occurrence, within/outside marriage and sex, 2000 **England and Wales**

Quarter/month of occurrence	Maternities	Live births			Stillbirths			Live births		Stillbirths	
		Total	Within marriage	Outside marriage	Total	Within marriage	Outside marriage	Male	Female	Male	Female
Annual Total	598,580	604,441	365,836	238,605	3,203	1,830	1,373	309,625	294,816	1,731	1,472
March quarter	147,259	**148,679**	89,726	58,953	**808**	479	329	75,973	72,706	439	369
June quarter	149,216	**150,700**	92,749	57,951	**776**	437	339	77,488	73,212	409	367
September quarter	153,559	**154,974**	93,303	61,671	**797**	442	355	79,372	75,602	454	343
December quarter	148,546	**150,088**	90,058	60,030	**822**	472	350	76,792	73,296	429	393
January	50,050	**50,547**	30,087	20,460	**301**	186	115	25,735	24,812	165	136
February	46,558	**47,017**	28,231	18,786	**232**	134	98	24,072	22,945	124	108
March	50,651	**51,115**	31,408	19,707	**275**	159	116	26,166	24,949	150	125
April	48,583	**49,031**	30,115	18,916	**269**	148	121	25,158	23,873	136	133
May	51,241	**51,752**	31,941	19,811	**264**	148	116	26,770	24,982	138	126
June	49,392	**49,917**	30,693	19,224	**243**	141	102	25,560	24,357	135	108
July	52,099	**52,609**	32,031	20,578	**268**	139	129	26,900	25,709	156	112
August	51,471	**51,922**	31,008	20,914	**265**	146	119	26,653	25,269	149	116
September	49,989	**50,443**	30,264	20,179	**264**	157	107	25,819	24,624	149	115
October	50,348	**50,862**	30,645	20,217	**293**	169	124	25,830	25,032	157	136
November	49,237	**49,771**	29,972	19,799	**261**	141	120	25,449	24,322	143	118
December	48,961	**49,455**	29,441	20,014	**268**	162	106	25,513	23,942	129	139

Table 2.5 Live birth occurrences* in 2000: quarter and month of occurrence and month of registration **England and Wales**

Quarter/month of occurrence in 2000	Month of registration*												Registrations from 1.1.01 to 11.2.01	Total
	January	February	March	April	May	June	July	August	September	October	November	December		
Annual Total	23,177	46,983	52,970	42,823	54,100	53,753	49,235	52,468	50,117	51,345	51,444	40,260	35,766	604,441
March	23,177	46,642	52,856	23,050	2,849	71	11	6	4	4	3	3	3	**148,679**
June	-	1	1	19,756	51,239	53,675	23,993	1,944	60	17	4	3	7	**150,700**
September	-	5	6	2	4	2	25,226	50,514	50,051	27,001	2,079	59	25	**154,974**
December	-	335	107	15	8	5	5	4	2	24,323	49,358	40,195	35,731	**150,088**
January	23,177	24,985	2,316	45	8	4	4	2	1	1	-	2	2	**50,547**
February	-	21,656	23,851	1,446	56	4	2	-	1	-	1	-	-	**47,017**
March	-	1	26,689	21,559	2,785	63	5	4	2	3	2	1	1	**51,115**
April	-	-	1	19,756	27,178	2,039	44	8	4	1	-	-	-	**49,031**
May	-	-	-	-	24,061	25,917	1,695	70	5	1	1	1	1	**51,752**
June	-	1	-	-	-	25,719	22,254	1,866	51	15	3	2	6	**49,917**
July	-	1	1	-	2	-	25,226	25,350	1,947	68	9	4	1	**52,609**
August	-	1	4	-	-	1	-	25,164	24,518	2,153	63	10	8	**51,922**
September	-	3	1	2	2	1	-	-	23,586	24,780	2,007	45	16	**50,443**
October	-	8	10	1	-	1	3	2	1	24,323	24,724	1,714	75	**50,862**
November	-	33	15	7	2	2	1	-	-	-	24,634	22,040	3,037	**49,771**
December	-	294	82	7	6	2	1	2	1	-	-	16,441	32,619	**49,455**

* Including the small number of births which occurred earlier than 2000 and were registered after the 'cut off' date in 2001 - see Section 2.2

Table 3.1 Live births: age of mother and occurrence within/outside marriage, 1990-2000
a. numbers

England and Wales

Year	Age of mother at birth							
	All ages	Under 20	20-24	25-29	30-34	35-39	40-44	45 and over
	All live births							
1990	**706,140**	55,541	180,136	252,577	156,264	51,905	9,220	497
1991	**699,217**	52,396	173,356	248,727	161,259	53,644	9,316	519
1992	**689,656**	47,861	163,311	244,798	166,839	56,650	9,696	501
1993	**673,467**	45,121	151,975	235,961	171,061	58,824	9,986	539
1994	**664,726**	42,026	140,240	229,102	179,568	63,061	10,241	488
1995	**648,138**	41,938	130,744	217,418	181,202	65,517	10,779	540
1996	**649,485**	44,667	125,732	211,103	186,377	69,503	11,516	587
1997	**643,095**	46,372	118,589	202,792	187,528	74,900	12,332	582
1998	**635,901**	48,285	113,537	193,144	188,499	78,881	12,980	575
1999	**621,872**	48,375	110,722	181,931	185,311	81,281	13,617	635
2000	**604,441**	45,846	107,741	170,701	180,113	84,974	14,403	663
	Live births within marriage							
1990	**506,141**	10,958	106,188	204,701	133,384	43,179	7,302	429
1991	**487,923**	8,948	95,605	196,281	135,542	43,810	7,294	443
1992	**474,431**	7,787	86,220	188,928	137,904	45,733	7,456	403
1993	**456,919**	6,875	76,950	178,456	139,671	46,919	7,621	427
1994	**449,190**	6,099	69,227	170,605	145,563	49,668	7,662	366
1995	**428,189**	5,623	61,029	157,855	144,200	51,129	7,944	409
1996	**416,822**	5,365	54,651	148,770	145,898	53,265	8,421	452
1997	**404,873**	5,233	49,068	139,383	145,293	56,671	8,797	428
1998	**395,290**	5,278	45,724	130,747	144,599	59,320	9,189	433
1999	**379,983**	5,333	43,190	120,716	140,330	60,470	9,466	478
2000	**365,836**	4,742	40,262	111,606	136,165	62,671	9,910	480
	Live births outside marriage							
1990	**199,999**	44,583	73,948	47,876	22,880	8,726	1,918	68
1991	**211,294**	43,448	77,751	52,446	25,717	9,834	2,022	76
1992	**215,225**	40,074	77,091	55,870	28,935	10,917	2,240	98
1993	**216,548**	38,246	75,025	57,505	31,390	11,905	2,365	112
1994	**215,536**	35,927	71,013	58,497	34,005	13,393	2,579	122
1995	**219,949**	36,315	69,715	59,563	37,002	14,388	2,835	131
1996	**232,663**	39,302	71,081	62,333	40,479	16,238	3,095	135
1997	**238,222**	41,139	69,521	63,409	42,235	18,229	3,535	154
1998	**240,611**	43,007	67,813	62,397	43,900	19,561	3,791	142
1999	**241,889**	43,042	67,532	61,215	44,981	20,811	4,151	157
2000	**238,605**	41,104	67,479	59,095	43,948	22,303	4,493	183

Table 3.1 Live births: age of mother and occurrence within/outside marriage, 1990-2000   **England and Wales**
    b. rates*

Year	Age of mother at birth							
	All ages	Under 20	20-24	25-29	30-34	35-39	40-44	45 and over
	All live births per 1,000 women							
1990	64.2	33.3	91.4	122.6	86.9	31.1	5.0	0.3
1991	63.6	33.0	89.3	119.4	86.7	32.1	5.1	0.3
1992	63.5	31.7	86.2	117.3	87.2	33.4	5.5	0.3
1993	62.6	31.0	82.7	114.1	87.0	34.1	5.9	0.3
1994	61.9	29.0	79.4	112.1	88.7	35.8	6.1	0.3
1995	60.4	28.5	76.8	108.6	87.3	36.2	6.5	0.3
1996	60.5	29.8	77.5	106.9	88.6	37.2	6.9	0.3
1997	59.8	30.2	76.6	104.8	88.8	38.9	7.3	0.3
1998	59.0	30.9	75.5	102.2	89.9	39.8	7.5	0.3
1999	57.6	30.8	73.7	99.2	89.2	39.8	7.7	0.4
2000	55.7	29.2	70.6	95.4	88.0	40.5	7.9	0.4
	Live births within marriage per 1,000 married women†							
1990	86.7	277.0	197.3	175.3	101.8	33.2	4.9	0.4
1991	84.6	277.1	195.3	169.5	101.9	34.0	5.0	0.4
1992	85.1	327.2	198.7	169.8	103.2	35.5	5.4	0.3
1993	84.4	381.5	201.7	168.0	104.4	36.3	5.8	0.3
1994	85.0	424.5	210.0	168.7	108.6	38.2	6.0	0.3
1995	83.3	444.0	216.6	166.6	108.2	39.0	6.3	0.3
1996	82.9	445.2	229.2	167.7	110.8	40.1	6.7	0.3
1997	82.4	456.3	240.7	170.3	112.9	42.2	7.0	0.3
1998	82.3	462.8	253.8	174.3	115.9	43.8	7.3	0.3
1999	80.8	500.8	261.8	176.0	116.5	44.3	7.5	0.4
2000	79.3	517.3	261.3	176.6	117.6	45.8	7.7	0.4
	Live births outside marriage per 1,000 single, widowed and divorced women†							
1990	38.9	27.4	51.9	53.5	47.7	24.1	5.4	0.2
1991	40.5	28.0	53.6	56.7	48.6	25.7	5.4	0.2
1992	40.8	27.0	52.8	57.3	50.1	26.9	5.9	0.3
1993	40.5	26.6	51.5	57.1	49.9	27.5	6.1	0.3
1994	39.5	25.0	49.4	56.7	49.6	28.9	6.5	0.3
1995	39.4	24.9	49.0	56.5	49.9	28.8	6.9	0.3
1996	40.7	26.4	51.4	57.3	51.5	30.0	7.2	0.3
1997	40.8	27.0	51.7	56.8	51.2	31.2	7.9	0.4
1998	40.3	27.7	51.2	54.8	51.6	31.2	8.0	0.3
1999	39.7	27.6	50.5	53.3	51.5	30.7	8.3	0.4
2000	38.2	26.4	49.2	51.1	49.4	30.6	8.4	0.4

* The rates for women of all ages, under 20 and 45 and over are based upon the population of women aged 15-44, 15-19 and 45-49 respectively
† See Section 2.1

**Table 3.2 Maternities (total), live births and stillbirths (total and female):
age of mother and occurrence within/outside marriage, 2000**

Age of mother at birth	Maternities			Births			
	Total	Within marriage	Outside marriage	Live		Still	
				Total	Female	Total	Female
All ages	**598,580**	**361,469**	**237,111**	**604,441**	**294,816**	**3,203**	**1,472**
11	**8**	-	8	8	1	-	-
12	**5**	-	5	5	1	-	-
13	**37**	1	36	37	22	-	-
14	**245**	2	243	246	109	-	-
15	**1,187**	5	1,182	1,186	572	6	4
16	**3,840**	89	3,751	3,825	1,855	33	9
17	**8,908**	442	8,466	8,906	4,254	53	20
18	**13,724**	1,305	12,419	13,726	6,689	83	40
19	**17,873**	2,892	14,981	17,907	8,842	108	49
Under 20	**45,827**	**4,736**	**41,091**	**45,846**	**22,345**	**283**	**122**
20	**20,153**	4,704	15,449	20,197	9,749	116	52
21	**20,616**	6,324	14,292	20,689	10,145	104	48
22	**20,573**	7,644	12,929	20,616	10,084	130	65
23	**21,715**	9,441	12,274	21,815	10,617	101	43
24	**24,279**	12,011	12,268	24,424	11,894	119	59
20-24	**107,336**	**40,124**	**67,212**	**107,741**	**52,489**	**570**	**267**
25	**27,246**	15,071	12,175	27,401	13,342	151	70
26	**30,294**	18,447	11,847	30,484	14,750	148	70
27	**33,604**	21,974	11,630	33,884	16,505	157	74
28	**37,669**	25,982	11,687	37,968	18,550	197	97
29	**40,506**	29,163	11,343	40,964	20,085	190	85
25-29	**169,319**	**110,637**	**58,682**	**170,701**	**83,232**	**843**	**396**
30	**39,734**	29,441	10,293	40,216	19,675	187	88
31	**38,997**	29,423	9,574	39,475	19,213	189	89
32	**36,498**	27,727	8,771	37,019	18,016	193	83
33	**32,943**	25,262	7,681	33,450	16,401	166	78
34	**29,463**	22,313	7,150	29,953	14,619	152	69
30-34	**177,635**	**134,166**	**43,469**	**180,113**	**87,924**	**887**	**407**
35	**25,517**	19,102	6,415	25,951	12,584	148	68
36	**21,036**	15,536	5,500	21,424	10,448	116	44
37	**16,189**	11,806	4,383	16,482	8,017	94	44
38	**12,007**	8,747	3,260	12,157	5,991	84	40
39	**8,822**	6,367	2,455	8,960	4,430	59	27
35-39	**83,571**	**61,558**	**22,013**	**84,974**	**41,470**	**501**	**223**
40	**5,945**	4,160	1,785	6,024	2,945	37	18
41	**3,926**	2,651	1,275	3,967	1,930	32	19
42	**2,367**	1,630	737	2,383	1,170	24	9
43	**1,333**	898	435	1,347	666	15	7
44	**677**	449	228	682	322	5	-
40-44	**14,248**	**9,788**	**4,460**	**14,403**	**7,033**	**113**	**53**
45	**333**	232	101	343	176	-	-
46	**153**	111	42	156	75	1	-
47	**59**	39	20	61	31	1	1
48	**33**	21	12	36	15	-	-
49	**23**	18	5	23	11	1	1
45-49	**601**	**421**	**180**	**619**	**308**	**3**	**2**
50 and over	**43**	39	4	44	15	3	2

England and Wales

| Births within marriage | | | | Births outside marriage | | | | Age of mother at birth |
| Live | | Still | | Live | | Still | | |
Total	Female	Total	Female	Total	Female	Total	Female	
365,836	178,469	1,830	851	238,605	116,347	1,373	621	All ages
-	-	-	-	8	1	-	-	11
-	-	-	-	5	1	-	-	12
1	1	-	-	36	21	-	-	13
2	1	-	-	244	108	-	-	14
5	1	-	-	1,181	571	6	4	15
89	48	-	-	3,736	1,807	33	9	16
443	211	3	-	8,463	4,043	50	20	17
1,306	621	8	3	12,420	6,068	75	37	18
2,896	1,433	18	7	15,011	7,409	90	42	19
4,742	2,316	29	10	41,104	20,029	254	112	Under 20
4,708	2,333	33	12	15,489	7,416	83	40	20
6,351	3,140	29	15	14,338	7,005	75	33	21
7,646	3,773	56	28	12,970	6,311	74	37	22
9,477	4,606	42	20	12,338	6,011	59	23	23
12,080	5,846	56	30	12,344	6,048	63	29	24
40,262	19,698	216	105	67,479	32,791	354	162	20-24
15,156	7,377	79	35	12,245	5,965	72	35	25
18,579	8,999	79	35	11,905	5,751	69	35	26
22,166	10,830	101	46	11,718	5,675	56	28	27
26,199	12,807	133	66	11,769	5,743	64	31	28
29,506	14,406	122	58	11,458	5,679	68	27	29
111,606	54,419	514	240	59,095	28,813	329	156	25-29
29,805	14,588	133	67	10,411	5,087	54	21	30
29,811	14,557	139	64	9,664	4,656	50	25	31
28,154	13,670	140	61	8,865	4,346	53	22	32
25,675	12,542	116	52	7,775	3,859	50	26	33
22,720	11,047	110	52	7,233	3,572	42	17	34
136,165	66,404	638	296	43,948	21,520	249	111	30-34
19,460	9,408	110	51	6,491	3,176	38	17	35
15,853	7,768	74	29	5,571	2,680	42	15	36
12,022	5,831	68	30	4,460	2,186	26	14	37
8,863	4,360	57	29	3,294	1,631	27	11	38
6,473	3,170	44	21	2,487	1,260	15	6	39
62,671	30,537	353	160	22,303	10,933	148	63	35-39
4,212	2,081	26	12	1,812	864	11	6	40
2,689	1,315	22	14	1,278	615	10	5	41
1,643	811	16	7	740	359	8	2	42
910	439	10	4	437	227	5	3	43
456	217	2	-	226	105	3	-	44
9,910	4,863	76	37	4,493	2,170	37	16	40-44
241	121	-	-	102	55	-	-	45
115	54	-	-	41	21	1	-	46
41	24	1	1	20	7	-	-	47
24	9	-	-	12	6	-	-	48
18	9	1	1	5	2	-	-	49
439	217	2	2	180	91	1	-	45-49
41	15	2	1	3	-	1	1	50 and over

Table 3.3 Live births within marriage (numbers and rates): age of father, 1990-2000   England and Wale

Year	Age of father at birth											
	All ages	Under 20	20-24	25-29	30-34	35-39	40-44	45-49	50-54	55-59	60-64	65 and ove
	Numbers											
1990	**506,141**	2,549	55,251	171,895	161,251	74,916	27,586	7,942	3,015	1,138	420	178
1991	**487,923**	1,975	48,647	161,668	160,871	74,835	27,466	7,833	2,906	1,117	435	170
1992	**474,431**	1,622	42,960	152,158	161,450	76,398	26,980	8,589	2,587	1,071	435	181
1993	**456,919**	1,363	37,948	140,674	159,845	77,470	26,673	8,584	2,645	1,071	420	226
1994	**449,190**	1,156	33,372	132,213	161,509	80,723	27,362	8,721	2,540	1,047	376	171
1995	**428,189**	1,015	28,873	120,070	157,518	80,946	26,934	8,826	2,475	1,008	364	160
1996	**416,822**	867	25,013	112,012	155,022	83,279	27,819	8,775	2,584	933	347	171
1997	**404,873**	940	21,895	103,320	151,162	86,097	28,579	8,684	2,794	894	350	158
1998	**395,290**	964	19,755	96,415	148,267	87,684	29,345	8,701	2,807	820	368	164
1999	**379,837**	1,028	18,703	87,896	141,629	88,329	29,986	8,328	2,756	878	304	146
2000	**365,836**	907	16,762	79,351	135,810	89,607	30,782	8,446	2,861	843	330	137
	Rates: live births within marriage per 1,000 married men by age*											
1990	**43.1**	335.4	205.6	197.1	137.0	60.5	19.2	6.6	2.7	1.1	0.4	0.1
1991	**41.5**	245.6	195.3	180.9	133.4	61.0	19.2	6.3	2.6	1.1	0.4	0.1
1992	**40.7**	297.6	200.5	178.5	134.3	62.4	20.2	6.4	2.4	1.0	0.4	0.1
1993	**39.5**	342.5	208.1	174.2	133.9	63.4	20.9	6.2	2.4	1.0	0.4	0.1
1994	**39.1**	396.2	219.3	175.2	136.1	66.1	22.0	6.3	2.2	1.0	0.4	0.1
1995	**37.5**	402.9	227.8	172.4	133.9	65.7	22.2	6.3	2.1	0.9	0.4	0.1
1996	**36.8**	380.8	238.8	175.4	134.2	66.7	23.2	6.4	2.2	0.9	0.4	0.1
1997	**36.0**	425.1	250.5	179.0	134.4	68.6	23.8	6.7	2.2	0.9	0.4	0.1
1998	**35.3**	443.8	260.3	185.4	136.7	69.6	24.3	7.0	2.1	0.8	0.4	0.1
1999	**34.1**	489.8	273.6	187.4	136.0	69.6	24.7	6.9	2.1	0.8	0.3	0.1
2000	**33.0**	465.1	267.0	186.2	136.8	70.5	25.0	7.1	2.1	0.8	0.3	0.1

* See Section 2.1

Table 3.4 Paternities (total), live births and stillbirths (total and male): age of father and occurrence within/outside marriage, 2000 **England and Wales**

Age of father at birth	Paternities within marriage	Births within marriage				Births outside marriage registered* on joint information of parents			
		Live		Still		Live		Still	
		Total	Male	Total	Male	Total	Male	Total	Male
All ages	361,469	365,836	187,367	1,830	979	192,832	98,997	1,080	595
13	-	-	-	-	-	1	1	-	-
14	-	-	-	-	-	28	18	-	-
15	-	-	-	-	-	158	79	-	-
16	11	11	5	-	-	641	331	4	2
17	53	53	28	-	-	1,538	810	15	7
18	205	205	101	3	2	3,076	1,628	27	16
19	639	638	309	8	4	5,268	2,734	23	13
Under 20	908	907	443	11	6	10,710	5,601	69	38
20	1,297	1,296	644	13	7	6,933	3,605	37	25
21	2,153	2,156	1,069	14	9	7,815	4,051	54	32
22	3,039	3,052	1,560	14	6	8,081	4,086	60	35
23	4,236	4,240	2,119	22	13	8,214	4,293	43	21
24	6,007	6,018	3,124	34	16	8,979	4,614	48	24
20-24	16,732	16,762	8,516	97	51	40,022	20,649	242	137
25	8,332	8,375	4,205	43	22	9,654	4,860	58	30
26	11,592	11,670	5,950	52	30	10,014	5,264	53	26
27	15,309	15,412	7,906	74	44	10,586	5,482	47	24
28	19,673	19,774	10,145	112	59	11,038	5,619	53	27
29	23,847	24,120	12,420	106	59	11,007	5,688	73	40
25-29	78,753	79,351	40,626	387	214	52,299	26,913	284	147
30	25,763	25,972	13,307	132	71	10,589	5,439	51	24
31	27,935	28,229	14,425	125	61	10,213	5,225	48	28
32	27,837	28,204	14,622	122	64	9,303	4,814	48	26
33	27,264	27,644	14,218	144	78	8,724	4,357	41	21
34	25,389	25,761	13,098	108	53	7,959	4,057	39	24
30-34	134,188	135,810	69,670	631	327	46,788	23,892	227	123
35	23,707	24,093	12,435	100	56	7,219	3,689	36	17
36	20,757	21,076	10,793	116	63	6,239	3,189	38	22
37	17,433	17,704	9,041	82	49	5,342	2,663	31	20
38	14,487	14,731	7,574	68	42	4,497	2,309	36	20
39	11,790	12,003	6,161	56	27	3,891	1,950	20	14
35-39	88,174	89,607	46,004	422	237	27,188	13,800	161	93
40	9,432	9,552	4,877	51	27	3,018	1,554	19	11
41	7,416	7,546	3,881	43	23	2,493	1,264	14	8
42	5,809	5,888	3,032	40	11	1,935	1,004	11	9
43	4,399	4,461	2,207	28	15	1,585	795	12	5
44	3,283	3,335	1,740	24	12	1,240	635	9	7
40-44	30,339	30,782	15,737	186	88	10,271	5,252	65	40
45	2,590	2,648	1,379	18	10	1,014	529	6	1
46	2,018	2,062	1,028	19	12	854	442	4	2
47	1,573	1,608	850	8	5	694	353	6	4
48	1,150	1,176	574	7	4	602	317	4	3
49	941	952	487	10	6	482	263	2	2
45-49	8,272	8,446	4,318	62	37	3,646	1,904	22	12
50-54	2,817	2,861	1,421	24	13	1,332	685	7	3
55-59	820	843	415	2	1	407	206	2	1
60-64	332	330	147	7	5	139	79	-	-
65-69	101	103	54	1	-	30	16	1	1
70-74	29	30	14	-	-	-	-	-	-
75 and over	4	4	2	-	-	-	-	-	-

* 45,773 live births and 293 stillbirths which occurred outside marriage and were registered without any information on the child's father are excluded from this table

Table 3.5 Rates of paternities within marriage by age of father, and rates of   England and Wales
            live births and stillbirths within marriage by age of father, 2000

Age of father at birth	Paternities within marriage per 1,000 married men*	Births within marriage per 1,000 married men*			
		Live		Still	
		Total	Male	Total	Male
All ages	**32.6**	**33.0**	**16.92**	**0.17**	**0.09**
Under 20	465.6	465.1	227.18	*5.64*	*3.08*
20-24	266.5	267.0	135.66	1.55	0.81
25-29	184.8	186.2	95.34	0.91	0.50
30-34	135.2	136.8	70.18	0.64	0.33
35-39	69.4	70.5	36.21	0.33	0.19
40-44	24.6	25.0	12.77	0.15	0.07
45-49	7.0	7.1	3.65	0.05	0.03
50-54	2.1	2.1	1.06	0.02	*0.01*
55-59	0.7	0.8	0.38	*0.00*	*0.00*
60-64	0.3	0.3	0.15	*0.01*	*0.01*
65 and over	0.1	0.1	0.03	*0.00*	-

* See Section 2.1
Note: For information on the use of italics - see Section 2.21.

Table 3.6 Live births within marriage: age of mother   England and Wales
            and of father, 2000

Age of father at birth	Age of mother at birth								
	All ages	Under 20	20-24	25-29	30-34	35-39	40-44	45-49	50 and over
All ages	**365,836**	**4,742**	**40,262**	**111,606**	**136,165**	**62,671**	**9,910**	**439**	**41**
Under 20	**907**	482	342	55	21	6	1	-	-
20-24	**16,762**	2,207	10,319	3,242	800	177	17	-	1
25-29	**79,351**	1,447	18,471	43,935	13,202	2,077	207	11	1
30-34	**135,810**	427	7,998	46,157	67,693	12,542	961	29	3
35-39	**89,607**	123	2,219	13,805	41,236	29,726	2,435	56	7
40-44	**30,782**	36	621	3,164	9,807	13,228	3,828	93	5
45-49	**8,446**	15	176	774	2,269	3,386	1,661	158	7
50-54	**2,861**	3	79	311	758	1,105	535	57	13
55-59	**843**	1	23	111	228	293	169	16	2
60-64	**330**	1	11	38	107	94	67	10	2
65 and over	**137**	-	3	14	44	37	29	9	1

Table 3.7 Stillbirths within marriage: age of mother   England and Wale
            and of father, 2000

Age of father at birth	Age of mother at birth								
	All ages	Under 20	20-24	25-29	30-34	35-39	40-44	45-49	50 and over
All ages	**1,830**	**29**	**216**	**514**	**638**	**353**	**76**	**2**	**2**
Under 20	**11**	4	1	2	2	2	-	-	-
20-24	**97**	8	62	18	8	1	-	-	-
25-29	**387**	12	83	200	70	22	-	-	-
30-34	**631**	3	54	202	308	60	4	-	-
35-39	**422**	2	11	64	174	152	19	-	-
40-44	**186**	-	2	19	59	77	29	-	-
45-49	**62**	-	2	4	11	30	12	1	2
50-54	**24**	-	1	5	3	6	8	1	-
55-59	**2**	-	-	-	1	1	-	-	-
60-64	**7**	-	-	-	2	2	3	-	-
65 and over	**1**	-	-	-	-	-	1	-	-

Table 3.8   Live births outside marriage: age of mother and of father and whether sole or joint registration, 2000

England and Wales

Age of father at birth	Age of mother at birth							
	All ages	Under 20	20-24	25-29	30-34	35-39	40-44	45 and over
	Total live births outside marriage							
	238,605	41,104	67,479	59,095	43,948	22,303	4,493	183
	Solely registered							
	45,773	12,459	13,919	9,213	6,116	3,309	732	25
	Jointly registered							
All ages	**192,832**	**28,645**	**53,560**	**49,882**	**37,832**	**18,994**	**3,761**	**158**
Under 20	**10,710**	8,129	2,030	392	119	33	7	-
20-24	**40,022**	13,490	19,773	4,887	1,445	367	59	1
25-29	**52,299**	4,563	19,514	19,423	6,843	1,746	203	7
30-34	**46,788**	1,656	8,268	16,209	15,141	4,874	621	19
35-39	**27,188**	565	2,794	6,284	9,641	6,831	1,037	36
40-44	**10,271**	168	831	1,799	3,193	3,246	1,000	34
45-49	**3,646**	52	245	601	970	1,226	517	35
50-54	**1,332**	17	69	198	336	474	220	18
55-59	**407**	3	24	65	114	130	65	6
60 and over	**169**	2	12	24	30	67	32	2

Note: Figures for jointly registered live births outside marriage include a small number of cases registered by the mother alone, for which the father's name was included in the birth register.

Table 3.9   Live births outside marriage (numbers and percentages):   **England and Wales**
             age of mother and whether sole or joint registration, 1990-2000

Year		Age of mother at birth											
		All ages	Under 20	20-24	25-29	30-34	35 and over	All ages	Under 20	20-24	25-29	30-34	35 and over
		Number (thousands)						Percentage by age					
1990	Total	200.0	44.6	73.9	47.9	22.9	10.7						
	Sole	54.8	16.2	20.1	11.1	5.0	2.4	27.4	36.3	27.2	23.3	21.9	22.0
	Joint	145.2	28.4	53.8	36.7	17.9	8.4	72.6	63.7	72.8	76.7	78.1	78.0
1991	Total	211.3	43.4	77.8	52.4	25.7	11.9						
	Sole	54.1	15.2	19.7	11.4	5.4	2.4	25.6	35.0	25.3	21.7	21.0	20.3
	Joint	157.2	28.2	58.1	41.1	20.3	9.5	74.4	65.0	74.7	78.3	79.0	79.7
1992	Total	215.2	40.1	77.1	55.9	28.9	13.3						
	Sole	51.5	13.5	18.4	11.4	5.6	2.6	23.9	33.6	23.8	20.4	19.5	19.5
	Joint	163.8	26.6	58.7	44.4	23.3	10.7	76.1	66.4	76.2	79.6	80.5	80.5
1993	Total	216.5	38.2	75.0	57.5	31.4	14.4						
	Sole	50.2	12.5	17.5	11.4	6.0	2.8	23.2	32.8	23.3	19.9	19.0	19.8
	Joint	166.3	25.7	57.5	46.1	25.4	11.5	76.8	67.2	76.7	80.1	81.0	80.2
1994	Total	215.5	35.9	71.0	58.5	34.0	16.1						
	Sole	49.0	12.0	16.4	11.4	6.2	3.0	22.7	33.4	23.1	19.5	18.2	18.8
	Joint	166.5	23.9	54.6	47.1	27.8	13.1	77.3	66.6	76.9	80.5	81.8	81.2
1995	Total	219.9	36.3	69.7	59.6	37.0	17.4						
	Sole	47.9	11.9	15.6	10.9	6.5	3.1	21.8	32.7	22.4	18.2	17.5	17.6
	Joint	172.0	24.4	54.1	48.7	30.5	14.3	78.2	67.3	77.6	81.8	82.5	82.4
1996	Total	232.7	39.3	71.1	62.3	40.5	19.5						
	Sole	51.0	12.9	16.2	11.4	7.0	3.5	21.9	32.9	22.9	18.2	17.2	18.0
	Joint	181.6	26.4	54.8	51.0	33.5	16.0	78.1	67.1	77.1	81.8	82.8	82.0
1997	Total	238.2	41.1	69.5	63.4	42.2	21.9						
	Sole	50.6	13.2	15.6	11.0	7.0	3.8	21.2	32.1	22.4	17.4	16.6	17.1
	Joint	187.6	27.9	53.9	52.4	35.2	18.2	78.8	67.9	77.6	82.6	83.4	82.9
1998	Total	240.6	43.0	67.8	62.4	43.9	23.5						
	Sole	50.0	13.8	14.8	10.7	6.8	3.9	20.8	32.2	21.9	17.1	15.4	16.4
	Joint	190.7	29.2	53.0	51.7	37.1	19.6	79.2	67.8	78.1	82.9	84.6	83.6
1999	Total	241.9	43.0	67.5	61.2	45.0	25.1						
	Sole	48.2	13.2	14.5	9.9	6.6	4.0	19.9	30.7	21.4	16.2	14.7	15.8
	Joint	193.7	29.8	53.1	51.3	38.4	21.1	80.1	69.3	78.6	83.8	85.3	84.2
2000	Total	238.6	41.1	67.5	59.1	43.9	27.0						
	Sole	45.8	12.5	13.9	9.2	6.1	4.1	19.2	30.3	20.6	15.6	13.9	15.1
	Joint	192.8	28.6	53.6	49.9	37.8	22.9	80.8	69.7	79.4	84.4	86.1	84.9

Note: Figures for jointly registered live births outside marriage include a small number of cases registered by the mother alone, for which the father's name was included in the birth register.

Table 3.10 Jointly registered live births outside marriage (numbers and percentages): age of mother and whether parents were usually resident at the same or different addresses, 1990-2000

England and Wales

Year	Addresses of mother and father	Age of mother at birth										
		All ages	Under 20	20-24	25-29	30-34	35 and over	All ages	Under 20	20-24	25-29	30-34	35 and over
		Numbers of jointly registered births outside marriage						Percentage by age					
1990	Total	145,168	28,392	53,813	36,736	17,874	8,353						
	Same	106,001	16,311	39,062	29,181	14,585	6,862	73.0	57.4	72.6	79.4	81.6	82.2
	Different	39,167	12,081	14,751	7,555	3,289	1,491	27.0	42.6	27.4	20.6	18.4	17.8
1991	Total	157,163	28,199	58,080	41,050	20,319	9,515						
	Same	115,298	16,351	42,245	32,532	16,468	7,702	73.4	58.0	72.7	79.2	81.0	80.9
	Different	41,865	11,848	15,835	8,518	3,851	1,813	26.6	42.0	27.3	20.8	19.0	19.1
1992	Total	163,753	26,617	58,721	44,449	23,293	10,673						
	Same	119,239	15,236	42,063	34,756	18,673	8,511	72.8	57.2	71.6	78.2	80.2	79.7
	Different	44,514	11,381	16,658	9,693	4,620	2,162	27.2	42.8	28.4	21.8	19.8	20.3
1993	Total	166,306	25,711	57,549	46,087	25,423	11,536						
	Same	118,758	14,134	40,168	35,307	20,084	9,065	71.4	55.0	69.8	76.6	79.0	78.6
	Different	47,548	11,577	17,381	10,780	5,339	2,471	28.6	45.0	30.2	23.4	21.0	21.4
1994	Total	166,506	23,920	54,605	47,107	27,801	13,073						
	Same	123,874	14,168	39,827	37,168	22,288	10,423	74.4	59.2	72.9	78.9	80.2	79.7
	Different	42,632	9,752	14,778	9,939	5,513	2,650	25.6	40.8	27.1	21.1	19.8	20.3
1995	Total	172,033	24,435	54,089	48,699	30,517	14,293						
	Same	127,789	14,424	39,274	38,376	24,376	11,339	74.3	59.0	72.6	78.8	79.9	79.3
	Different	44,244	10,011	14,815	10,323	6,141	2,954	25.7	41.0	27.4	21.2	20.1	20.7
1996	Total	181,647	26,356	54,836	50,983	33,501	15,971						
	Same	135,282	15,410	39,978	40,384	26,875	12,635	74.5	58.5	72.9	79.2	80.2	79.1
	Different	46,365	10,946	14,858	10,599	6,626	3,336	25.5	41.5	27.1	20.8	19.8	20.9
1997	Total	187,640	27,916	53,931	52,394	35,238	18,161						
	Same	141,740	16,551	39,784	42,020	28,715	14,670	75.5	59.3	73.8	80.2	81.5	80.8
	Different	45,900	11,365	14,147	10,374	6,523	3,491	24.5	40.7	26.2	19.8	18.5	19.2
1998	Total	190,651	29,177	52,975	51,725	37,132	19,642						
	Same	146,521	17,589	39,818	42,212	30,938	15,964	76.9	60.3	75.2	81.6	83.3	81.3
	Different	44,130	11,588	13,157	9,513	6,194	3,678	23.1	39.7	24.8	18.4	16.7	18.7
1999	Total	193,686	29,848	53,055	51,279	38,366	21,138						
	Same	149,584	17,833	40,190	42,126	32,152	17,283	77.2	59.7	75.8	82.2	83.8	81.8
	Different	44,102	12,015	12,865	9,153	6,214	3,855	22.8	40.3	24.2	17.8	16.2	18.2
2000	Total	192,832	28,645	53,560	49,882	37,832	22,913						
	Same	149,510	17,011	40,450	41,236	31,795	19,018	77.5	59.4	75.5	82.7	84.0	83.0
	Different	43,322	11,634	13,110	8,646	6,037	3,895	22.5	40.6	24.5	17.3	16.0	17.0

Note: Figures for jointly registered live births outside marriage include a small number of cases registered by the mother alone, for which the father's name was included in the birth register.

Table 4.1 Live births within marriage: number of previous liveborn children and age of mother (five-year age-groups), 1990-2000
a. all married women

England and Wales

All ages of mother at birth

Year	Total	0	1	2	3	4 or more
1990	506,141	200,394	185,334	79,040	25,984	15,389
1991	487,923	193,665	178,317	76,146	25,082	14,713
1992	474,431	187,342	173,981	74,241	24,528	14,339
1993	456,919	178,141	169,445	71,789	23,781	13,763
1994	449,190	176,046	166,343	69,735	23,582	13,484
1995	428,189	168,118	158,102	66,692	22,320	12,957
1996	416,822	163,020	153,780	65,291	22,038	12,693
1997	404,873	157,049	150,404	63,220	21,515	12,685
1998	395,290	155,708	146,850	60,391	20,327	12,014
1999	379,983	153,423	139,490	56,375	19,517	11,178
2000	365,836	146,509	134,691	54,920	18,590	11,126

Under 20

Year	Total	0	1	2	3	4 or more
1990	10,958	8,334	2,409	205	9	1
1991	8,948	6,726	2,048	164	7	3
1992	7,787	5,956	1,673	144	11	3
1993	6,875	5,196	1,523	142	12	2
1994	6,099	4,687	1,268	132	9	3
1995	5,623	4,308	1,187	116	10	2
1996	5,365	4,223	1,034	102	5	1
1997	5,233	4,121	1,018	84	9	1
1998	5,278	4,188	1,001	85	4	-
1999	5,333	4,290	930	99	13	1
2000	4,742	3,810	842	81	7	2

20-24

Year	Total	0	1	2	3	4 or more
1990	106,188	56,995	36,532	10,144	2,118	399
1991	95,605	51,157	32,782	9,358	1,957	351
1992	86,220	45,900	29,589	8,604	1,794	333
1993	76,950	40,399	26,827	7,915	1,516	293
1994	69,227	36,421	23,926	7,115	1,484	281
1995	61,029	32,340	20,634	6,453	1,367	235
1996	54,651	28,925	18,481	5,789	1,231	225
1997	49,068	25,891	16,558	5,257	1,153	209
1998	45,724	24,303	15,537	4,679	993	212
1999	43,190	23,474	14,443	4,175	910	188
2000	40,262	21,571	13,744	3,950	827	170

25-29

Year	Total	0	1	2	3	4 or more
1990	204,701	86,432	77,678	28,684	8,431	3,476
1991	196,281	84,524	73,861	26,835	7,886	3,175
1992	188,928	81,727	70,733	25,744	7,773	2,951
1993	178,456	77,612	66,682	24,023	7,356	2,783
1994	170,605	75,660	62,721	22,550	6,854	2,820
1995	157,855	71,036	57,282	20,513	6,472	2,552
1996	148,770	67,178	53,445	19,576	6,153	2,418
1997	139,383	63,139	50,024	18,108	5,793	2,319
1998	130,747	60,602	46,404	16,375	5,198	2,168
1999	120,716	57,385	41,763	14,735	4,907	1,926
2000	111,606	52,673	38,376	14,129	4,594	1,834

30-34

Year	Total	0	1	2	3	4 or more
1990	133,384	38,277	52,462	27,616	9,422	5,607
1991	135,542	40,227	52,989	27,493	9,302	5,531
1992	137,904	41,840	54,492	27,240	9,029	5,303
1993	139,671	42,665	55,939	26,948	9,002	5,117
1994	145,563	46,110	58,615	26,779	8,989	5,070
1995	144,200	46,573	58,458	26,098	8,335	4,736
1996	145,898	47,742	59,084	25,968	8,426	4,678
1997	145,293	48,090	59,414	25,112	8,116	4,561
1998	144,599	49,529	58,944	23,998	7,740	4,388
1999	140,330	50,031	56,622	22,314	7,293	4,070
2000	136,165	49,400	54,760	21,120	6,832	4,053

35 and over

Year	Total	0	1	2	3	4 or more
1990	50,910	10,356	16,253	12,391	6,004	5,906
1991	51,547	11,031	16,637	12,296	5,930	5,653
1992	53,592	11,919	17,494	12,509	5,921	5,749
1993	54,967	12,269	18,474	12,761	5,895	5,568
1994	57,696	13,168	19,813	13,159	6,246	5,310
1995	59,482	13,861	20,541	13,512	6,136	5,432
1996	62,138	14,952	21,736	13,856	6,223	5,371
1997	65,896	15,808	23,390	14,659	6,444	5,595
1998	68,942	17,086	24,964	15,254	6,392	5,246
1999	70,414	18,243	25,732	15,052	6,394	4,993
2000	73,061	19,055	26,969	15,640	6,330	5,067

* See Section 2.15.

Table 4.1 Live births within marriage: number of previous liveborn children and age of mother (five-year age-groups), 1990-2000 **England and Wales**
  b. women married once only

Year	Number of previous liveborn children*						Year	Number of previous liveborn children*					
	Total	0	1	2	3	4 or more		**Total**	0	1	2	3	4 or more
	All ages of mother at birth							**25-29**					
1990	**464,830**	189,322	171,848	69,562	21,368	12,730	1990	**192,837**	82,564	73,765	26,179	7,349	2,980
1991	**448,507**	182,931	165,499	67,128	20,857	12,092	1991	**185,504**	80,931	70,200	24,598	6,999	2,776
1992	**436,331**	176,962	161,626	65,632	20,364	11,747	1992	**178,995**	78,518	67,377	23,683	6,867	2,550
1993	**421,059**	168,624	157,843	63,587	19,759	11,246	1993	**169,746**	74,896	63,733	22,159	6,528	2,430
1994	**413,994**	166,466	154,855	61,954	19,696	11,023	1994	**162,526**	73,011	60,001	20,925	6,137	2,452
1995	**394,904**	158,963	147,266	59,295	18,705	10,675	1995	**150,644**	68,634	54,897	19,020	5,814	2,279
1996	**384,240**	153,994	143,223	58,094	18,546	10,383	1996	**142,375**	65,075	51,296	18,258	5,592	2,154
1997	**373,428**	148,419	140,155	56,425	18,023	10,406	1997	**133,555**	61,201	48,104	16,953	5,223	2,074
1998	**365,105**	147,207	136,867	53,797	17,292	9,942	1998	**125,642**	58,883	44,644	15,357	4,790	1,968
1999	**352,494**	145,500	130,434	50,644	16,645	9,271	1999	**116,462**	55,900	40,375	13,890	4,525	1,772
2000	**340,054**	139,210	126,117	49,451	15,999	9,277	2000	**107,887**	51,426	37,148	13,379	4,274	1,660
	Under 20							**30-34**					
1990	**10,935**	8,323	2,400	202	9	1	1990	**117,147**	33,930	46,962	23,927	7,689	4,639
1991	**8,935**	6,723	2,039	164	7	2	1991	**119,751**	35,901	47,738	23,925	7,646	4,541
1992	**7,776**	5,950	1,671	142	11	2	1992	**122,517**	37,574	49,349	23,784	7,441	4,369
1993	**6,867**	5,194	1,521	141	10	1	1993	**124,850**	38,626	51,012	23,624	7,398	4,190
1994	**6,092**	4,682	1,266	132	9	3	1994	**130,643**	41,841	53,612	23,590	7,460	4,140
1995	**5,609**	4,300	1,183	114	10	2	1995	**130,170**	42,557	53,710	23,095	6,923	3,885
1996	**5,355**	4,218	1,031	100	5	1	1996	**131,973**	43,639	54,427	23,009	7,039	3,859
1997	**5,226**	4,116	1,016	84	9	1	1997	**132,225**	44,292	54,982	22,343	6,803	3,805
1998	**5,273**	4,186	999	85	3	-	1998	**132,210**	45,773	54,755	21,354	6,634	3,694
1999	**5,329**	4,287	929	99	13	1	1999	**129,006**	46,439	52,704	20,112	6,286	3,465
2000	**4,737**	3,806	841	81	7	2	2000	**125,811**	46,204	51,177	18,990	5,960	3,480
	20-24							**35 and over**					
1990	**104,294**	56,358	35,810	9,762	1,990	374	1990	**39,617**	8,147	12,911	9,492	4,331	4,736
1991	**93,984**	50,601	32,194	9,016	1,849	324	1991	**40,333**	8,775	13,328	9,425	4,356	4,449
1992	**84,849**	45,398	29,098	8,342	1,703	308	1992	**42,194**	9,522	14,131	9,681	4,342	4,518
1993	**75,750**	39,994	26,409	7,644	1,442	261	1993	**43,846**	9,914	15,168	10,019	4,381	4,364
1994	**68,262**	36,117	23,556	6,897	1,427	265	1994	**46,471**	10,815	16,420	10,410	4,663	4,163
1995	**60,190**	32,056	20,331	6,278	1,309	216	1995	**48,291**	11,416	17,145	10,788	4,649	4,293
1996	**53,956**	28,676	18,252	5,643	1,179	206	1996	**50,581**	12,386	18,217	11,084	4,731	4,163
1997	**48,423**	25,655	16,339	5,117	1,113	199	1997	**53,999**	13,155	19,714	11,928	4,875	4,327
1998	**45,159**	24,111	15,333	4,570	947	198	1998	**56,821**	14,254	21,136	12,431	4,918	4,082
1999	**42,765**	23,303	14,293	4,104	882	183	1999	**58,932**	15,571	22,133	12,439	4,939	3,850
2000	**39,861**	21,422	13,596	3,880	799	164	2000	**61,758**	16,352	23,355	13,121	4,959	3,971

* See Section 2.15.

Table 4.1 Live births within marriage: number of previous liveborn children and age of mother (five-year age-groups), 1990-2000
c. remarried women

England and Wale

Year	Number of previous liveborn children*						Year	Number of previous liveborn children*					
	Total	0	1	2	3	4 or more		Total	0	1	2	3	4 or more
	All ages of mother at birth						**25-29**						
1990	**41,311**	11,072	13,486	9,478	4,616	2,659	1990	**11,864**	3,868	3,913	2,505	1,082	496
1991	**39,416**	10,734	12,818	9,018	4,225	2,621	1991	**10,777**	3,593	3,661	2,237	887	399
1992	**38,100**	10,380	12,355	8,609	4,164	2,592	1992	**9,933**	3,209	3,356	2,061	906	401
1993	**35,860**	9,517	11,602	8,202	4,022	2,517	1993	**8,710**	2,716	2,949	1,864	828	353
1994	**35,196**	9,580	11,488	7,781	3,886	2,461	1994	**8,079**	2,649	2,720	1,625	717	368
1995	**33,285**	9,155	10,836	7,397	3,615	2,282	1995	**7,211**	2,402	2,385	1,493	658	273
1996	**32,582**	9,026	10,557	7,197	3,492	2,310	1996	**6,395**	2,103	2,149	1,318	561	264
1997	**31,445**	8,630	10,249	6,795	3,492	2,279	1997	**5,828**	1,938	1,920	1,155	570	245
1998	**30,185**	8,501	9,983	6,594	3,035	2,072	1998	**5,105**	1,719	1,760	1,018	408	200
1999	**27,489**	7,923	9,056	5,731	2,872	1,907	1999	**4,254**	1,485	1,388	845	382	154
2000	**25,782**	7,299	8,574	5,469	2,591	1,849	2000	**3,719**	1,247	1,228	750	320	174
	Under 20						**30-34**						
1990	**23**	11	9	3	-	-	1990	**16,237**	4,347	5,500	3,689	1,733	968
1991	**13**	3	9	-	-	1	1991	**15,791**	4,326	5,251	3,568	1,656	990
1992	**11**	6	2	2	-	1	1992	**15,387**	4,266	5,143	3,456	1,588	934
1993	**8**	2	2	1	2	1	1993	**14,821**	4,039	4,927	3,324	1,604	927
1994	**7**	5	2	-	-	-	1994	**14,920**	4,269	5,003	3,189	1,529	930
1995	**14**	8	4	2	-	-	1995	**14,030**	4,016	4,748	3,003	1,412	851
1996	**10**	5	3	2	-	-	1996	**13,925**	4,103	4,657	2,959	1,387	819
1997	**7**	5	2	-	-	-	1997	**13,068**	3,798	4,432	2,769	1,313	756
1998	**5**	2	2	-	1	-	1998	**12,389**	3,756	4,189	2,644	1,106	694
1999	**4**	3	1	-	-	-	1999	**11,324**	3,592	3,918	2,202	1,007	605
2000	**5**	4	1	-	-	-	2000	**10,354**	3,196	3,583	2,130	872	573
	20-24						**35 and over**						
1990	**1,894**	637	722	382	128	25	1990	**11,293**	2,209	3,342	2,899	1,673	1,170
1991	**1,621**	556	588	342	108	27	1991	**11,214**	2,256	3,309	2,871	1,574	1,204
1992	**1,371**	502	491	262	91	25	1992	**11,398**	2,397	3,363	2,828	1,579	1,231
1993	**1,200**	405	418	271	74	32	1993	**11,121**	2,355	3,306	2,742	1,514	1,204
1994	**965**	304	370	218	57	16	1994	**11,225**	2,353	3,393	2,749	1,583	1,147
1995	**839**	284	303	175	58	19	1995	**11,191**	2,445	3,396	2,724	1,487	1,139
1996	**695**	249	229	146	52	19	1996	**11,557**	2,566	3,519	2,772	1,492	1,208
1997	**645**	236	219	140	40	10	1997	**11,897**	2,653	3,676	2,731	1,569	1,268
1998	**565**	192	204	109	46	14	1998	**12,121**	2,832	3,828	2,823	1,474	1,164
1999	**425**	171	150	71	28	5	1999	**11,482**	2,672	3,599	2,613	1,455	1,143
2000	**401**	149	148	70	28	6	2000	**11,303**	2,703	3,614	2,519	1,371	1,096

* See Section 2.15.

Table 4.2   Live births within marriage: number of previous liveborn children and age of mother (single years), 2000
a. all married women

England and Wales

Age of mother at birth	Number of previous liveborn children*												
	Total	0	1	2	3	4	5	6	7	8	9	10-14†	15 and† over
All ages	**365,836**	**146,509**	**134,691**	**54,920**	**18,590**	**6,480**	**2,528**	**1,080**	**524**	**258**	**127**	**126**	**3**
Under 16	**8**	8	-	-	-	-	-	-	-	-	-	-	-
16	**89**	85	4	-	-	-	-	-	-	-	-	-	-
17	**443**	397	45	1	-	-	-	-	-	-	-	-	-
18	**1,306**	1,127	161	15	3	-	-	-	-	-	-	-	-
19	**2,896**	2,193	632	65	4	2	-	-	-	-	-	-	-
Under 20	**4,742**	**3,810**	**842**	**81**	**7**	**2**	**-**	**-**	**-**	**-**	**-**	**-**	**-**
20	**4,708**	3,181	1,309	188	26	3	-	1	-	-	-	-	-
21	**6,351**	3,732	2,117	433	57	10	1	1	-	-	-	-	-
22	**7,646**	4,019	2,743	745	118	17	4	-	-	-	-	-	-
23	**9,477**	4,714	3,409	1,070	230	47	6	1	-	-	-	-	-
24	**12,080**	5,925	4,166	1,514	396	66	12	1	-	-	-	-	-
20-24	**40,262**	**21,571**	**13,744**	**3,950**	**827**	**143**	**23**	**4**	**-**	**-**	**-**	**-**	**-**
25	**15,156**	7,417	5,052	1,961	569	129	24	3	1	-	-	-	-
26	**18,579**	9,132	5,980	2,428	795	192	41	7	3	-	-	1	-
27	**22,166**	10,585	7,481	2,834	924	253	73	12	3	-	-	1	-
28	**26,199**	12,372	9,012	3,262	1,056	366	104	16	9	2	-	-	-
29	**29,506**	13,167	10,851	3,644	1,250	420	115	44	14	1	-	-	-
25-29	**111,606**	**52,673**	**38,376**	**14,129**	**4,594**	**1,360**	**357**	**82**	**30**	**3**	**-**	**2**	**-**
30	**29,805**	12,599	11,207	4,000	1,318	433	173	54	12	6	2	1	-
31	**29,811**	11,559	11,916	4,167	1,390	484	189	59	30	9	5	3	-
32	**28,154**	10,004	11,646	4,304	1,391	479	195	98	27	4	6	-	-
33	**25,675**	8,460	10,669	4,338	1,337	502	212	91	42	16	5	3	-
34	**22,720**	6,778	9,322	4,311	1,396	506	216	102	48	26	10	5	-
30-34	**136,165**	**49,400**	**54,760**	**21,120**	**6,832**	**2,404**	**985**	**404**	**159**	**61**	**28**	**12**	**-**
35	**19,460**	5,599	7,670	3,984	1,345	490	202	94	37	20	11	8	-
36	**15,853**	4,263	6,188	3,369	1,214	438	209	82	42	29	15	4	-
37	**12,022**	3,045	4,444	2,730	1,072	393	168	81	48	20	12	9	-
38	**8,863**	2,169	3,272	1,963	834	299	140	84	48	22	12	20	-
39	**6,473**	1,556	2,234	1,438	655	292	129	69	42	32	11	15	-
35-39	**62,671**	**16,632**	**23,808**	**13,484**	**5,120**	**1,912**	**848**	**410**	**217**	**123**	**61**	**56**	**-**
40	**4,212**	997	1,365	906	447	230	122	68	36	20	7	14	-
41	**2,689**	602	855	542	337	192	59	39	28	15	10	9	1
42	**1,643**	396	484	325	191	117	50	31	20	15	6	8	-
43	**910**	211	236	191	121	55	37	19	15	5	6	13	1
44	**456**	100	119	93	50	33	30	10	5	6	4	5	1
40-44	**9,910**	**2,306**	**3,059**	**2,057**	**1,146**	**627**	**298**	**167**	**104**	**61**	**33**	**49**	**3**
45	**241**	48	56	56	37	13	7	6	5	6	2	5	-
46	**115**	30	22	23	18	6	5	3	3	3	1	1	-
47	**41**	13	7	6	6	3	3	2	-	-	1	-	-
48	**24**	5	6	4	-	6	1	-	1	1	-	-	-
49 and over	**59**	21	11	10	3	4	1	2	5	-	1	1	-
45 and over	**480**	**117**	**102**	**99**	**64**	**32**	**17**	**13**	**14**	**10**	**5**	**7**	**-**

Note: 1,834 cases in which age of mother at birth, and 76 cases in which the number of previous liveborn children was not stated have been included with the stated cases (for method of distribution - see Sections 3.2 and 3.3).

* See Section 2.15.

† Detailed distribution for these groups is as follows:

Number of previous liveborn children	Number of live births
10	65
11	29
12	19
13	10
14	3
15	2
16	1

Table 4.2 **Live births within marriage: number of previous liveborn children and age of mother (single years), 2000**
b. women married once only

Age of mother at birth	Number of previous liveborn children*												
	Total	0	1	2	3	4	5	6	7	8	9	10-14†	15 and over†
All ages	**340,054**	**139,210**	**126,117**	**49,451**	**15,999**	**5,382**	**2,104**	**908**	**424**	**226**	**112**	**118**	**3**
Under 16	**8**	8	-	-	-	-	-	-	-	-	-	-	-
16	**89**	85	4	-	-	-	-	-	-	-	-	-	-
17	**443**	397	45	1	-	-	-	-	-	-	-	-	-
18	**1,304**	1,125	161	15	3	-	-	-	-	-	-	-	-
19	**2,893**	2,191	631	65	4	2	-	-	-	-	-	-	-
Under 20	**4,737**	**3,806**	**841**	**81**	**7**	**2**	**-**	**-**	**-**	**-**	**-**	**-**	**-**
20	**4,693**	3,176	1,305	183	25	3	-	1	-	-	-	-	-
21	**6,323**	3,722	2,105	428	56	10	1	1	-	-	-	-	-
22	**7,587**	3,991	2,730	735	110	17	4	-	-	-	-	-	-
23	**9,374**	4,675	3,371	1,051	225	45	6	1	-	-	-	-	-
24	**11,884**	5,858	4,085	1,483	383	63	11	1	-	-	-	-	-
20-24	**39,861**	**21,422**	**13,596**	**3,880**	**799**	**138**	**22**	**4**	**-**	**-**	**-**	**-**	**-**
25	**14,842**	7,307	4,952	1,893	537	125	24	3	1	-	-	-	-
26	**18,087**	8,971	5,837	2,317	748	170	36	5	2	-	-	1	-
27	**21,464**	10,339	7,255	2,689	868	231	67	12	2	-	-	1	-
28	**25,290**	12,095	8,675	3,083	984	336	95	13	7	2	-	-	-
29	**28,204**	12,714	10,429	3,397	1,137	372	105	39	10	1	-	-	-
25-29	**107,887**	**51,426**	**37,148**	**13,379**	**4,274**	**1,234**	**327**	**72**	**22**	**3**	**-**	**2**	**-**
30	**28,159**	12,026	10,659	3,684	1,189	378	158	47	10	5	2	1	-
31	**27,886**	10,930	11,276	3,762	1,242	413	173	48	28	7	4	3	-
32	**26,041**	9,347	10,904	3,886	1,199	427	162	82	24	4	6	-	-
33	**23,313**	7,747	9,830	3,845	1,153	419	190	72	35	14	5	3	-
34	**20,412**	6,154	8,508	3,813	1,177	425	171	86	42	24	7	5	-
30-34	**125,811**	**46,204**	**51,177**	**18,990**	**5,960**	**2,062**	**854**	**335**	**139**	**54**	**24**	**12**	**-**
35	**17,163**	4,944	6,909	3,491	1,130	387	155	81	29	18	11	8	-
36	**13,751**	3,718	5,490	2,893	990	342	172	71	36	24	12	3	-
37	**10,253**	2,635	3,853	2,320	870	300	134	65	39	17	11	9	-
38	**7,346**	1,826	2,761	1,635	635	215	111	74	40	20	10	19	-
39	**5,246**	1,289	1,855	1,163	483	221	92	58	31	29	11	14	-
35-39	**53,759**	**14,412**	**20,868**	**11,502**	**4,108**	**1,465**	**664**	**349**	**175**	**108**	**55**	**53**	**-**
40	**3,316**	817	1,088	715	329	165	94	53	23	14	5	13	-
41	**2,073**	483	671	409	245	135	40	32	25	14	9	9	1
42	**1,234**	306	372	235	127	89	40	26	14	14	4	7	-
43	**672**	164	186	130	75	42	26	16	10	5	6	11	1
44	**347**	79	89	68	31	27	24	9	5	6	4	4	1
40-44	**7,642**	**1,849**	**2,406**	**1,557**	**807**	**458**	**224**	**136**	**77**	**53**	**28**	**44**	**3**
45	**172**	35	41	37	25	8	5	6	3	5	2	5	-
46	**92**	26	21	14	12	5	4	3	3	2	1	1	-
47	**31**	11	5	3	5	3	2	1	-	-	1	-	-
48	**19**	3	4	3	-	6	1	-	1	1	-	-	-
49 and over	**43**	16	10	5	2	1	1	2	4	-	1	1	-
45 and over	**357**	**91**	**81**	**62**	**44**	**23**	**13**	**12**	**11**	**8**	**5**	**7**	**-**

Note: 1,809 cases in which age of mother at birth, and 72 cases in which the number of previous liveborn children was not stated have been included with the stated cases (for method of distribution - see Sections 3.2 and 3.3).

* See Section 2.15.

† Detailed distribution for these groups is as follows:

Number of previous liveborn children	Number of live births
10	62
11	27
12	17
13	9
14	3
15	2
16	1

Table 4.2   Live births within marriage: number of previous liveborn children and age of mother (single years), 2000
c. remarried women

England and Wales

| Age of mother at birth | Number of previous liveborn children* | | | | | | | | | | | | |
	Total	0	1	2	3	4	5	6	7	8	9	10-14†	15 and† over
All ages	25,782	7,299	8,574	5,469	2,591	1,098	424	172	100	32	15	8	-
Under 16	-	-	-	-	-	-	-	-	-	-	-	-	-
16	·	-	-	-	-	-	-	-	-	-	-	-	-
17	·	-	-	-	-	-	-	-	-	-	-	-	-
18	2	2	-	-	-	-	-	-	-	-	-	-	-
19	3	2	1	-	-	-	-	-	-	-	-	-	-
Under 20	**5**	**4**	**1**	·	-	-	-	-	-	-	-	-	-
20	15	5	4	5	1	-	-	-	-	-	-	-	-
21	28	10	12	5	1	-	-	-	-	-	-	-	-
22	59	28	13	10	8	-	-	-	-	-	-	-	-
23	103	39	38	19	5	2	-	-	-	-	-	-	-
24	196	67	81	31	13	3	1	-	-	-	-	-	-
20-24	**401**	**149**	**148**	**70**	**28**	**5**	**1**	·	-	-	-	-	-
25	314	110	100	68	32	4	-	-	-	-	-	-	-
26	492	161	143	111	47	22	5	2	1	-	-	-	-
27	702	246	226	145	56	22	6	-	1	-	-	-	-
28	909	277	337	179	72	30	9	3	2	-	-	-	-
29	1,302	453	422	247	113	48	10	5	4	-	-	-	-
25-29	**3,719**	**1,247**	**1,228**	**750**	**320**	**126**	**30**	**10**	**8**	·	-	-	-
30	1,646	573	548	316	129	55	15	7	2	1	-	-	-
31	1,925	629	640	405	148	71	16	11	2	2	1	-	-
32	2,113	657	742	418	192	52	33	16	3	-	-	-	-
33	2,362	713	839	493	184	83	22	19	7	2	-	-	-
34	2,308	624	814	498	219	81	45	16	6	2	3	-	-
30-34	**10,354**	**3,196**	**3,583**	**2,130**	**872**	**342**	**131**	**69**	**20**	**7**	**4**	·	-
35	2,297	655	761	493	215	103	47	13	8	2	-	-	-
36	2,102	545	698	476	224	96	37	11	6	5	3	1	-
37	1,769	410	591	410	202	93	34	16	9	3	1	-	-
38	1,517	343	511	328	199	84	29	10	8	2	2	1	-
39	1,227	267	379	275	172	71	37	11	11	3	-	1	-
35-39	**8,912**	**2,220**	**2,940**	**1,982**	**1,012**	**447**	**184**	**61**	**42**	**15**	**6**	**3**	-
40	896	180	277	191	118	65	28	15	13	6	2	1	-
41	616	119	184	133	92	57	19	7	3	1	1	-	-
42	409	90	112	90	64	28	10	5	6	1	2	1	-
43	238	47	50	61	46	13	11	3	5	-	-	2	-
44	109	21	30	25	19	6	6	1	-	-	-	1	-
40-44	**2,268**	**457**	**653**	**500**	**339**	**169**	**74**	**31**	**27**	**8**	**5**	**5**	-
45	69	13	15	19	12	5	2	-	2	1	-	-	-
46	23	4	1	9	6	1	1	-	-	1	-	-	-
47	10	2	2	3	1	-	1	1	-	-	-	-	-
48	5	2	2	1	-	-	-	-	-	-	-	-	-
49 and over	16	5	1	5	1	3	-	-	1	-	-	-	-
45 and over	**123**	**26**	**21**	**37**	**20**	**9**	**4**	**1**	**3**	**2**	·	·	-

Note: 25 cases in which age of mother at birth, and 4 cases in which the number of previous liveborn children was not stated have been included with the stated cases (for method of distribution - see Sections 3.2 and 3.3).

* See Section 2.15.

† Detailed distribution for these groups is as follows:

Number of previous liveborn children	Number of live births
10	3
11	2
12	2
13	1

Table 4.3 Live births and stillbirths within marriage (numbers and sex ratios):
number of previous liveborn children, age of mother and sex, 2000   England and Wales

Numbers

Age of mother at birth	Sex	Total	0	1	2	3	4	5	6	7	8	9	10-14†	15 and over†
All ages	M	188,346	75,331	69,197	28,384	9,698	3,370	1,316	541	256	127	66	59	1
	F	179,320	71,850	66,099	26,857	9,022	3,150	1,242	556	276	133	64	69	2
Under 20	M	2,445	1,977	422	38	5	2	1	-	-	-	-	-	-
	F	2,326	1,852	425	44	3	-	1	-	-	1	-	-	-
20-24	M	20,675	11,139	6,980	2,014	449	78	14	1	-	-	-	-	-
	F	19,803	10,542	6,835	1,965	380	68	10	3	-	-	-	-	-
25-29	M	57,461	27,091	19,747	7,283	2,397	696	191	37	16	2	-	1	-
	F	54,659	25,802	18,791	6,932	2,231	670	172	45	14	1	-	1	-
30-34	M	70,103	25,361	28,165	10,994	3,541	1,231	487	203	73	30	12	6	-
	F	66,700	24,244	26,820	10,249	3,346	1,186	504	211	87	31	16	6	-
35-39	M	32,327	8,534	12,274	6,947	2,648	1,024	449	214	110	62	37	28	-
	F	30,697	8,204	11,652	6,595	2,504	903	410	201	112	62	26	28	-
40-44	M	5,086	1,176	1,561	1,051	620	318	164	81	49	30	14	21	1
	F	4,900	1,141	1,521	1,029	532	312	137	88	57	31	20	30	2
45 and over	M	249	53	48	57	38	21	10	5	8	3	3	3	-
	F	235	65	55	43	26	11	8	8	6	7	2	4	-

Ratio: male births inside marriage per 1,000 female births inside marriage

Age of mother at birth	Total	0	1	2	3	4	5	6	7	8	9	10-14†	15 and over†
All ages	1,050	1,048	1,047	1,057	1,075	1,070	1,060	973	928	955	1,031	855	*500*
Under 20	1,051	1,067	993	864	*1,667*	-	*1,000*	-	-	-	-	-	-
20-24	1,044	1,057	1,021	1,025	1,182	1,147	1,400	*333*	-	-	-	-	-
25-29	1,051	1,050	1,051	1,051	1,074	1,039	1,110	822	1,143	*2,000*	-	*1,000*	-
30-34	1,051	1,046	1,050	1,073	1,058	1,038	966	962	839	968	750	*1,000*	-
35-39	1,053	1,040	1,053	1,053	1,058	1,134	1,095	1,065	982	1,000	1,423	1,000	-
40-44	1,038	1,031	1,026	1,021	1,165	1,019	1,197	920	860	968	700	700	*500*
45 and over	1,060	815	873	1,326	1,462	1,909	*1,250*	625	*1,333*	429	*1,500*	750	-

Note: 1.   1,920 cases in which the age of mother at birth, and 600 cases in which the number of previous liveborn children
was not stated have been included with the stated cases (for method of distribution - see Sections 3.2 and 3.3).
     2.   For information on the use of italics - see Section 2.21.
* See Section 2.15.
† Detailed distribution for these groups is as follows:

Number of previous liveborn children	Number of live births and stillbirths
10	65
11	29
12	20
13	10
14	4
15	2
16	1

Table 5.1 First live births within marriage: duration of marriage and age of mother, 1990-2000
a. all married women

England and Wales

Year	All durations	Completed months		Completed years											10-14	15-19	20 and over
		0-7	8-11	0	1	2	3	4	5	6	7	8	9			
All ages of mother at birth																	
1990	**200,394**	27,130	18,024	45,154	46,764	32,856	23,345	15,762	11,117	7,533	5,158	3,633	2,705	5,410	871	86
1991	**193,665**	23,541	16,998	40,539	46,793	32,255	22,539	15,745	10,769	7,320	5,115	3,586	2,523	5,429	941	111
1992	**187,342**	21,685	16,152	37,837	44,664	32,506	21,732	15,557	10,621	7,054	4,948	3,273	2,368	5,780	877	125
1993	**178,141**	19,816	16,205	36,021	41,431	30,084	21,823	15,042	10,550	7,040	4,733	3,332	2,263	4,727	870	90
1994	**176,046**	18,578	15,765	34,343	42,371	29,388	20,874	15,368	10,403	7,153	4,914	3,179	2,281	4,823	830	119
1995	**168,118**	17,332	15,611	32,943	40,542	28,659	19,683	13,947	10,115	6,788	4,763	3,098	2,262	4,411	797	110
1996	**163,020**	17,300	15,489	32,789	39,521	27,283	18,951	13,225	9,333	6,806	4,622	3,129	2,173	4,274	807	107
1997	**157,049**	16,760	15,199	31,959	38,650	26,225	18,075	12,479	8,680	6,243	4,632	3,043	2,181	4,044	728	110
1998	**155,708**	16,582	15,617	32,199	38,631	26,169	17,648	12,097	8,643	5,886	4,350	3,091	2,006	4,165	720	103
1999	**153,423**	16,193	15,346	31,539	38,723	25,803	17,267	11,989	8,271	5,797	4,004	2,964	2,223	4,085	670	88
2000	**146,509**	14,423	14,838	29,261	38,069	25,331	16,239	11,166	7,561	5,422	3,858	2,734	2,046	4,165	575	82
Under 20																	
1990	**8,334**	4,429	1,534	5,963	1,970	333	64	4	-	-	-	-	-	-	-	-
1991	**6,726**	3,267	1,369	4,636	1,741	290	57	1	1	-	-	-	-	-	-	-
1992	**5,956**	2,636	1,287	3,923	1,638	331	57	7	-	-	-	-	-	-	-	-
1993	**5,196**	2,157	1,179	3,336	1,496	278	60	4	3	1	-	-	-	-	-	-
1994	**4,687**	1,872	1,094	2,966	1,384	267	59	10	-	1	-	-	-	-	-	-
1995	**4,308**	1,605	1,128	2,733	1,228	282	56	7	-	1	1	-	-	-	-	-
1996	**4,223**	1,567	1,149	2,716	1,180	256	61	8	2	-	-	-	-	-	-	-
1997	**4,121**	1,505	1,031	2,536	1,237	272	71	4	1	-	-	-	-	-	-	-
1998	**4,188**	1,490	1,123	2,613	1,223	280	63	7	2	-	-	-	-	-	-	-
1999	**4,290**	1,455	996	2,451	1,430	333	69	6	1	-	-	-	-	-	-	-
2000	**3,810**	1,225	903	2,128	1,221	383	75	3	-	-	-	-	-	-	-	-
20-24																	
1990	**56,995**	11,029	7,457	18,486	18,952	11,068	5,541	2,115	618	160	33	15	7	-	-	-
1991	**51,157**	9,279	6,650	15,929	17,663	10,046	4,817	1,956	572	140	21	10	2	1	-	-
1992	**45,900**	8,282	5,931	14,213	15,683	9,265	4,288	1,744	530	141	25	1	6	4	-	-
1993	**40,399**	7,192	5,678	12,870	13,345	7,812	3,995	1,611	546	141	33	8	4	8	-	-
1994	**36,421**	6,339	5,117	11,456	12,375	6,956	3,468	1,491	473	153	23	9	1	16	-	-
1995	**32,340**	5,783	4,755	10,538	10,893	6,153	2,964	1,215	407	122	32	6	4	4	-	-
1996	**28,925**	5,408	4,469	9,877	9,780	5,227	2,510	1,033	347	107	34	4	1	5	-	-
1997	**25,891**	4,913	4,135	9,048	8,733	4,629	2,113	910	305	112	28	8	3	2	-	-
1998	**24,303**	4,494	3,885	8,379	8,270	4,386	1,973	832	299	112	35	8	-	9	-	-
1999	**23,474**	4,336	3,706	8,042	8,000	4,165	1,952	803	353	100	36	7	7	9	-	-
2000	**21,571**	3,896	3,415	7,311	7,507	4,016	1,665	681	263	78	28	15	-	7	-	-
25-29																	
1990	**86,432**	7,422	5,929	13,351	17,839	15,659	13,166	9,937	7,078	4,486	2,554	1,371	678	313	-	-
1991	**84,524**	6,784	5,835	12,619	18,538	15,630	12,929	9,676	6,631	4,036	2,363	1,222	549	329	2	-
1992	**81,727**	6,482	5,707	12,189	17,961	15,765	12,122	9,555	6,449	3,772	2,112	975	478	349	-	-
1993	**77,612**	6,161	5,772	11,933	16,998	14,639	11,954	8,810	6,126	3,586	1,920	923	412	263	3	-
1994	**75,660**	5,760	5,826	11,586	17,636	13,990	11,238	8,670	5,741	3,478	1,865	827	402	224	3	-
1995	**71,036**	5,391	5,850	11,241	17,299	13,629	10,082	7,518	5,234	3,071	1,709	758	309	186	-	-
1996	**67,178**	5,396	5,695	11,091	16,590	12,889	9,552	6,846	4,604	2,915	1,530	699	286	176	-	-
1997	**63,139**	5,280	5,620	10,900	16,230	12,182	8,905	6,052	4,055	2,405	1,397	649	236	127	1	-
1998	**60,602**	5,377	5,804	11,181	15,895	11,552	8,269	5,593	3,746	2,137	1,238	609	230	148	4	-
1999	**57,385**	5,152	5,611	10,763	15,467	11,093	7,596	5,229	3,298	1,961	1,073	561	226	117	1	-
2000	**52,673**	4,352	5,306	9,658	14,859	10,595	7,010	4,538	2,740	1,606	871	427	220	149	-	-
30 and over																	
1990	**48,633**	4,250	3,104	7,354	8,003	5,796	4,574	3,706	3,421	2,887	2,571	2,247	2,020	5,097	871	86
1991	**51,258**	4,211	3,144	7,355	8,851	6,289	4,736	4,112	3,565	3,144	2,731	2,354	1,972	5,099	939	111
1992	**53,759**	4,285	3,227	7,512	9,382	7,145	5,265	4,251	3,642	3,141	2,811	2,297	1,884	5,427	877	125
1993	**54,934**	4,306	3,576	7,882	9,592	7,355	5,814	4,617	3,875	3,312	2,780	2,401	1,847	4,456	867	90
1994	**59,278**	4,607	3,728	8,335	10,976	8,175	6,109	5,197	4,189	3,521	3,026	2,343	1,878	4,583	827	119
1995	**60,434**	4,553	3,878	8,431	11,122	8,595	6,581	5,207	4,474	3,594	3,021	2,334	1,947	4,221	797	110
1996	**62,694**	4,929	4,176	9,105	11,971	8,911	6,828	5,338	4,380	3,784	3,058	2,426	1,886	4,093	807	107
1997	**63,898**	5,062	4,413	9,475	12,450	9,142	6,986	5,513	4,319	3,726	3,207	2,386	1,942	3,915	727	110
1998	**66,615**	5,221	4,805	10,026	13,243	9,951	7,343	5,665	4,596	3,637	3,077	2,474	1,776	4,008	716	103
1999	**68,274**	5,250	5,033	10,283	13,826	10,212	7,650	5,951	4,619	3,736	2,895	2,396	1,990	3,959	669	88
2000	**68,455**	4,950	5,214	10,164	14,482	10,337	7,489	5,944	4,558	3,738	2,959	2,292	1,826	4,009	575	82

Table 5.1 First live births within marriage: duration of marriage and age of mother, 1990-2000
b. women married once only

England and Wales

| Year | All durations | Completed months | | Completed years | | | | | | | | | | | | |
		0-7	8-11	0	1	2	3	4	5	6	7	8	9	10-14	15-19	20 and over
All ages of mother at birth																
1990	**189,322**	24,304	16,547	40,851	43,751	31,374	22,498	15,280	10,778	7,320	5,024	3,547	2,655	5,296	862	86
1991	**182,931**	21,049	15,552	36,601	43,696	30,819	21,733	15,240	10,447	7,109	4,997	3,476	2,455	5,313	934	111
1992	**176,962**	19,333	14,846	34,179	41,629	31,009	20,946	15,057	10,317	6,849	4,823	3,180	2,326	5,652	871	124
1993	**168,624**	17,678	14,928	32,606	38,823	28,756	21,037	14,558	10,262	6,847	4,589	3,247	2,205	4,620	860	90
1994	**166,466**	16,476	14,500	30,976	39,643	28,004	20,138	14,867	10,105	6,983	4,755	3,105	2,237	4,714	820	119
1995	**158,963**	15,368	14,320	29,688	38,073	27,298	18,947	13,461	9,799	6,609	4,660	3,023	2,200	4,304	791	110
1996	**153,994**	15,351	14,225	29,576	36,982	26,052	18,207	12,779	9,040	6,616	4,491	3,059	2,124	4,166	797	105
1997	**148,419**	14,878	14,049	28,927	36,178	24,992	17,418	12,048	8,401	6,069	4,526	2,966	2,128	3,938	719	109
1998	**147,207**	14,745	14,365	29,110	36,324	24,909	16,981	11,691	8,390	5,715	4,223	3,023	1,964	4,059	716	102
1999	**145,500**	14,545	14,186	28,731	36,489	24,678	16,594	11,595	8,010	5,653	3,914	2,895	2,181	4,007	665	88
2000	**139,210**	12,980	13,791	26,771	35,999	24,278	15,601	10,786	7,318	5,268	3,766	2,655	2,012	4,105	570	81
Under 20																
1990	**8,323**	4,422	1,531	5,953	1,970	332	64	4	-	-	-	-	-	-	-	-
1991	**6,723**	3,266	1,369	4,635	1,739	290	57	1	1	-	-	-	-	-	-	-
1992	**5,950**	2,634	1,285	3,919	1,636	331	57	7	-	-	-	-	-	-	-	-
1993	**5,194**	2,155	1,179	3,334	1,496	278	60	4	3	1	-	-	-	-	-	-
1994	**4,682**	1,870	1,094	2,964	1,381	267	59	10	-	1	-	-	-	-	-	-
1995	**4,300**	1,600	1,128	2,728	1,225	282	56	7	-	1	1	-	-	-	-	-
1996	**4,218**	1,565	1,146	2,711	1,180	256	61	8	2	-	-	-	-	-	-	-
1997	**4,116**	1,502	1,029	2,531	1,237	272	71	4	1	-	-	-	-	-	-	-
1998	**4,186**	1,489	1,123	2,612	1,222	280	63	7	2	-	-	-	-	-	-	-
1999	**4,287**	1,454	994	2,448	1,430	333	69	6	1	-	-	-	-	-	-	-
2000	**3,806**	1,223	902	2,125	1,220	383	75	3	-	-	-	-	-	-	-	-
20-24																
1990	**56,358**	10,751	7,327	18,078	18,774	11,031	5,531	2,112	617	160	33	15	7	-	-	-
1991	**50,601**	9,035	6,549	15,584	17,503	10,012	4,805	1,952	571	140	21	10	2	1	-	-
1992	**45,398**	8,065	5,823	13,888	15,556	9,224	4,280	1,743	530	141	25	1	6	4	-	-
1993	**39,994**	7,008	5,594	12,602	13,245	7,792	3,982	1,609	545	141	33	8	4	8	-	-
1994	**36,117**	6,214	5,058	11,272	12,290	6,929	3,462	1,490	472	153	23	9	1	16	-	-
1995	**32,056**	5,672	4,682	10,354	10,820	6,134	2,958	1,214	406	122	32	6	6	4	-	-
1996	**28,676**	5,299	4,421	9,720	9,713	5,210	2,502	1,033	347	107	34	4	1	5	-	-
1997	**25,655**	4,824	4,085	8,909	8,662	4,613	2,107	907	304	112	28	8	3	2	-	-
1998	**24,111**	4,423	3,836	8,259	8,221	4,368	1,969	831	299	112	35	8	-	9	-	-
1999	**23,303**	4,269	3,660	7,929	7,956	4,158	1,946	802	353	100	36	7	7	9	-	-
2000	**21,422**	3,848	3,375	7,223	7,461	4,006	1,661	680	263	78	28	15	-	7	-	-
25-29																
1990	**82,564**	6,237	5,324	11,561	16,674	15,143	12,932	9,836	7,039	4,474	2,552	1,368	676	309	-	-
1991	**80,931**	5,805	5,244	11,049	17,380	15,168	12,712	9,572	6,585	4,014	2,356	1,219	548	326	2	-
1992	**75,518**	5,622	5,194	10,816	16,894	15,331	11,937	9,463	6,418	3,756	2,108	971	478	346	-	-
1993	**74,896**	5,419	5,318	10,737	16,111	14,286	11,797	8,739	6,095	3,572	1,914	920	411	263	3	-
1994	**73,011**	5,078	5,346	10,424	16,782	13,619	11,101	8,594	5,711	3,465	1,862	827	401	222	3	-
1995	**68,634**	4,744	5,414	10,158	16,525	13,309	9,970	7,447	5,208	3,060	1,707	757	308	185	-	-
1996	**65,075**	4,817	5,310	10,127	15,934	12,625	9,427	6,791	4,585	2,905	1,526	699	285	171	-	-
1997	**61,201**	4,754	5,280	10,034	15,572	11,940	8,809	6,012	4,036	2,395	1,393	648	236	125	1	-
1998	**58,883**	4,890	5,458	10,348	15,386	11,338	8,169	5,557	3,734	2,130	1,233	609	230	145	4	-
1999	**55,900**	4,734	5,289	10,023	15,027	10,914	7,530	5,196	3,278	1,956	1,071	561	226	117	1	-
2000	**51,426**	4,035	5,067	9,102	14,457	10,428	6,945	4,502	2,729	1,601	869	426	220	147	-	-
30 and over																
1990	**42,077**	2,894	2,365	5,259	6,333	4,868	3,971	3,328	3,122	2,686	2,439	2,164	1,972	4,987	862	86
1991	**44,676**	2,943	2,390	5,333	7,074	5,349	4,159	3,715	3,290	2,955	2,620	2,247	1,905	4,986	932	111
1992	**47,096**	3,012	2,544	5,556	7,543	6,123	4,672	3,844	3,369	2,952	2,690	2,208	1,842	5,302	871	124
1993	**48,540**	3,096	2,837	5,933	7,965	6,400	5,198	4,206	3,619	3,133	2,642	2,319	1,790	4,349	857	90
1994	**52,656**	3,314	3,002	6,316	9,190	7,189	5,516	4,773	3,922	3,364	2,870	2,269	1,835	4,476	817	119
1995	**53,973**	3,352	3,096	6,448	9,503	7,573	5,963	4,793	4,185	3,426	2,920	2,260	1,886	4,115	791	110
1996	**56,025**	3,670	3,348	7,018	10,155	7,961	6,217	4,947	4,106	3,604	2,931	2,356	1,838	3,990	797	105
1997	**57,447**	3,798	3,655	7,453	10,707	8,167	6,431	5,125	4,060	3,562	3,105	2,310	1,889	3,811	718	109
1998	**60,027**	3,943	3,948	7,891	11,495	8,923	6,780	5,296	4,355	3,473	2,955	2,406	1,734	3,905	712	102
1999	**62,010**	4,088	4,243	8,331	12,076	9,273	7,049	5,591	4,378	3,597	2,807	2,327	1,948	3,881	664	88
2000	**62,556**	3,874	4,447	8,321	12,861	9,461	6,920	5,601	4,326	3,589	2,869	2,214	1,792	3,951	570	81

Table 5.1 First live births within marriage: duration of marriage and age of mother, 1990-2000
c. remarried women

England and Wales

Year	Duration of current marriage															
		Completed months		Completed years												
	All durations	0-7	8-11	0	1	2	3	4	5	6	7	8	9	10-14	15-19	20 and over
All ages of mother at birth																
1990	**11,072**	2,826	1,477	4,303	3,013	1,482	847	482	339	213	134	86	50	114	9	-
1991	**10,734**	2,492	1,446	3,938	3,097	1,436	806	505	322	211	118	110	68	116	7	-
1992	**10,380**	2,352	1,306	3,658	3,035	1,497	786	500	304	205	125	93	42	128	6	1
1993	**9,517**	2,138	1,277	3,415	2,608	1,328	786	484	288	193	144	85	58	107	10	-
1994	**9,580**	2,102	1,265	3,367	2,728	1,384	736	501	298	170	159	74	44	109	10	-
1995	**9,155**	1,964	1,291	3,255	2,469	1,361	736	486	316	179	103	75	62	107	6	-
1996	**9,026**	1,949	1,264	3,213	2,539	1,231	744	446	293	190	131	70	49	108	10	2
1997	**8,630**	1,882	1,150	3,032	2,472	1,233	657	431	279	174	106	77	53	106	9	1
1998	**8,501**	1,837	1,252	3,089	2,307	1,260	667	406	253	171	127	68	42	106	4	1
1999	**7,923**	1,648	1,160	2,808	2,234	1,125	673	394	261	144	90	69	42	78	5	-
2000	**7,299**	1,443	1,047	2,490	2,070	1,053	638	380	243	154	92	79	34	60	5	1
Under 20																
1990	**11**	7	3	10	-	1	-	-	-	-	-	-	-	-	-	-
1991	**3**	1	-	1	2	-	-	-	-	-	-	-	-	-	-	-
1992	**6**	2	2	4	2	-	-	-	-	-	-	-	-	-	-	-
1993	**2**	2	-	2	-	-	-	-	-	-	-	-	-	-	-	-
1994	**5**	2	-	2	3	-	-	-	-	-	-	-	-	-	-	-
1995	**8**	5	-	5	3	-	-	-	-	-	-	-	-	-	-	-
1996	**5**	2	3	5	-	-	-	-	-	-	-	-	-	-	-	-
1997	**5**	3	2	5	-	-	-	-	-	-	-	-	-	-	-	-
1998	**2**	1	-	1	1	-	-	-	-	-	-	-	-	-	-	-
1999	**3**	1	2	3	-	-	-	-	-	-	-	-	-	-	-	-
2000	**4**	2	1	3	1	-	-	-	-	-	-	-	-	-	-	-
20-24																
1990	**637**	278	130	408	178	37	10	3	1	-	-	-	-	-	-	-
1991	**556**	244	101	345	160	34	12	4	1	-	-	-	-	-	-	-
1992	**502**	217	108	325	127	41	8	1	-	-	-	-	-	-	-	-
1993	**405**	184	84	268	100	20	13	2	1	-	-	-	-	-	-	-
1994	**304**	125	59	184	85	27	6	1	1	-	-	-	-	-	-	-
1995	**284**	111	73	184	73	19	6	1	1	-	-	1	1	1	-	-
1996	**249**	109	48	157	67	17	8	-	-	-	-	-	-	-	-	-
1997	**236**	89	50	139	71	16	6	3	1	-	-	-	-	-	-	-
1998	**192**	71	49	120	49	18	4	1	-	-	-	-	-	-	-	-
1999	**171**	67	46	113	44	7	6	1	-	-	-	-	-	-	-	-
2000	**149**	48	40	88	46	10	4	1	-	-	-	-	-	-	-	-
25-29																
1990	**3,868**	1,185	605	1,790	1,165	516	234	101	39	12	2	3	2	4	-	-
1991	**3,593**	979	591	1,570	1,158	462	217	104	46	22	7	3	1	3	-	-
1992	**3,209**	860	513	1,373	1,067	434	185	92	31	16	4	4	-	3	-	-
1993	**2,716**	742	454	1,196	881	353	157	71	31	14	6	3	1	-	-	-
1994	**2,649**	682	480	1,162	854	371	137	76	30	13	3	-	1	2	-	-
1995	**2,402**	647	436	1,083	774	320	112	71	26	11	2	1	1	1	-	-
1996	**2,103**	579	385	964	656	264	125	55	19	10	4	-	1	5	-	-
1997	**1,938**	526	340	866	658	242	96	40	19	10	4	1	-	2	-	-
1998	**1,719**	487	346	833	509	214	100	36	12	7	5	-	-	3	-	-
1999	**1,485**	418	322	740	440	179	66	33	20	5	2	-	-	-	-	-
2000	**1,247**	317	239	556	402	167	65	36	11	5	2	1	-	2	-	-
30 and over																
1990	**6,556**	1,356	739	2,095	1,670	928	603	378	299	201	132	83	48	110	9	-
1991	**6,582**	1,268	754	2,022	1,777	940	577	397	275	189	111	107	67	113	7	-
1992	**6,663**	1,273	683	1,956	1,839	1,022	593	407	273	189	121	89	42	125	6	1
1993	**6,394**	1,210	739	1,949	1,627	955	616	411	256	179	138	82	57	107	10	-
1994	**6,622**	1,293	726	2,019	1,786	986	593	424	267	157	156	74	43	107	10	-
1995	**6,461**	1,201	782	1,983	1,619	1,022	618	414	289	168	101	74	61	106	6	-
1996	**6,669**	1,259	828	2,087	1,816	950	611	391	274	180	127	70	48	103	10	2
1997	**6,451**	1,264	758	2,022	1,743	975	555	388	259	164	102	76	53	104	9	1
1998	**6,588**	1,278	857	2,135	1,748	1,028	563	369	241	164	122	68	42	103	4	1
1999	**6,264**	1,162	790	1,952	1,750	939	601	360	241	139	88	69	42	78	5	-
2000	**5,899**	1,076	767	1,843	1,621	876	569	343	232	149	90	78	34	58	5	1

Table 5.2   Live births within 8 months of marriage: order of marriage and age of mother, 1990-2000   England and Wales

Age of mother at birth	1990	1991	1992	1993	1994	1995	1996	1997	1998	1999	2000
All married women											
All ages	**36,167**	**32,037**	**30,510**	**28,249**	**27,242**	**25,454**	**25,265**	**24,467**	**24,042**	**23,196**	**20,806**
Under 16	1	5	-	4	3	2	1	4	1	1	-
16	166	108	97	96	78	61	86	73	48	54	42
17	627	455	410	308	269	250	225	221	223	201	156
18	1,590	1,168	997	788	731	587	546	595	569	552	467
19	2,472	1,926	1,512	1,291	1,052	960	925	818	861	842	737
Under 20	**4,856**	**3,662**	**3,016**	**2,487**	**2,133**	**1,860**	**1,783**	**1,711**	**1,702**	**1,650**	**1,402**
20	2,769	2,363	1,993	1,588	1,413	1,238	1,139	1,010	913	988	904
21	2,880	2,350	2,225	1,915	1,660	1,416	1,306	1,167	1,145	1,059	1,033
22	2,802	2,454	2,125	1,984	1,793	1,590	1,448	1,274	1,202	1,080	975
23	2,754	2,374	2,239	1,964	1,918	1,681	1,608	1,408	1,296	1,204	1,043
24	2,553	2,216	2,178	2,016	1,786	1,762	1,684	1,603	1,453	1,353	1,163
20-24	**13,758**	**11,757**	**10,760**	**9,467**	**8,570**	**7,687**	**7,185**	**6,462**	**6,009**	**5,684**	**5,118**
25-29	10,274	9,430	9,323	8,967	8,622	7,979	8,035	7,708	7,612	7,294	6,266
30-34	4,999	4,908	5,038	4,961	5,498	5,370	5,531	5,766	5,656	5,541	5,087
35-39	1,891	1,853	2,012	1,922	2,029	2,121	2,264	2,310	2,546	2,501	2,432
40 and over	389	427	361	445	390	437	467	510	517	526	501
Women married once only											
All ages	**29,114**	**25,765**	**24,364**	**22,673**	**21,683**	**20,250**	**20,175**	**19,596**	**19,438**	**19,169**	**17,210**
Under 16	1	5	-	4	3	2	1	4	1	1	-
16	165	108	97	96	78	61	86	73	48	54	42
17	624	454	409	308	269	250	225	220	222	201	156
18	1,587	1,168	995	786	731	584	546	595	568	552	467
19	2,465	1,920	1,510	1,288	1,049	956	919	815	861	841	735
Under 20	**4,842**	**3,655**	**3,011**	**2,482**	**2,130**	**1,853**	**1,777**	**1,707**	**1,700**	**1,649**	**1,400**
20	2,741	2,345	1,973	1,574	1,405	1,232	1,134	1,003	906	980	899
21	2,826	2,305	2,181	1,884	1,621	1,395	1,280	1,146	1,130	1,045	1,024
22	2,696	2,356	2,048	1,911	1,733	1,548	1,406	1,251	1,177	1,061	948
23	2,569	2,207	2,099	1,851	1,820	1,582	1,523	1,357	1,252	1,162	1,011
24	2,257	1,973	1,984	1,812	1,647	1,628	1,570	1,500	1,367	1,285	1,099
20-24	**13,089**	**11,186**	**10,285**	**9,032**	**8,226**	**7,385**	**6,913**	**6,257**	**5,832**	**5,533**	**4,981**
25-29	7,646	7,266	7,199	7,140	6,877	6,440	6,604	6,461	6,511	6,370	5,516
30-34	2,690	2,802	2,932	2,977	3,371	3,362	3,538	3,796	3,856	3,935	3,634
35-39	742	723	844	858	944	1,023	1,143	1,158	1,344	1,443	1,434
40 and over	105	133	93	184	135	187	200	217	195	239	245
Remarried women											
All ages	**7,053**	**6,272**	**6,146**	**5,576**	**5,559**	**5,204**	**5,090**	**4,871**	**4,604**	**4,027**	**3,596**
Under 16	-	-	-	-	-	-	-	-	-	-	-
16	1	-	-	-	-	-	-	-	-	-	-
17	3	1	1	-	-	-	-	1	1	-	-
18	3	-	2	2	-	3	-	-	1	-	-
19	7	6	2	3	3	4	6	3	-	1	2
Under 20	**14**	**7**	**5**	**5**	**3**	**7**	**6**	**4**	**2**	**1**	**2**
20	28	18	20	14	8	6	5	7	7	8	5
21	54	45	44	31	39	21	26	21	15	14	9
22	106	98	77	73	60	42	42	23	25	19	27
23	185	167	140	113	98	99	85	51	44	42	32
24	296	243	194	204	139	134	114	103	86	68	64
20-24	**669**	**571**	**475**	**435**	**344**	**302**	**272**	**205**	**177**	**151**	**137**
25-29	2,628	2,164	2,124	1,827	1,745	1,539	1,431	1,247	1,101	924	750
30-34	2,309	2,106	2,106	1,984	2,127	2,008	1,993	1,970	1,800	1,606	1,453
35-39	1,149	1,130	1,168	1,064	1,085	1,098	1,121	1,152	1,202	1,058	998
40 and over	284	294	268	261	255	250	267	293	322	287	256

Table 5.3 Live births within 8 months of marriage: duration of marriage, order of marriage and age of mother, 2000 　　　　　　　　　　　　　　**England and Wales**

Age of mother at birth	Duration of current marriage - completed months								
	0-7	0	1	2	3	4	5	6	7
All married women									
All ages	**20,806**	838	1,417	1,967	2,704	3,508	3,897	3,407	3,068
Under 16	-	-	-	-	-	-	-	-	-
16	**42**	9	9	8	9	2	1	2	2
17	**156**	20	17	23	26	23	16	22	9
18	**467**	31	54	58	72	78	75	52	47
19	**737**	24	79	92	115	112	122	97	96
Under 20	**1,402**	**84**	**159**	**181**	**222**	**215**	**214**	**173**	**154**
20	**904**	58	72	94	145	164	149	117	105
21	**1,033**	46	78	107	146	191	174	162	129
22	**975**	43	71	101	138	178	178	140	126
23	**1,043**	34	76	97	153	164	185	180	154
24	**1,163**	34	76	94	148	210	234	200	167
20-24	**5,118**	**215**	**373**	**493**	**730**	**907**	**920**	**799**	**681**
25-29	**6,266**	212	383	524	739	1,048	1,212	1,110	1,038
30-34	**5,087**	192	289	472	600	834	1,010	867	823
35-39	**2,432**	104	174	248	330	419	457	379	321
40 and over	**501**	31	39	49	83	85	84	79	51
Women married once only									
All ages	**17,210**	681	1,135	1,577	2,293	2,901	3,238	2,823	2,562
Under 16	-	-	-	-	-	-	-	-	-
16	**42**	9	9	8	9	2	1	2	2
17	**156**	20	17	23	26	23	16	22	9
18	**467**	31	54	58	72	78	75	52	47
19	**735**	24	79	92	115	110	122	97	96
Under 20	**1,400**	**84**	**159**	**181**	**222**	**213**	**214**	**173**	**154**
20	**899**	58	71	92	145	163	149	117	104
21	**1,024**	46	78	106	144	189	173	159	129
22	**948**	42	69	97	137	173	173	135	122
23	**1,011**	32	74	93	147	160	177	176	152
24	**1,099**	30	66	89	144	200	225	187	158
20-24	**4,981**	**208**	**358**	**477**	**717**	**885**	**897**	**774**	**665**
25-29	**5,516**	182	324	432	654	923	1,082	994	925
30-34	**3,634**	131	175	318	452	602	735	606	615
35-39	**1,434**	60	102	147	208	232	269	241	175
40 and over	**245**	16	17	22	40	46	41	35	28
Remarried women									
All ages	**3,596**	157	282	390	411	607	659	584	506
Under 16	-	-	-	-	-	-	-	-	-
16	-	-	-	-	-	-	-	-	-
17	-	-	-	-	-	-	-	-	-
18	-	-	-	-	-	-	-	-	-
19	**2**	-	-	-	-	2	-	-	-
Under 20	**2**	**-**	**-**	**-**	**-**	**2**	**-**	**-**	**-**
20	**5**	-	1	2	-	1	-	-	1
21	**9**	-	-	1	2	2	1	3	-
22	**27**	1	2	4	1	5	5	5	4
23	**32**	2	2	4	6	4	8	4	2
24	**64**	4	10	5	4	10	9	13	9
20-24	**137**	**7**	**15**	**16**	**13**	**22**	**23**	**25**	**16**
25-29	**750**	30	59	92	85	125	130	116	113
30-34	**1,453**	61	114	154	148	232	275	261	208
35-39	**998**	44	72	101	122	187	188	138	146
40 and over	**256**	15	22	27	43	39	43	44	23

Table 6.1   Maternities with multiple births: occurrence within/outside marriage   **England and Wales**
            and age of mother, 1990-2000
            a. numbers

Year	Age of mother at birth							
	All ages	Under 20	20-24	25-29	30-34	35-39	40-44	45 and over
	All maternities with multiple births							
1990	**8,145**	333	1,600	2,892	2,287	920	108	5
1991	**8,380**	298	1,561	2,833	2,558	994	125	11
1992	**8,525**	271	1,447	2,962	2,627	1,068	145	5
1993	**8,549**	286	1,407	2,800	2,794	1,096	154	12
1994	**8,719**	277	1,269	2,836	2,914	1,263	150	10
1995	**9,038**	291	1,306	2,906	2,993	1,348	175	19
1996	**8,883**	273	1,152	2,643	3,192	1,408	194	21
1997	**9,217**	263	1,124	2,615	3,360	1,599	233	23
1998	**9,080**	303	1,078	2,457	3,332	1,627	252	31
1999	**8,907**	291	958	2,412	3,250	1,728	239	29
2000	**8,792**	297	962	2,163	3,246	1,835	264	25
	Maternities within marriage with multiple births							
1990	**6,181**	76	956	2,347	1,940	767	90	5
1991	**6,182**	50	855	2,206	2,146	818	98	9
1992	**6,241**	53	799	2,245	2,155	868	116	5
1993	**6,209**	39	729	2,123	2,284	909	115	10
1994	**6,271**	34	656	2,094	2,362	1,003	112	10
1995	**6,498**	50	623	2,146	2,437	1,100	126	16
1996	**6,323**	28	501	1,914	2,590	1,120	152	18
1997	**6,369**	31	458	1,813	2,653	1,227	174	13
1998	**6,227**	41	427	1,668	2,606	1,269	192	24
1999	**6,011**	41	397	1,593	2,466	1,322	169	23
2000	**5,980**	35	347	1,432	2,539	1,408	195	24
	Maternities outside marriage with multiple births							
1990	**1,964**	257	644	545	347	153	18	-
1991	**2,198**	248	706	627	412	176	27	2
1992	**2,284**	218	648	717	472	200	29	-
1993	**2,340**	247	678	677	510	187	39	2
1994	**2,448**	243	613	742	552	260	38	-
1995	**2,540**	241	683	760	556	248	49	3
1996	**2,560**	245	651	729	602	288	42	3
1997	**2,848**	232	666	802	707	372	59	10
1998	**2,853**	262	651	789	726	358	60	7
1999	**2,896**	250	561	819	784	406	70	6
2000	**2,812**	262	615	731	707	427	69	1

Note: The figures include maternities where live births and/or stillbirths occurred.

Table 6.1 Maternities with multiple births: occurrence within/outside marriage and age of mother, 1990-2000
b. rates

England and Wales

Year	Age of mother at birth							
	All ages	Under 20	20-24	25-29	30-34	35-39	40-44	45 and over
	All maternities with multiple births per 1,000 all maternities							
1990	**11.6**	6.0	8.9	11.5	14.8	17.9	11.7	*9.9*
1991	**12.1**	5.7	9.0	11.5	16.1	18.8	13.5	*21.5*
1992	**12.5**	5.7	8.9	12.2	15.9	19.1	15.1	*10.0*
1993	**12.8**	6.3	9.3	12.0	16.5	18.9	15.5	*22.3*
1994	**13.2**	6.6	9.1	12.5	16.4	20.3	14.7	*20.7*
1995	**14.1**	6.9	10.0	13.5	16.7	20.9	16.3	*36.5*
1996	**13.8**	6.1	9.2	12.6	17.4	20.6	17.0	36.9
1997	**14.5**	5.7	9.5	13.0	18.2	21.7	19.1	40.6
1998	**14.4**	6.3	9.5	12.8	17.9	21.0	19.7	56.7
1999	**14.5**	6.0	8.7	13.4	17.8	21.6	17.7	47.4
2000	**14.7**	6.5	9.0	12.8	18.3	22.0	18.5	38.8
	Maternities within marriage with multiple births per 1,000 maternities within marriage							
1990	**12.3**	6.9	9.0	11.6	14.7	18.0	12.4	*11.5*
1991	**12.8**	5.6	9.0	11.3	16.0	18.9	13.5	*20.5*
1992	**13.3**	6.8	9.3	12.0	15.8	19.3	15.7	*12.5*
1993	**13.7**	5.7	9.5	12.0	16.5	19.6	15.2	*23.4*
1994	**14.1**	5.6	9.5	12.4	16.4	20.5	14.7	*27.9*
1995	**15.3**	8.9	10.3	13.7	17.1	21.9	15.9	*40.9*
1996	**15.3**	5.2	9.2	13.0	18.0	21.4	18.2	*41.3*
1997	**15.9**	5.9	9.4	13.1	18.5	22.0	20.0	*31.0*
1998	**15.9**	7.8	9.4	12.9	18.3	21.8	21.2	58.4
1999	**16.0**	7.7	9.2	13.3	17.8	22.2	18.0	49.9
2000	**16.5**	7.4	8.6	12.9	18.9	22.9	19.9	52.2
	Maternities outside marriage with multiple births per 1,000 maternities outside marriage							
1990	**9.9**	5.8	8.7	11.5	15.3	17.7	*9.4*	-
1991	**10.5**	5.7	9.1	12.0	16.2	18.1	13.4	*27.0*
1992	**10.7**	5.4	8.4	12.9	16.5	18.5	13.0	-
1993	**10.9**	6.5	9.1	11.8	16.4	15.8	16.6	*18.0*
1994	**11.4**	6.8	8.6	12.8	16.4	19.6	14.8	-
1995	**11.6**	6.6	9.8	12.9	15.2	17.4	17.4	*23.3*
1996	**11.1**	6.2	9.2	11.8	15.0	17.9	13.6	22.6
1997	**12.0**	5.6	9.6	12.7	16.9	20.7	16.8	68.5
1998	**11.9**	6.1	9.6	12.7	16.7	18.5	16.0	*51.5*
1999	**12.0**	5.8	8.3	13.5	17.6	19.8	17.0	*39.7*
2000	**11.9**	6.4	9.2	12.5	16.3	19.4	15.5	5.4

Note: 1. The figures include maternities where live births and/or stillbirths occurred.
       2. For information on the use of italics - see Section 2.21.

Table 6.2   Maternities with multiple births: whether live births or stillbirths, multiplicity, age of mother and sex, 2000   England and Wales

Age of mother at birth	Maternities	Births					
	Total	Live			Still		
		Total	Male	Female	Total	Male	Female
All maternities with multiple births*							
All ages	**8,792**	**17,573**	**8,805**	**8,768**	**283**	**148**	**135**
Under 20	297	**579**	285	294	**20**	10	10
20-24	962	**1,904**	955	949	**33**	16	17
25-29	2,163	**4,315**	2,191	2,124	**73**	33	40
30-34	3,246	**6,526**	3,226	3,300	**85**	49	36
35-39	1,835	**3,675**	1,878	1,797	**64**	35	29
40-44	264	**525**	244	281	**7**	4	3
45 and over	25	**49**	26	23	**1**	1	-
Twins only							
All ages	**8,526**	**16,785**	**8,422**	**8,363**	**269**	**143**	**126**
Under 20	292	**565**	281	284	**19**	9	10
20-24	951	**1,871**	938	933	**32**	16	16
25-29	2,103	**4,136**	2,099	2,037	**69**	32	37
30-34	3,128	**6,177**	3,060	3,117	**80**	49	31
35-39	1,767	**3,474**	1,779	1,695	**61**	32	29
40-44	260	**513**	239	274	**7**	4	3
45 and over	25	**49**	26	23	**1**	1	-
Triplets only							
All ages	**262**	**772**	**373**	**399**	**14**	**5**	**9**
Under 20	5	**14**	4	10	**1**	1	-
20-24	10	**29**	15	14	**1**	-	1
25-29	57	**167**	84	83	**4**	1	3
30-34	118	**349**	166	183	**5**	-	5
35-39	68	**201**	99	102	**3**	3	-
40-44	4	**12**	5	7	**-**	-	-
45 and over	-	**-**	-	-	**-**	-	-

* Includes quads and above

Table 6.3   Maternities within marriage with multiple births (numbers and rates): age of mother and number of previous liveborn children, 2000   England and Wale●

Number of previous liveborn children	Age of mother at birth							
	All ages	Under 20	20-24	25-29	30-34	35-39	40-44	45 and over
Numbers								
Total	**5,980**	**35**	**347**	**1,432**	**2,539**	**1,408**	**195**	**24**
0	**2,868**	27	172	756	1,238	584	78	13
1	**1,917**	8	132	415	818	474	65	5
2	**778**	-	35	173	316	230	21	3
3	**256**	-	6	62	100	74	12	2
4 and over	**161**	-	2	26	67	46	19	1
Rates: maternities with multiple births per 1,000 maternities within marriage								
Total	**16.5**	**7.4**	**8.6**	**12.9**	**18.9**	**22.9**	**19.9**	**52.2**
0	**19.9**	7.1	8.0	14.5	25.6	36.2	34.9	*123.8*
1	**14.4**	9.5	9.6	10.9	15.1	20.2	21.5	*51.0*
2	**14.3**	-	8.9	12.3	15.1	17.3	10.2	*30.9*
3	**13.9**	-	*7.3*	13.6	14.7	14.6	*10.5*	*32.3*
4 and over	**14.6**	-	*11.6*	14.3	16.7	12.7	*14.2*	*10.2*

Note: 1. The figures include maternities where live births and/or stillbirths occurred.
        2. For information on the use of italics - see Section 2.21.

Table 6.4 All maternities: age of mother, multiplicity and type of outcome, 2000   **England and Wales**

Outcome	All maternities							
	All ages	Under 20	20-24	25-29	30-34	35-39	40-44	45 and over
All maternities	**598,580**	**45,827**	**107,336**	**169,319**	**177,635**	**83,571**	**14,248**	**644**
Singleton maternities	**589,788**	**45,530**	**106,374**	**167,156**	**174,389**	**81,736**	**13,984**	**619**
1 LM	**300,820**	23,216	54,297	85,278	88,963	41,626	7,126	314
1 LF	**286,048**	22,051	51,540	81,108	84,624	39,673	6,752	300
1 SM	**1,583**	151	287	414	431	243	56	1
1 SF	**1,337**	112	250	356	371	194	50	4
All multiple maternities	**8,792**	**297**	**962**	**2,163**	**3,246**	**1,835**	**264**	**25**
Twins	**8,526**	**292**	**951**	**2,103**	**3,128**	**1,767**	**260**	**25**
2 LM	**2,746**	111	335	698	980	544	71	7
1 LM and 1 LF	**2,832**	54	255	676	1,079	663	93	12
2 LF	**2,714**	110	335	666	1,002	506	90	5
1 LM and 1 SM	**79**	5	12	19	20	19	4	-
1 LM and 1 SF	**18**	-	1	8	1	8	-	-
1 LF and 1 SM	**35**	2	1	9	12	10	-	1
1 LF and 1 SF	**68**	8	7	20	22	10	1	-
2 SM	**13**	1	1	2	8	1	-	-
1 SM and 1 SF	**1**	-	-	-	-	1	-	-
2 SF	**20**	1	4	5	4	5	1	-
Triplets	**262**	**5**	**10**	**57**	**118**	**68**	**4**	**-**
3 LM	**49**	-	4	13	18	13	1	-
2 LM and 1 LF	**73**	-	1	14	39	18	1	-
1 LM and 2 LF	**70**	2	1	13	33	21	-	-
3 LF	**58**	2	3	13	24	14	2	-
2 LM and 1 SM	**3**	1	-	1	-	1	-	-
2 LM and 1 SF	**1**	-	-	1	-	-	-	-
1 LM, 1 LF and 1 SM	**-**	-	-	-	-	-	-	-
1 LM, 1 LF and 1 SF	**-**	-	-	-	-	-	-	-
2 LF and 1 SM	**-**	-	-	-	-	-	-	-
2 LF and 1 SF	**6**	-	1	2	3	-	-	-
1 LM and 2 SM	**1**	-	-	-	-	1	-	-
1 LM, 1 SM and 1 SF	**-**	-	-	-	-	-	-	-
1 LM and 2 SF	**1**	-	-	-	1	-	-	-
1 LF and 2 SM	**-**	-	-	-	-	-	-	-
1 LF, 1 SM and 1 SF	**-**	-	-	-	-	-	-	-
1 LF and 2 SF	**-**	-	-	-	-	-	-	-
3 SM	**-**	-	-	-	-	-	-	-
2 SM and 1 SF	**-**	-	-	-	-	-	-	-
1 SM and 2 SF	**-**	-	-	-	-	-	-	-
3 SF	**-**	-	-	-	-	-	-	-
Quads and above	**4**	**-**	**1**	**3**	**-**	**-**	**-**	**-**
2 LM and 2 LF	**3**	-	1	2	-	-	-	-
4 LM	**1**	-	-	1	-	-	-	-

LM - Liveborn male   SM - Stillborn male   LF - Liveborn female   SF - Stillborn female

Table 7.1 Live births and stillbirths (numbers, rates, general fertility rate, and total fertility rate), and population: occurrence within/outside marriage, and area of usual residence, 2000

England and Wales and elsewhere, England, Wales, elsewhere, government office regions, Greater London, metropolitan counties, health regional office areas

Area of usual residence of mother	Estimated number of women aged 15-44	Live births			Stillbirths			Live births outside marriage per 1,000 live births	Stillbirths per 1,000 live and still births	General fertility rate (GFR)	Total fertility rate (TFR)
		Total	Within marrriage	Outside marriage	Total	Within marriage	Outside marriage				
England and Wales and elsewhere	**10,851.3**	**604,441**	**365,836**	**238,605**	**3,203**	**1,830**	**1,373**	**395**	**5.3**	**55.7**	**1.66**
England	10,279.6	**572,826**	349,059	223,767	**3,029**	1,743	1,286	391	5.3	55.7	1.65
Wales	571.8	**31,304**	16,541	14,763	**145**	72	73	472	4.6	54.8	1.70
Elsewhere	:	**311**	236	75	**29**	15	14	241	85.3	:	:
Government Office Regions											
North East	525.7	**26,499**	13,114	13,385	**140**	66	74	505	5.3	50.4	1.57
North West	1,402.2	**76,675**	41,163	35,512	**418**	204	214	463	5.4	54.7	1.67
Yorkshire and the Humber	1,022.0	**55,966**	31,966	24,000	**338**	181	157	429	6.0	54.8	1.69
East Midlands	846.9	**45,787**	26,901	18,886	**218**	131	87	412	4.7	54.1	1.64
West Midlands	1,067.2	**61,497**	36,989	24,508	**348**	189	159	399	5.6	57.6	1.75
East	1,099.5	**61,186**	39,584	21,602	**296**	172	124	353	4.8	55.6	1.63
London	1,719.1	**104,695**	68,564	36,131	**663**	415	248	345	6.3	60.9	1.72
South East	1,644.0	**90,445**	59,637	30,808	**398**	249	149	341	4.4	55.0	1.61
South West	953.1	**50,076**	31,141	18,935	**210**	136	74	378	4.2	52.5	1.58
Metropolitan Counties											
Greater London	1,719.1	**104,695**	68,564	36,131	**663**	415	248	345	6.3	60.9	1.72
Greater Manchester	543.7	**30,401**	16,117	14,284	**186**	97	89	470	6.1	55.9	1.68
Merseyside	290.1	**15,216**	6,792	8,424	**67**	20	47	554	4.4	52.4	1.61
South Yorkshire	264.6	**14,077**	7,334	6,743	**83**	39	44	479	5.9	53.2	1.64
Tyne and Wear	229.9	**11,489**	5,556	5,933	**59**	29	30	516	5.1	50.0	1.55
West Midlands	541.4	**33,398**	19,771	13,627	**212**	117	95	408	6.3	61.7	1.87
West Yorkshire	443.8	**25,379**	15,195	10,184	**169**	99	70	401	6.6	57.2	1.75
Health Regional Office Areas											
Northern and Yorkshire	1,283.1	**68,117**	37,895	30,222	**384**	205	179	444	5.6	53.1	1.64
Trent	1,034.7	**55,248**	31,238	24,010	**293**	160	133	435	5.3	53.4	1.63
Eastern	1,099.5	**61,186**	39,584	21,602	**296**	172	124	353	4.8	55.6	1.63
London	1,719.1	**104,695**	68,564	36,131	**663**	415	248	345	6.3	60.9	1.72
South East	1,773.1	**98,121**	64,140	33,981	**432**	268	164	346	4.4	55.3	1.63
South West	953.1	**50,076**	31,141	18,935	**210**	136	74	378	4.2	52.5	1.58
West Midlands	1,067.2	**61,497**	36,989	24,508	**348**	189	159	399	5.6	57.6	1.75
North West	1,349.8	**73,886**	39,508	34,378	**403**	198	205	465	5.4	54.7	1.67

Table 7.2   Live births (numbers and rates): age of mother and area of usual residence, 2000

England and Wales and elsewhere, England,
Wales, elsewhere, government office regions,
Greater London, metropolitan counties,
health regional office areas

Area of usual residence of mother	Age of mother at birth							Age of mother at birth						
	All ages	Under 20	20-24	25-29	30-34	35-39	40 and over	All ages*	Under 20	20-24	25-29	30-34	35-39	40 and over
	Numbers							Rates per 1,000 women in age-group						
England and Wales and elsewhere	**604,441**	**45,846**	**107,741**	**170,701**	**180,113**	**84,974**	**15,066**	**55.7**	**29.2**	**70.6**	**95.4**	**88.0**	**40.5**	**8.3**
England	**572,826**	42,527	101,322	161,449	171,793	81,331	14,404	**55.7**	28.8	70.2	94.9	88.3	40.9	8.4
Wales	**31,304**	3,306	6,383	9,158	8,229	3,579	649	**54.8**	35.2	78.5	104.5	80.5	33.0	6.6
Elsewhere	**311**	13	36	94	91	64	13	**:**	:	:	:	:	:	:
Government Office Regions														
North East	**26,499**	3,061	5,834	7,370	6,861	2,894	479	**50.4**	37.2	78.2	91.6	73.4	28.4	5.2
North West	**76,675**	7,229	15,512	21,859	21,069	9,421	1,585	**54.7**	33.4	80.1	96.3	81.8	34.8	6.7
Yorkshire and the Humber	**55,966**	5,386	11,873	16,668	14,922	6,103	1,014	**54.8**	34.5	79.5	107.2	79.2	30.8	5.8
East Midlands	**45,787**	3,737	8,538	13,522	13,207	5,830	953	**54.1**	29.4	74.2	99.6	82.7	35.5	6.6
West Midlands	**61,497**	5,371	12,433	18,008	17,093	7,310	1,282	**57.6**	32.6	84.0	106.1	84.8	35.7	7.2
East	**61,186**	3,694	9,763	17,732	19,589	8,987	1,421	**55.6**	23.9	71.6	90.2	90.0	42.8	7.7
London	**104,695**	5,470	16,156	27,335	33,655	18,399	3,680	**60.9**	27.8	55.9	89.4	102.2	55.1	14.0
South East	**90,445**	5,203	13,176	24,544	29,894	15,022	2,606	**55.0**	22.2	62.0	88.5	93.7	47.0	9.3
South West	**50,076**	3,376	8,037	14,411	15,503	7,365	1,384	**52.5**	23.7	64.1	93.5	87.0	39.7	8.2
Metropolitan Counties														
Greater London	**104,695**	5,470	16,156	27,335	33,655	18,399	3,680	**60.9**	27.8	55.9	89.4	102.2	55.1	14.0
Greater Manchester	**30,401**	3,033	6,614	8,730	7,919	3,492	613	**55.9**	36.6	82.0	98.0	78.6	33.8	7.1
Merseyside	**15,216**	1,551	3,089	4,201	4,145	1,909	321	**52.4**	33.7	72.7	93.7	82.5	33.5	6.5
South Yorkshire	**14,077**	1,486	3,067	4,170	3,650	1,454	250	**53.2**	37.8	82.5	100.3	73.2	28.1	5.6
Tyne and Wear	**11,489**	1,318	2,574	3,212	2,940	1,232	213	**50.0**	37.1	69.2	96.6	74.4	27.6	5.4
West Midlands	**33,398**	3,244	7,686	9,835	8,430	3,539	664	**61.7**	37.9	89.2	119.0	84.6	34.6	7.8
West Yorkshire	**25,379**	2,471	5,704	7,648	6,497	2,642	417	**57.2**	36.5	78.9	116.3	80.2	31.3	5.7
Health Regional Office Areas														
Northern and Yorkshire	**68,117**	6,813	14,358	19,789	18,263	7,626	1,268	**53.1**	34.3	76.9	101.6	78.7	30.7	5.7
Trent	**55,248**	5,011	10,999	16,316	15,281	6,557	1,084	**53.4**	32.2	78.3	99.0	78.2	32.7	6.1
Eastern	**61,186**	3,694	9,763	17,732	19,589	8,987	1,421	**55.6**	23.9	71.6	90.2	90.0	42.8	7.7
London	**104,695**	5,470	16,156	27,335	33,655	18,399	3,680	**60.9**	27.8	55.9	89.4	102.2	55.1	14.0
South East	**98,121**	5,801	14,539	26,854	32,172	15,993	2,762	**55.3**	22.9	63.3	90.0	93.6	46.3	9.1
South West	**50,076**	3,376	8,037	14,411	15,503	7,365	1,384	**52.5**	23.7	64.1	93.5	87.0	39.7	8.2
West Midlands	**61,497**	5,371	12,433	18,008	17,093	7,310	1,282	**57.6**	32.6	84.0	106.1	84.8	35.7	7.2
North West	**73,886**	6,991	15,037	21,004	20,237	9,094	1,523	**54.7**	33.5	79.8	96.3	81.8	34.9	6.7

* The rates for women of all ages, under 20 and 40 and over are based on women aged 15-44, 15-19 and 40-44 respectively

Table 7.3 Live births (numbers and percentages): birthweight and area of usual residence, 2000

England and Wales and elsewhere, England, Wales, elsewhere, government office regions, Greater London, metropolitan counties, health regional office areas

Area of usual residence of mother	Birthweight (grams)												
	All weights	Under 1,500	1,500-1,999	2,000-2,499	2,500-2,999	3,000-3,499	3,500 and over	All weights	Under 1,500	1,500-1,999	2,000-2,499	2,500-2,999	3,000-3,499	3,500 and over
	Numbers							Percentages						
England and Wales and elsewhere	604,441	7,536	9,234	28,957	99,738	215,898	242,058	100	1.2	1.5	4.8	16.5	35.7	40.0
England	572,826	7,143	8,738	27,457	94,747	204,532	229,227	100	1.2	1.5	4.8	16.5	35.7	40.0
Wales	31,304	375	484	1,483	4,928	11,275	12,723	100	1.2	1.5	4.7	15.7	36.0	40.6
Elsewhere	311	18	12	17	63	91	108	100	5.8	3.9	5.5	20.3	29.3	34.7
Government Office Regions														
North East	26,499	311	423	1,317	4,418	9,324	10,685	100	1.2	1.6	5.0	16.7	35.2	40.3
North West	76,675	1,010	1,199	3,808	12,597	26,982	30,993	100	1.3	1.6	5.0	16.4	35.2	40.4
Yorkshire and the Humber	55,966	746	886	2,870	9,898	19,921	21,607	100	1.3	1.6	5.1	17.7	35.6	38.6
East Midlands	45,787	586	775	2,212	7,550	16,108	18,511	100	1.3	1.7	4.8	16.5	35.2	40.4
West Midlands	61,497	841	985	3,325	11,027	22,192	23,094	100	1.4	1.6	5.4	17.9	36.1	37.6
East	61,186	644	902	2,606	9,578	21,642	25,675	100	1.1	1.5	4.3	15.7	35.4	42.0
London	104,695	1,505	1,603	5,396	18,517	39,060	38,116	100	1.4	1.5	5.2	17.7	37.3	36.4
South East	90,445	953	1,297	3,834	13,724	31,710	38,821	100	1.1	1.4	4.2	15.2	35.1	42.9
South West	50,076	547	668	2,089	7,438	17,593	21,725	100	1.1	1.3	4.2	14.9	35.1	43.4
Metropolitan Counties														
Greater London	104,695	1,505	1,603	5,396	18,517	39,060	38,116	100	1.4	1.5	5.2	17.7	37.3	36.4
Greater Manchester	30,401	427	487	1,653	5,250	10,927	11,623	100	1.4	1.6	5.4	17.3	35.9	38.2
Merseyside	15,216	188	229	735	2,355	5,288	6,414	100	1.2	1.5	4.8	15.5	34.8	42.2
South Yorkshire	14,077	186	215	761	2,408	5,016	5,482	100	1.3	1.5	5.4	17.1	35.6	38.9
Tyne and Wear	11,489	115	203	608	1,920	4,024	4,614	100	1.0	1.8	5.3	16.7	35.0	40.2
West Midlands	33,398	482	601	2,063	6,658	12,201	11,376	100	1.4	1.8	6.2	19.9	36.5	34.1
West Yorkshire	25,379	358	415	1,431	4,990	9,122	9,040	100	1.4	1.6	5.6	19.7	35.9	35.6
Health Regional Office Areas														
Northern and Yorkshire	68,117	855	1,080	3,392	11,833	24,141	26,763	100	1.3	1.6	5.0	17.4	35.4	39.3
Trent	55,248	710	918	2,745	9,276	19,470	22,081	100	1.3	1.7	5.0	16.8	35.2	40.0
Eastern	61,186	644	902	2,606	9,578	21,642	25,675	100	1.1	1.5	4.3	15.7	35.4	42.0
London	104,695	1,505	1,603	5,396	18,517	39,060	38,116	100	1.4	1.5	5.2	17.7	37.3	36.4
South East	98,121	1,061	1,418	4,198	14,914	34,437	41,980	100	1.1	1.4	4.3	15.2	35.1	42.8
South West	50,076	547	668	2,089	7,438	17,593	21,725	100	1.1	1.3	4.2	14.9	35.1	43.4
West Midlands	61,497	841	985	3,325	11,027	22,192	23,094	100	1.4	1.6	5.4	17.9	36.1	37.6
North West	73,886	980	1,164	3,706	12,164	25,997	29,793	100	1.3	1.6	5.0	16.5	35.2	40.3

Note: Births where the birthweight was not stated are included in 'All weights' but are otherwise excluded.

Table 7.4 Stillbirths (numbers and percentages): birthweight and area of usual residence, 2000

England and Wales and elsewhere, England, Wales, elsewhere, government office regions, Greater London, metropolitan counties, health regional office areas

Area of usual residence of mother	Birthweight (grams)													
	All weights	Under 1,500	1,500-1,999	2,000-2,499	2,500-2,999	3,000-3,499	3,500 and over	All weights	Under 1,500	1,500-1,999	2,000-2,499	2,500-2,999	3,000-3,499	3,500 and over
	Numbers							**Percentages**						
England and Wales and elsewhere	3,203	1,345	316	367	371	311	244	100	42.0	9.9	11.5	11.6	9.7	7.6
England	3,029	1,261	294	348	354	297	239	100	41.6	9.7	11.5	11.7	9.8	7.9
Wales	145	65	17	17	16	14	5	100	44.8	11.7	11.7	11.0	9.7	3.4
Elsewhere	29	19	5	2	1	-	-	100	65.5	17.2	6.9	3.4	-	-
Government Office Regions														
North East	140	57	13	24	14	14	10	100	40.7	9.3	17.1	10.0	10.0	7.1
North West	418	158	47	44	42	47	33	100	37.8	11.2	10.5	10.0	11.2	7.9
Yorkshire and the Humber	338	141	41	37	40	36	24	100	41.7	12.1	10.9	11.8	10.7	7.1
East Midlands	218	75	22	24	30	29	18	100	34.4	10.1	11.0	13.8	13.3	8.3
West Midlands	348	154	31	49	40	33	24	100	44.3	8.9	14.1	11.5	9.5	6.9
East	296	130	36	27	31	31	24	100	43.9	12.2	9.1	10.5	10.5	8.1
London	663	309	51	62	76	58	48	100	46.6	7.7	9.4	11.5	8.7	7.2
South East	398	160	30	52	54	31	37	100	40.2	7.5	13.1	13.6	7.8	9.3
South West	210	77	23	29	27	18	21	100	36.7	11.0	13.8	12.9	8.6	10.0
Metropolitan Counties														
Greater London	663	309	51	62	76	58	48	100	46.6	7.7	9.4	11.5	8.7	7.2
Greater Manchester	186	69	22	21	17	20	14	100	37.1	11.8	11.3	9.1	10.8	7.5
Merseyside	67	22	11	10	5	7	4	100	32.8	16.4	14.9	7.5	10.4	6.0
South Yorkshire	83	34	6	11	10	8	8	100	41.0	7.2	13.3	12.0	9.6	9.6
Tyne and Wear	59	23	5	10	6	5	5	100	39.0	8.5	16.9	10.2	8.5	8.5
West Midlands	212	91	20	33	21	17	15	100	42.9	9.4	15.6	9.9	8.0	7.1
West Yorkshire	169	74	22	17	18	19	12	100	43.8	13.0	10.1	10.7	11.2	7.1
Health Regional Office Areas														
Northern and Yorkshire	384	160	42	50	46	40	27	100	41.7	10.9	13.0	12.0	10.4	7.0
Trent	293	105	31	35	40	34	24	100	35.8	10.6	11.9	13.7	11.6	8.2
Eastern	296	130	36	27	31	31	24	100	43.9	12.2	9.1	10.5	10.5	8.1
London	663	309	51	62	76	58	48	100	46.6	7.7	9.4	11.5	8.7	7.2
South East	432	172	33	55	58	37	39	100	39.8	7.6	12.7	13.4	8.6	9.0
South West	210	77	23	29	27	18	21	100	36.7	11.0	13.8	12.9	8.6	10.0
West Midlands	348	154	31	49	40	33	24	100	44.3	8.9	14.1	11.5	9.5	6.9
North West	403	154	47	41	36	46	32	100	38.2	11.7	10.2	8.9	11.4	7.9

Note: Births where the birthweight was not stated are included in 'All weights' but are otherwise excluded.

Table 8.1 Maternities: age of mother, occurrence within/outside marriage, number of previous liveborn children* and place of confinement, 2000

England and Wales

	Place of confinement†	Age of mother at birth							
		All ages	Under 20	20-24	25-29	30-34	35-39	40-44	45 and over
Total	**Total**	**598,580**	**45,827**	**107,336**	**169,319**	**177,635**	**83,571**	**14,248**	**644**
	NHS Hospitals	**581,850**	**45,430**	**105,687**	**165,213**	**171,400**	**79,876**	**13,624**	**620**
	Non-NHS Hospitals	**3,310**	**31**	**253**	**692**	**1,307**	**844**	**173**	**10**
	At Home	**12,803**	**295**	**1,260**	**3,255**	**4,781**	**2,764**	**436**	**12**
	Elsewhere	**617**	**71**	**136**	**159**	**147**	**87**	**15**	**2**
All born within marriage	**Total**	**361,469**	**4,736**	**40,124**	**110,637**	**134,166**	**61,558**	**9,788**	**460**
	NHS Hospitals	**349,758**	4,677	39,365	107,922	129,292	58,712	9,348	442
	Non-NHS Hospitals	**3,031**	20	226	638	1,222	776	141	8
	At Home	**8,418**	34	498	2,012	3,562	2,013	289	10
	Elsewhere	**262**	5	35	65	90	57	10	-
Previous liveborn 0	**Total**	**144,169**	**3,802**	**21,504**	**52,101**	**48,306**	**16,115**	**2,236**	**105**
	NHS Hospitals	**141,720**	3,773	21,260	51,399	47,318	15,696	2,171	103
	Non-NHS Hospitals	**1,386**	16	131	368	561	264	44	2
	At Home	**1,031**	12	106	323	419	151	20	-
	Elsewhere	**32**	1	7	11	8	4	1	-
1	**Total**	**133,328**	**839**	**13,681**	**38,112**	**54,141**	**23,440**	**3,017**	**98**
	NHS Hospitals	**128,606**	812	13,329	36,972	52,089	22,410	2,904	90
	Non-NHS Hospitals	**1,035**	4	79	183	437	282	46	4
	At Home	**3,579**	19	256	935	1,574	727	64	4
	Elsewhere	**108**	4	17	22	41	21	3	-
2	**Total**	**54,447**	**82**	**3,944**	**14,038**	**20,918**	**13,309**	**2,059**	**97**
	NHS Hospitals	**51,456**	79	3,818	13,429	19,669	12,435	1,932	94
	Non-NHS Hospitals	**439**	-	14	68	165	161	31	-
	At Home	**2,481**	3	103	518	1,060	699	95	3
	Elsewhere	**71**	-	9	23	24	14	1	-
3	**Total**	**18,461**	**8**	**823**	**4,566**	**6,785**	**5,077**	**1,140**	**62**
	NHS Hospitals	**17,391**	8	790	4,372	6,386	4,716	1,060	59
	Non-NHS Hospitals	**113**	-	2	16	33	49	12	1
	At Home	**924**	-	29	173	354	301	65	2
	Elsewhere	**33**	-	2	5	12	11	3	-
4	**Total**	**6,428**	**2**	**144**	**1,347**	**2,383**	**1,904**	**617**	**31**
	NHS Hospitals	**6,112**	2	140	1,290	2,259	1,801	590	30
	Non-NHS Hospitals	**30**	-	-	1	15	7	6	1
	At Home	**276**	-	4	54	105	93	20	-
	Elsewhere	**10**	-	-	2	4	3	1	-
4 and over	**Total**	**11,064**	**5**	**172**	**1,820**	**4,016**	**3,617**	**1,336**	**98**
	NHS Hospitals	**10,585**	5	168	1,750	3,830	3,455	1,281	96
	Non-NHS Hospitals	**58**	-	-	3	26	20	8	1
	At Home	**403**	-	4	63	155	135	45	1
	Elsewhere	**18**	-	-	4	5	7	2	-
5-9	**Total**	**4,507**	**3**	**28**	**471**	**1,621**	**1,659**	**665**	**60**
	NHS Hospitals	**4,350**	3	28	458	1,559	1,604	639	59
	Non-NHS Hospitals	**25**	-	-	2	11	12	-	-
	At Home	**125**	-	-	9	50	40	25	1
	Elsewhere	**7**	-	-	2	1	3	1	-
10-14	**Total**	**126**	-	-	**2**	**12**	**54**	**51**	**7**
	NHS Hospitals	**120**	-	-	2	12	50	49	7
	Non-NHS Hospitals	**3**	-	-	-	-	1	2	-
	At Home	**2**	-	-	-	-	2	-	-
	Elsewhere	**1**	-	-	-	-	1	-	-
15 and over	**Total**	**3**	-	-	-	-	-	**3**	-
	NHS Hospitals	**3**	-	-	-	-	-	3	-
	Non-NHS Hospitals	**-**	-	-	-	-	-	-	-
	At Home	**-**	-	-	-	-	-	-	-
	Elsewhere	**-**	-	-	-	-	-	-	-
All born outside marriage	**Total**	**237,111**	**41,091**	**67,212**	**58,682**	**43,469**	**22,013**	**4,460**	**184**
	NHS Hospitals	**232,092**	40,753	66,322	57,291	42,108	21,164	4,276	178
	Non-NHS Hospitals	**279**	11	27	54	85	68	32	2
	At Home	**4,385**	261	762	1,243	1,219	751	147	2
	Elsewhere	**355**	66	101	94	57	30	5	2

* See Section 2.15.
† See Section 3.7.

Table 8.2 Maternities: place of confinement and whether area of occurrence is the same as area of usual residence, and area of usual residence, 2000

England and Wales and elsewhere,
England and Wales, England, elsewhere,
health regional office areas, health authorities

Area of usual residence	Place of confinement*					Health authority of occurrence		
	Total	NHS hospitals	Non-NHS hospitals	At home	Elsewhere	Same as usual residence	Other than usual residence	Not identified
England and Wales and elsewhere	598,580	581,850	3,310	12,803	617	496,805	101,775	-
England and Wales	598,247	581,593	3,243	12,803	608	496,796	101,451	-
England	567,297	551,390	3,242	12,108	557	469,256	98,041	-
Elsewhere	333	257	67	-	9	9	324	-
Northern and Yorkshire	67,522	66,554	2	906	60	65,923	633	966
Bradford	7,004	6,935	-	63	6	6,647	288	69
Calderdale and Kirklees	7,050	6,925	-	119	6	6,598	327	125
County Durham and Darlington	6,005	5,926	2	75	2	4,583	1,345	77
East Riding and Hull	5,626	5,498	-	118	10	4,805	693	128
Gateshead and South Tyneside	3,555	3,510	-	42	3	2,706	804	45
Leeds	7,703	7,587	-	111	5	7,028	559	116
Newcastle and North Tyneside	4,883	4,828	-	47	8	4,765	63	55
North Cumbria	3,094	3,029	-	61	4	2,886	143	65
Northumberland	2,762	2,747	-	12	3	2,168	579	15
North Yorkshire	7,332	7,194	-	134	4	6,249	945	138
Sunderland	2,937	2,906	-	26	5	2,539	367	31
Tees	6,123	6,070	-	50	3	5,999	71	53
Wakefield	3,448	3,399	-	48	1	3,066	333	49
Trent	54,716	53,545	4	1,097	70	50,289	3,260	1,167
Barnsley	2,326	2,298	-	22	6	2,021	277	28
Doncaster	3,155	3,115	-	37	3	2,941	174	40
Leicestershire	10,654	10,430	1	211	12	8,739	1,692	223
Lincolnshire	6,105	5,972	3	118	12	4,560	1,415	130
North Derbyshire	3,577	3,493	-	76	8	2,544	949	84
North Nottinghamshire	4,071	4,003	-	64	4	3,114	889	68
Nottingham	6,693	6,572	-	117	4	6,508	64	121
Rotherham	2,779	2,734	-	44	1	2,264	470	45
Sheffield	5,704	5,515	-	185	4	5,288	227	189
Southern Derbyshire	6,273	6,145	-	119	9	4,130	2,015	128
South Humber	3,379	3,268	-	104	7	3,166	102	111
Eastern	60,501	58,158	642	1,643	58	55,454	3,346	1,701
Bedfordshire	7,363	7,176	9	168	10	6,213	972	178
Cambridgeshire	8,005	7,741	72	182	10	7,266	547	192
East and North Hertfordshire	6,026	5,838	26	158	4	4,175	1,689	162
Norfolk	7,778	7,429	122	219	8	6,983	568	227
North Essex	9,737	9,399	38	291	9	8,284	1,153	300
South Essex	7,983	7,746	10	223	4	6,725	1,031	227
Suffolk	6,955	6,419	306	222	8	5,255	1,470	230
West Hertfordshire	6,654	6,410	59	180	5	5,187	1,282	185
London	103,728	99,246	2,187	2,199	96	99,841	1,592	2,295
Barking and Havering	4,584	4,510	1	69	4	3,088	1,423	73
Barnet	4,078	3,817	224	34	3	1,890	2,151	37
Bexley and Greenwich	5,848	5,642	16	183	7	5,219	439	190
Brent and Harrow	6,527	6,381	79	61	6	4,325	2,135	67
Bromley	3,504	3,393	17	92	2	2,563	847	94
Camden and Islington	5,398	4,960	317	117	4	4,427	850	121
Croydon	4,540	4,416	11	107	6	3,804	623	113
Ealing, Hammersmith and Hounslow	9,866	9,512	189	161	4	7,491	2,210	165
East London and The City	12,341	12,084	98	140	19	10,695	1,487	159

See Section 3.7

Table 8.2 - *continued*

Area of usual residence	Place of confinement*					Health authority of occurrence		
	Total	NHS hospitals	Non-NHS hospitals	At home	Elsewhere	Same as usual residence	Other than usual residence	Not identified
Enfield and Haringey	7,530	7,245	86	193	6	4,904	2,427	199
Hillingdon	3,289	3,211	24	53	1	2,691	544	54
Kensington & Chelsea and Westminster	4,538	3,675	805	54	4	3,919	561	58
Kingston and Richmond	4,141	3,975	88	77	1	2,819	1,244	78
Lambeth, Southwark and Lewisham	12,270	11,596	60	589	25	10,554	1,102	614
Merton, Sutton and Wandsworth	8,628	8,296	156	173	3	5,380	3,072	176
Redbridge and Waltham Forest	6,646	6,533	16	96	1	5,922	627	97
South East	**97,020**	**93,810**	**373**	**2,734**	**103**	**90,998**	**3,185**	**2,837**
Berkshire	10,188	9,836	111	229	12	8,144	1,803	241
Buckinghamshire	8,376	8,184	60	129	3	7,204	1,040	132
East Kent	6,271	6,039	2	220	10	5,938	103	230
East Surrey	4,685	4,531	33	118	3	3,583	981	121
East Sussex, Brighton and Hove	7,407	7,012	8	382	5	6,148	872	387
Isle of Wight	1,169	1,120	1	45	3	1,112	9	48
North and Mid Hampshire	6,398	6,200	16	175	7	3,632	2,584	182
Northamptonshire	7,565	7,400	5	150	10	6,610	795	160
Oxfordshire	7,122	6,902	12	201	7	6,336	578	208
Portsmouth and South East Hampshire	5,795	5,648	17	120	10	5,260	405	130
Southampton and South West Hampshire	5,613	5,417	13	174	9	4,221	1,209	183
West Kent	11,421	10,968	14	432	7	10,202	780	439
West Surrey	7,188	6,951	72	156	9	6,735	288	165
West Sussex	7,822	7,602	9	203	8	6,937	674	211
South West	**49,564**	**47,663**	**22**	**1,830**	**49**	**47,171**	**514**	**1,879**
Avon	10,950	10,531	2	409	8	10,427	106	417
Cornwall and Isles of Scilly	4,474	4,287	-	180	7	3,414	873	187
Dorset	6,194	5,969	4	216	5	5,475	498	221
Gloucestershire	6,015	5,876	1	135	3	5,342	535	138
North and East Devon	4,464	4,215	1	242	6	4,056	160	248
Somerset	4,963	4,767	2	188	6	4,010	759	194
South and West Devon	5,552	5,228	2	313	9	5,059	171	322
Wiltshire	6,952	6,790	10	147	5	5,068	1,732	152
West Midlands	**60,969**	**60,068**	**7**	**836**	**58**	**59,105**	**970**	**894**
Birmingham	14,231	14,094	-	121	16	12,769	1,325	137
Coventry	3,605	3,583	-	20	2	3,400	183	22
Dudley	3,509	3,452	-	55	2	3,049	403	57
Herefordshire	1,607	1,550	-	56	1	1,394	156	57
North Staffordshire	4,780	4,715	-	61	4	4,464	251	65
Sandwell	3,734	3,697	-	32	5	2,104	1,593	37
Shropshire	4,585	4,493	-	80	12	4,130	363	92
Solihull	1,965	1,946	-	18	1	1,175	771	19
South Staffordshire	5,930	5,818	1	103	8	3,951	1,868	111
Walsall	3,223	3,183	1	39	-	2,856	328	39
Warwickshire	5,321	5,180	-	138	3	3,927	1,253	141
Wolverhampton	2,878	2,850	-	27	1	2,641	209	28
Worcestershire	5,601	5,507	5	86	3	4,767	745	89
North West	**73,277**	**72,346**	**5**	**863**	**63**	**71,820**	**531**	**926**
Bury and Rochdale	4,688	4,648	-	36	4	3,478	1,170	40
East Lancashire	6,549	6,467	1	69	12	5,555	913	81
Liverpool	5,122	5,087	-	31	4	5,001	86	35
Manchester	5,508	5,414	-	90	4	5,175	239	94
Morecambe Bay	2,937	2,893	-	40	4	2,867	26	44
North Cheshire	3,663	3,628	-	32	3	2,693	935	35

* See Section 3.7

Table 8.2 - *continued*

Area of usual residence	Place of confinement*					Health authority of occurrence		
	Total	NHS hospitals	Non-NHS hospitals	At home	Elsewhere	Same as usual residence	Other than usual residence	Not identified
North West Lancashire	**4,637**	4,564	-	68	5	4,425	139	73
St Helen's and Knowsley	**3,857**	3,835	-	20	2	2,010	1,825	22
Salford and Trafford	**4,917**	4,872	-	42	3	3,344	1,528	45
Sefton	**2,675**	2,648	-	22	5	896	1,752	27
South Cheshire	**6,779**	6,643	3	125	8	5,865	781	133
South Lancashire	**3,125**	3,074	-	50	1	978	2,096	51
Stockport	**3,040**	2,982	-	57	1	2,496	486	58
West Pennine	**5,711**	5,612	-	97	2	4,878	734	99
Wigan and Bolton	**6,670**	6,607	-	60	3	5,966	641	63
Wirral	**3,399**	3,372	1	24	2	2,996	377	26
Wales	**30,950**	**30,203**	**1**	**695**	**51**	**29,173**	**1,031**	**746**
North Wales	**6,912**	6,775	1	124	12	6,216	560	136
Dyfed Powys	4,614	4,424	-	177	13	3,167	1,257	190
Morgannwg	5,148	5,055	-	88	5	4,979	76	93
Bro Taf	8,121	7,972	-	137	12	7,797	175	149
Gwent	6,155	5,977	-	169	9	5,381	596	178

* See Section 3.7

Table 8.3   Maternities in hospitals: live births and stillbirths, and area of occurrence*, 2000

England and Wales, England, Wales, government office regions, health regional office areas

Area of occurrence	Total maternities	Live births	Stillbirths	Stillbirths per 1,000 live births and stillbirths
England and Wales	**585,160**	**591,051**	**3,148**	**5.30**
England	**555,650**	**561,184**	**3,018**	**5.35**
Wales	**29,510**	**29,867**	**130**	**4.33**
Government Office Regions				
North East	**26,174**	26,429	135	5.08
North West	**76,344**	76,990	428	5.53
Yorkshire and the Humber	**54,904**	55,372	341	6.12
East Midlands	**40,281**	40,736	188	4.59
West Midlands	**61,230**	61,773	346	5.57
East	**57,389**	58,064	281	4.82
London	**104,789**	105,813	705	6.62
South East	**86,261**	87,197	384	4.38
South West	**48,278**	48,810	210	4.28
Health Regional Office Areas				
Northern and Yorkshire	**66,553**	67,165	376	5.57
Trent	**50,829**	51,329	275	5.33
Eastern	**57,389**	58,064	281	4.82
London	**104,789**	105,813	705	6.62
South East	**93,171**	94,206	410	4.33
South West	**48,278**	48,810	210	4.28
West Midlands	**61,230**	61,773	346	5.57
North West	**73,411**	74,024	415	5.58

* Area of occurrence is not equivalent to area of usual address as defined in Tables 7.1, 7.2 and 8.2

Table 9.1 Live births (numbers and percentages): country of birth of mother, 1990-2000   **England and Wales**

Country of birth of mother	1990	1995	1996	1997	1998	1999	2000
	Numbers						
Total	**706,140**	**648,138**	**649,485**	**643,095**	**635,901**	**621,872**	**604,441**
United Kingdom*	624,160	566,452	566,352	558,591	549,432	532,852	510,835
Total outside the United Kingdom	**81,946**	**81,677**	**83,123**	**84,497**	**86,456**	**89,000**	**93,588**
Irish Republic	6,424	5,167	4,968	4,903	4,673	4,470	4,050
Australia, Canada and New Zealand	2,998	3,051	3,182	3,319	3,393	3,531	3,635
New Commonwealth	**49,790**	**47,486**	**47,219**	**46,063**	**46,023**	**46,201**	**47,249**
India	8,570	6,684	6,608	6,553	6,513	6,497	6,650
Pakistan	12,359	12,324	12,319	12,571	13,069	13,472	13,561
Bangladesh	5,618	6,783	6,930	7,307	7,424	7,375	7,482
East Africa	6,590	5,128	5,121	4,745	4,498	4,159	3,959
Southern Africa	:	1,010	1,080	1,211	1,437	1,608	1,907
Rest of Africa	4,954	6,438	6,484	6,377	6,135	6,138	6,537
Caribbean	3,809	2,912	2,754	2,627	2,564	2,536	2,681
Far East†	3,963	3,311	3,122	1,805	1,682	1,539	1,538
Mediterranean≠	2,345	1,782	1,580	1,557	1,369	1,268	1,148
Rest of New Commonwealth	1,582	1,114	1,221	1,310	1,332	1,609	1,786
Other European Union**	5,859	8,763	9,299	9,848	10,414	10,845	11,105
Rest of Europe	3,448	3,178	3,538	3,894	4,522	5,635	7,362
United States of America	3,338	2,630	2,578	2,779	2,857	2,780	2,895
Rest of the World	10,089	11,402	12,339	13,691	14,574	15,538	17,292
Not stated	34	9	10	7	13	20	18
	Percentage of all live births						
Total	**100.0**	**100.0**	**100.0**	**100.0**	**100.0**	**100.0**	**100.0**
United Kingdom*	95.1	87.4	87.2	86.9	86.4	85.7	84.5
Total outside the United Kingdom	**12.5**	**12.6**	**12.8**	**13.1**	**13.6**	**14.3**	**15.5**
Irish Republic	1.0	0.8	0.8	0.8	0.7	0.7	0.7
Australia, Canada and New Zealand	0.5	0.5	0.5	0.5	0.5	0.6	0.6
New Commonwealth	**7.6**	**7.3**	**7.3**	**7.2**	**7.2**	**7.4**	**7.8**
India	1.3	1.0	1.0	1.0	1.0	1.0	1.1
Pakistan	1.9	1.9	1.9	2.0	2.1	2.2	2.2
Bangladesh	0.9	1.0	1.1	1.1	1.2	1.2	1.2
East Africa	1.0	0.8	0.8	0.7	0.7	0.7	0.7
Southern Africa	:	0.2	0.2	0.2	0.2	0.3	0.3
Rest of Africa	0.8	1.0	1.0	1.0	1.0	1.0	1.1
Caribbean	0.6	0.4	0.4	0.4	0.4	0.4	0.4
Far East†	0.6	0.5	0.5	0.3	0.3	0.2	0.3
Mediterranean≠	0.4	0.3	0.2	0.2	0.2	0.2	0.2
Rest of New Commonwealth	0.2	0.2	0.2	0.2	0.2	0.3	0.3
Other European Union**	0.8	1.4	1.4	1.5	1.6	1.7	1.8
Rest of Europe	0.5	0.5	0.5	0.6	0.7	0.9	1.2
United States of America	0.5	0.4	0.4	0.4	0.4	0.4	0.5
Rest of the World	1.5	1.8	1.9	2.1	2.3	2.5	2.9
Not stated	0.0	0.0	0.0	0.0	0.0	0.0	0.0

* Including Isle of Man and Channel Islands
† Brunei, Malaysia and Singapore, and Hong Kong for 1996 and earlier
≠ Cyprus, Gibraltar and Malta
** As now constituted

Table 9.2 Live births (numbers and percentages): birthplace of mother if outside United Kingdom, and area of usual residence, 2000

England and Wales, England, Wales, government office regions, Greater London, London boroughs, selected metropolitan and non-metropolitan districts (with more than 15 per cent non-UK born mothers)

Area of usual residence of mother	All live births	Birthplace of mother outside United Kingdom					
		New Commonwealth		Rest of the World		All outside United Kingdom	
		Number	Percentage	Number	Percentage	Number	Percentage
England and Wales*	**604,130**	**47,212**	**8**	**46,251**	**8**	**93,463**	**15**
England	**572,826**	46,561	8	45,300	8	91,861	16
Wales	**31,304**	651	2	951	3	1,602	5
Government Office Regions							
North East	**26,499**	702	3	734	3	1,436	5
North West	**76,675**	4,423	6	2,757	4	7,180	9
Yorkshire and the Humber	**55,966**	4,174	7	1,813	3	5,987	11
East Midlands	**45,787**	2,461	5	1,667	4	4,128	9
West Midlands	**61,497**	6,033	10	2,043	3	8,076	13
East	**61,186**	2,919	5	4,058	7	6,977	11
London	**104,695**	20,290	19	23,134	22	43,424	41
South East	**90,445**	4,344	5	6,669	7	11,013	12
South West	**50,076**	1,215	2	2,425	5	3,640	7
Greater London	**104,695**	**20,290**	**19**	**23,134**	**22**	**43,424**	**41**
Inner London	**44,989**	**10,504**	**23**	**12,484**	**28**	**22,988**	**51**
Camden	**2,749**	495	18	1,089	40	1,584	58
City of London	**53**	11	21	15	28	26	49
Hackney	**3,896**	910	23	990	25	1,900	49
Hammersmith and Fulham	**2,479**	222	9	898	36	1,120	45
Haringey	**3,734**	672	18	1,374	37	2,046	55
Islington	**2,709**	339	13	865	32	1,204	44
Kensington and Chelsea	**2,020**	146	7	1,134	56	1,280	63
Lambeth	**4,344**	880	20	1,112	26	1,992	46
Lewisham	**3,887**	729	19	693	18	1,422	37
Newham	**4,927**	2,045	42	992	20	3,037	62
Southwark	**4,122**	1,185	29	802	19	1,987	48
Tower Hamlets	**3,541**	1,920	54	394	11	2,314	65
Wandsworth	**3,948**	576	15	847	21	1,423	36
Westminster City	**2,580**	374	14	1,279	50	1,653	64
Outer London	**59,706**	**9,786**	**16**	**10,650**	**18**	**20,436**	**34**
Barking and Dagenham	**2,321**	249	11	291	13	540	23
Barnet	**4,130**	646	16	1,083	26	1,729	42
Bexley	**2,677**	157	6	172	6	329	12
Brent	**4,021**	1,212	30	1,224	30	2,436	61
Bromley	**3,551**	210	6	357	10	567	16
Croydon	**4,572**	789	17	562	12	1,351	30
Ealing	**4,396**	967	22	1,263	29	2,230	51
Enfield	**3,872**	612	16	885	23	1,497	39
Greenwich	**3,240**	465	14	471	15	936	29
Harrow	**2,560**	789	31	440	17	1,229	48
Havering	**2,305**	64	3	103	4	167	7
Hillingdon	**3,297**	462	14	469	14	931	28
Hounslow	**3,088**	631	20	683	22	1,314	43
Kingston upon Thames	**1,818**	167	9	323	18	490	27
Merton	**2,602**	461	18	450	17	911	35
Redbridge	**3,185**	832	26	471	15	1,303	41
Richmond upon Thames	**2,384**	120	5	522	22	642	27
Sutton	**2,166**	130	6	185	9	315	15
Waltham Forest	**3,521**	823	23	696	20	1,519	43

* This table excludes births to mothers whose usual residence was outside of England and Wales.

Table 9.2 - *continued*

Area of usual residence of mother	All live births	Birthplace of mother outside United Kingdom					
		New Commonwealth		Rest of the World		All outside United Kingdom	
		Number	Percentage	Number	Percentage	Number	Percentage
Metropolitan districts*							
Greater Manchester	**30,401**	**2,750**	**9**	**1,348**	**4**	**4,098**	**13**
Manchester	**5,537**	691	12	519	9	1,210	22
Oldham	**2,962**	673	23	49	2	722	24
Rochdale	**2,634**	424	16	59	2	483	18
West Midlands	**33,398**	**5,235**	**16**	**1,216**	**4**	**6,451**	**19**
Birmingham	**14,308**	3,387	24	637	4	4,024	28
Coventry	**3,641**	371	10	198	5	569	16
Sandwell	**3,753**	540	14	95	3	635	17
West Yorkshire	**25,379**	**3,336**	**13**	**712**	**3**	**4,048**	**16**
Bradford	**7,051**	1,762	25	176	2	1,938	27
Kirklees	**4,850**	717	15	110	2	827	17
Non-Metropolitan districts*							
Bedfordshire	**4,558**	**267**	**6**	**271**	**6**	**538**	**12**
Bedford	**1,772**	209	12	131	7	340	19
Buckinghamshire	**5,578**	**526**	**9**	**394**	**7**	**920**	**16**
South Bucks	**607**	40	7	71	12	111	18
Wycombe	**2,040**	278	14	130	6	408	20
Cambridgeshire	**6,035**	**197**	**3**	**614**	**10**	**811**	**13**
Cambridge	**1,128**	81	7	240	21	321	28
East Cambridgeshire	**792**	25	3	93	12	118	15
Hertfordshire	**12,838**	**721**	**6**	**935**	**7**	**1,656**	**13**
Hertsmere	**1,160**	58	5	114	10	172	15
St. Albans	**1,700**	134	8	168	10	302	18
Watford	**1,129**	169	15	101	9	270	24
Lancashire	**12,132**	**838**	**7**	**330**	**3**	**1,168**	**10**
Burnley	**1,009**	125	12	22	2	147	15
Hyndburn	**1,052**	150	14	19	2	169	16
Pendle	**1,131**	246	22	19	2	265	23
Oxfordshire	**7,217**	**357**	**5**	**697**	**10**	**1,054**	**15**
Oxford	**1,536**	187	12	283	18	470	31
Suffolk	**7,032**	**150**	**2**	**580**	**8**	**730**	**10**
Forest Heath	**766**	11	1	287	37	298	39
Surrey	**12,035**	**623**	**5**	**1,194**	**10**	**1,817**	**15**
Elmbridge	**1,488**	80	5	212	14	292	20
Epsom and Ewell	**762**	49	6	74	10	123	16
Runnymede	**894**	41	5	95	11	136	15
Spelthorne	**984**	47	5	105	11	152	15
Surrey Heath	**947**	34	4	109	12	143	15
Woking	**1,129**	117	10	124	11	241	21
West Sussex	**7,904**	**304**	**4**	**488**	**6**	**792**	**10**
Crawley	**1,331**	136	10	88	7	224	17

* Where at least 15 per cent of the total live births were to mothers born outside the United Kingdom

Table 9.3 Live births: country of birth of mother and of father, 2000   **England and Wales**

Country of birth of father	Country of birth of mother					New Commonwealth				
	Total	United Kingdom*	**Total outside United Kingdom**	Irish Republic	Australia Canada and New Zealand	**Total**	India	Pakistan	Bangladesh	East Africa
Total	**604,441**	**510,835**	**93,588**	**4,050**	**3,635**	**47,249**	**6,650**	**13,561**	**7,482**	**3,959**
United Kingdom*	**467,120**	434,843	**32,273**	2,596	2,566	**13,631**	2,293	4,207	402	1,259
Total outside United Kingdom	**91,521**	34,405	**57,112**	**1,208**	**956**	**31,725**	**4,322**	**9,282**	**7,056**	**2,435**
Irish Republic	**3,722**	2,552	**1,170**	842	25	**94**	8	1	1	20
Australia, Canada and New Zealand	**3,165**	2,101	**1,063**	42	602	**104**	7	1	-	9
New Commonwealth	**51,235**	18,956	**32,278**	143	118	**30,536**	**4,167**	**9,199**	**7,046**	**2,259**
India	**6,001**	2,299	**3,701**	15	10	**3,512**	3,056	47	11	311
Pakistan	**15,550**	6,165	**9,385**	12	6	**9,199**	43	8,988	21	119
Bangladesh	**8,090**	1,004	**7,086**	-	-	**7,052**	23	8	7,001	10
East Africa	**4,697**	1,556	**3,141**	20	18	**2,853**	892	137	11	1,660
Southern Africa	**1,708**	871	**837**	11	16	**710**	16	4	-	22
Rest of Africa	**6,798**	2,419	**4,379**	39	32	**3,958**	43	4	-	94
Caribbean	**3,619**	2,426	**1,193**	17	10	**1,043**	5	1	1	19
Far East†	**1,428**	918	**510**	8	7	**372**	39	5	-	11
Mediterranean≠	**1,443**	1,122	**321**	13	7	**180**	2	4	-	2
Rest of New Commonwealth	**1,901**	176	**1,725**	8	12	**1,657**	48	1	1	11
Other European Union**	**8,315**	5,043	**3,272**	60	88	**252**	17	15	1	47
Rest of Europe	**6,178**	1,209	**4,969**	12	21	**101**	5	5	1	9
United States of America	**2,687**	1,151	**1,536**	23	34	**55**	4	-	1	4
Rest of the World	**16,219**	3,393	**12,824**	86	68	**583**	114	61	6	87
Not stated	**45,800**	41,587	**4,203**	246	113	**1,893**	35	72	24	265

Country of birth of father	Country of birth of mother						Other European Union**	Rest of Europe	Rest of the World	United States of America	Not Stated
	New Commonwealth - *continued*										
	Southern Africa	Rest of Africa	Caribbean	Far East†	Mediterranean≠	Rest of New Commonwealth					
Total	**1,907**	**6,537**	**2,681**	**1,538**	**1,148**	**1,786**	**11,105**	**7,362**	**17,292**	**2,895**	**18**
United Kingdom*	987	1,613	926	945	852	147	6,714	1,654	3,790	1,322	4
Total outside United Kingdom	**852**	**4,144**	**1,195**	**569**	**248**	**1,622**	**3,840**	**5,428**	**12,431**	**1,524**	**4**
Irish Republic	20	20	7	14	2	1	83	27	65	34	-
Australia, Canada and New Zealand	37	14	11	11	4	10	142	43	71	59	1
New Commonwealth	**719**	**3,901**	**1,094**	**378**	**175**	**1,598**	**536**	**257**	**598**	**90**	**1**
India	7	36	6	27	-	11	50	29	76	9	1
Pakistan	4	10	5	6	-	3	67	22	70	9	-
Bangladesh	1	3	-	2	3	1	14	6	14	-	-
East Africa	34	85	16	9	2	7	75	26	138	11	-
Southern Africa	593	65	3	5	1	1	48	15	26	11	-
Rest of Africa	68	3,632	100	7	3	7	152	56	119	23	-
Caribbean	3	56	951	1	2	4	45	22	48	8	-
Far East†	3	2	5	295	7	5	34	6	71	12	-
Mediterranean≠	4	1	4	6	157	-	31	70	14	6	-
Rest of New Commonwealth	2	11	4	20	-	1,559	20	5	22	1	-
Other European Union**	33	70	22	25	15	7	2,205	192	368	107	-
Rest of Europe	11	18	7	7	38	-	143	4,601	68	23	-
United States of America	8	9	15	10	2	2	124	47	136	1,117	-
Rest of the World	24	112	39	124	12	4	607	261	11,125	94	2
Not stated	68	780	560	24	48	17	551	280	1,071	49	10

*   Including Isle of Man and Channel Islands
†   Brunei, Malaysia and Singapore
≠   Cyprus, Gibraltar and Malta
**   As now constituted

Table 9.4   Live births: age of mother and country of birth of mother, 2000   **England and Wales**

Country of birth of mother	Age of mother at birth							
	All ages	Under 20	20-24	25-29	30-34	35-39	40-44	45 and over
	Numbers of live births							
Total*	**604,441**	**45,846**	**107,741**	**170,701**	**180,113**	**84,974**	**14,403**	**663**
United Kingdom†	**510,835**	42,566	89,936	142,644	152,785	71,115	11,330	459
Total outside UK	**93,588**	**3,280**	**17,802**	**28,050**	**27,322**	**13,858**	**3,072**	**204**
New Commonwealth	**47,249**	**1,512**	**10,800**	**14,924**	**12,248**	**6,079**	**1,573**	**113**
India	**6,650**	106	1,483	2,459	1,616	815	157	14
Pakistan	**13,561**	494	4,235	4,600	2,843	1,068	285	36
Bangladesh	**7,482**	366	2,937	2,601	1,078	386	104	10
East Africa	**3,959**	56	317	1,012	1,522	869	176	7
Southern Africa	**1,907**	54	256	657	647	238	54	1
Rest of Africa	**6,537**	150	709	1,762	2,244	1,341	316	15
Caribbean	**2,681**	222	449	588	615	497	296	14
Far East ≠	**1,538**	3	53	318	729	347	81	7
Mediterranean**	**1,148**	50	129	301	371	247	49	1
Rest of New Commonwealth	**1,786**	11	232	626	583	271	55	8
Rest of the World	**46,339**	1,768	7,002	13,126	15,074	7,779	1,499	91

*   Includes 18 births to women whose country of birth was not stated
†   Including Isle of Man and Channel Islands
≠   Brunei, Malaysia and Singapore
**   Cyprus, Gibraltar and Malta

Table 9.5 Live births (numbers and percentages): occurrence within/outside marriage, number of previous liveborn children and country of birth of mother, 1990-2000　　　　　　England and Wales

Country of birth of mother	Year	All live births (= 100%) (numbers)	All live births within marriage (percentages)	Number of previous liveborn children within marriage						Births outside marriage (percentages)
				0	1	2 (percentages)	3	4	5 and over	
Total*	**1990**	**706,140**	**71.7**	**28.4**	**26.2**	**11.2**	**3.7**	**1.2**	**1.0**	**28.3**
	1998	**635,901**	**62.2**	**24.5**	**23.1**	**9.5**	**3.2**	**1.1**	**0.8**	**37.8**
	1999	**621,872**	**61.1**	**24.7**	**22.4**	**9.1**	**3.1**	**1.0**	**0.8**	**38.9**
	2000	**604,441**	**60.5**	**24.2**	**22.3**	**9.1**	**3.1**	**1.1**	**0.8**	**39.5**
United Kingdom†	1990	624,160	69.7	28.0	26.2	10.8	3.3	0.9	0.5	30.3
	1998	549,432	58.8	23.3	22.5	8.9	2.8	0.8	0.6	41.2
	1999	532,852	57.4	23.2	21.8	8.4	2.7	0.8	0.5	42.6
	2000	510,835	56.5	22.6	21.6	8.3	2.6	0.8	0.5	43.5
Irish Republic	1990	6,424	69.7	26.7	21.5	12.1	4.6	2.1	2.7	30.3
	1998	4,673	68.6	28.3	24.4	9.5	3.3	1.2	2.0	31.4
	1999	4,470	67.4	28.5	23.6	9.5	3.0	1.3	1.5	32.6
	2000	4,050	68.8	29.3	23.8	9.8	3.4	1.0	1.5	31.2
New Commonwealth total	**1990**	**49,790**	**89.8**	**28.5**	**26.4**	**15.6**	**8.2**	**4.9**	**6.1**	**10.2**
	1998	**46,023**	**88.0**	**30.5**	**27.1**	**16.0**	**7.6**	**3.7**	**3.2**	**12.0**
	1999	**46,201**	**88.2**	**32.3**	**27.0**	**15.3**	**7.5**	**3.2**	**2.8**	**11.8**
	2000	**47,249**	**87.6**	**31.5**	**26.9**	**15.6**	**7.5**	**3.3**	**2.6**	**12.4**
India	1990	8,570	97.6	32.3	33.6	18.8	7.6	3.0	2.3	2.4
	1998	6,513	97.4	40.4	33.2	15.5	5.2	1.9	1.2	2.6
	1999	6,497	97.6	43.7	32.6	13.8	4.8	1.6	1.0	2.4
	2000	6,650	97.7	44.1	32.8	13.7	4.9	1.4	0.8	2.3
Pakistan	1990	12,359	98.7	24.7	20.8	16.9	13.4	10.2	12.8	1.3
	1998	13,069	98.2	29.3	25.0	19.7	12.0	6.5	5.9	1.8
	1999	13,472	98.4	32.0	24.7	19.3	11.8	5.8	5.0	1.6
	2000	13,561	98.5	29.5	27.0	19.7	11.8	6.0	4.5	1.5
Bangladesh	1990	5,618	99.5	24.2	19.5	13.9	12.5	10.7	18.8	0.5
	1998	7,424	99.1	30.2	27.9	18.1	10.2	6.3	6.4	0.9
	1999	7,375	99.1	29.0	29.1	18.7	11.2	5.1	6.0	0.9
	2000	7,482	99.1	28.2	27.7	20.6	11.0	5.7	5.9	0.9
East Africa	1990	6,590	93.8	35.1	35.2	16.8	4.6	1.4	0.6	6.2
	1998	4,498	85.0	30.5	31.8	15.5	4.9	1.4	0.8	15.0
	1999	4,159	83.4	31.6	31.5	13.8	4.7	1.3	0.6	16.6
	2000	3,959	82.5	31.4	30.0	14.0	5.0	1.3	0.8	17.5
Southern Africa	1990	:	:	:	:	:	:	:	:	:
	1998	1,437	77.2	38.6	27.3	7.8	2.2	1.0	0.3	22.8
	1999	1,608	80.9	42.5	26.9	8.4	2.0	0.6	0.6	19.1
	2000	1,907	80.7	43.6	26.5	7.5	2.0	0.5	0.5	19.3
Rest of Africa	1990	4,954	68.9	25.9	21.9	12.9	5.1	2.1	0.9	31.1
	1998	6,135	64.8	23.1	22.1	12.5	5.2	1.4	0.6	35.2
	1999	6,138	66.0	23.8	22.1	12.5	5.3	1.6	0.7	34.0
	2000	6,537	65.6	23.4	21.2	13.2	5.4	1.6	0.7	34.4
Caribbean	1990	3,809	52.2	15.8	16.9	11.7	4.9	1.5	1.4	47.8
	1998	2,564	52.3	17.9	17.2	10.3	3.9	2.0	1.1	47.7
	1999	2,536	50.0	18.5	17.0	8.4	3.0	1.9	1.1	50.0
	2000	2,681	45.4	17.9	14.9	7.6	2.7	1.2	1.0	54.6
Far East≠	1990	3,963	88.4	37.7	31.8	13.2	4.0	1.2	0.6	11.6
	1998	1,682	83.5	33.1	29.8	13.2	4.3	2.1	0.9	16.5
	1999	1,539	84.3	36.5	29.0	13.0	3.8	1.0	0.9	15.7
	2000	1,538	84.9	36.5	30.5	11.8	4.3	1.4	0.5	15.1
Mediterranean**	1990	2,345	85.0	29.9	31.6	16.5	5.2	1.2	0.6	15.0
	1998	1,369	77.1	27.2	28.1	15.6	4.2	0.9	1.1	22.9
	1999	1,268	74.2	28.3	27.6	13.6	3.5	1.1	0.2	25.8
	2000	1,148	73.5	31.5	25.3	11.5	3.7	1.4	0.2	26.5
Rest of New Commonwealth	1990	1,582	91.5	40.1	34.4	12.7	3.0	0.9	0.3	8.5
	1998	1,332	92.7	43.7	35.1	11.1	2.3	0.5	0.2	7.3
	1999	1,609	93.3	48.3	33.7	9.4	1.6	0.2	0.2	6.7
	2000	1,786	92.7	47.5	32.0	10.1	2.4	0.4	0.3	7.3
Rest of the World	1990	25,732	84.5	37.0	28.7	11.6	4.3	1.4	1.5	15.5
	1998	35,773	79.2	35.3	26.6	10.4	3.9	1.4	1.6	20.8
	1999	38,349	78.5	35.2	25.9	10.6	3.8	1.5	1.4	21.5
	2000	42,307	78.0	35.2	25.5	10.7	3.6	1.6	1.4	22.0

*　Including births to women whose country of birth was not stated
†　Including Isle of Man and Channel Islands
≠　Brunei, Malaysia and Singapore, and Hong Kong in 1990
**　Cyprus, Gibraltar and Malta

Table 10.1 Age-specific fertility rates: age and year of birth of woman, 1920-1985

Year of birth of woman/female birth cohort	Age of woman - completed years														
	15	16	17	18	19	20	21	22	23	24	25	26	27	28	29
1920	0	3	10	23	40	59	84	104	117	131	119	159	165	136	123
1925	0	2	9	22	43	67	101	147	157	156	147	141	134	131	118
1926	1	3	9	23	44	72	124	142	151	150	148	148	142	133	121
1927	1	3	10	24	45	86	124	138	144	149	148	152	142	134	128
1928	1	3	11	24	54	88	123	134	146	152	155	150	143	143	135
1929	1	4	10	27	59	90	117	132	146	158	156	151	148	148	137
1930	1	3	11	30	60	87	117	138	155	162	161	165	160	154	141
1931	1	3	12	32	58	85	119	143	156	162	169	170	162	153	146
1932	1	3	14	31	57	87	123	142	154	171	175	173	160	156	147
1933	1	4	13	31	58	90	125	146	167	180	183	178	172	165	151
1934	1	3	12	32	61	92	128	157	175	188	190	189	179	173	155
1935	1	3	13	33	61	94	137	162	180	190	198	193	181	173	158
1936	1	3	13	35	63	103	141	167	179	191	201	196	184	174	151
1937	1	3	14	34	70	107	147	168	184	198	206	199	188	167	142
1938	1	3	15	40	75	112	150	174	194	204	210	202	181	162	135
1939	1	4	18	44	79	116	155	180	200	208	213	193	174	154	131
1940	1	5	20	48	83	123	162	189	204	214	208	191	169	152	127
1941	1	5	22	52	91	127	169	193	209	210	201	183	162	144	123
1942	1	6	24	54	91	132	169	192	202	202	193	178	159	139	121
1943	1	7	27	57	95	132	167	187	197	191	187	172	154	139	112
1944	1	8	31	63	98	135	166	183	188	189	180	168	154	128	105
1945	2	11	35	66	103	136	166	176	181	181	178	168	145	121	101
1946	2	12	36	67	104	136	161	172	175	179	178	159	139	119	100
1947	2	12	36	66	99	128	151	158	165	169	159	145	130	111	97
1948	3	13	38	67	102	127	147	161	167	160	153	142	127	114	100
1949	2	13	38	71	101	124	144	155	152	148	144	134	125	113	106
1950	3	14	41	73	101	124	142	141	142	141	137	131	123	118	114
1951	3	15	43	75	102	125	129	130	133	130	131	126	126	127	115
1952	3	16	45	77	104	115	121	126	125	128	129	132	136	129	114
1953	3	17	46	78	97	107	115	118	121	122	133	141	138	125	114
1954	4	17	47	73	89	99	105	111	114	127	139	142	133	122	113
1955	4	18	47	68	83	92	101	107	119	134	144	135	129	123	114
1956	4	19	42	62	76	86	95	110	126	136	138	133	129	124	117
1957	4	18	41	57	70	81	98	115	128	131	133	134	130	126	116
1958	4	16	35	50	63	81	100	116	119	127	132	133	131	123	118
1959	4	13	30	46	63	83	102	107	116	124	129	132	128	125	119
1960	3	12	28	45	66	85	96	105	114	123	129	128	130	125	117
1961	3	11	27	47	66	78	90	102	110	119	124	129	127	122	120
1962	3	11	28	47	61	74	86	98	108	115	123	126	124	125	117
1963	3	11	27	42	58	71	83	96	105	114	122	122	127	122	117
1964	3	11	24	41	55	68	83	93	104	114	117	123	123	120	115
1965	3	10	24	39	55	69	81	93	104	109	119	120	120	118	115
1966	2	10	24	40	58	70	82	94	101	109	115	118	117	116	112
1967	2	10	25	43	59	71	85	92	100	107	112	114	115	112	111
1968	3	11	27	45	61	74	83	91	99	104	107	111	112	112	111
1969	3	12	28	46	63	72	82	89	94	99	103	106	109	110	109
1970	3	12	28	48	61	72	80	86	91	95	99	104	107	108	107
1971	3	12	30	46	62	71	76	81	86	90	97	101	104	104	103
1972	3	13	29	47	61	68	73	78	82	88	93	98	100	101	
1973	3	13	31	47	59	66	70	76	82	87	91	95	95		
1974	4	13	30	45	58	65	70	77	80	86	88	91			
1975	4	14	30	44	55	63	71	75	79	82	85				
1976	4	13	30	43	56	67	71	76	77	80					
1977	4	14	28	44	59	67	70	74	75						
1978	4	13	28	45	58	65	69	71							
1979	4	13	31	46	58	65	67								
1980	4	14	31	46	59	62									
1981	4	14	31	46	57										
1982	4	14	30	44											
1983	4	13	29												
1984	4	12													
1985	4														

* Includes births at ages 45 and over achieved up to the end of 2000 by women born in 1955 and earlier years.
Notes: 1. The age-specific fertility rates refer to 'all live births per 1,000 women' at the age shown.
2. Live births to women aged under 15 are not included in the calculation of the rate for age 15.

England and Wales

30	31	32	33	34	35	36	37	38	39	40	41	42	43	44	45*	Year of birth of woman/female birth cohort
109	93	87	76	67	58	52	44	38	32	25	17	13	8	5	4	1920
108	97	90	78	72	65	56	47	40	32	23	15	11	6	3	3	1925
113	100	94	80	76	67	58	48	43	31	22	15	10	5	3	3	1926
119	103	95	85	77	67	57	49	40	29	21	13	9	5	3	2	1927
123	104	101	86	78	67	59	46	38	28	20	12	8	5	2	2	1928
125	109	102	86	79	68	55	43	36	26	18	11	7	4	2	2	1929
136	117	109	91	83	68	54	43	34	24	17	11	7	4	2	2	1930
134	117	107	91	77	63	51	39	30	21	16	10	6	3	2	2	1931
132	116	111	88	72	60	47	36	28	20	13	8	5	3	2	2	1932
137	117	105	85	70	57	44	34	26	18	11	7	4	2	1	2	1933
140	112	97	79	67	53	42	32	22	15	10	6	4	2	1	2	1934
134	104	92	73	62	50	39	28	19	13	9	6	4	2	2	2	1935
127	101	88	70	57	47	34	23	17	12	8	5	4	2	2	2	1936
121	97	83	66	54	41	29	21	16	11	7	5	4	2	1	2	1937
117	94	78	64	47	35	25	19	14	11	8	5	4	2	1	2	1938
111	90	75	56	41	31	24	18	14	10	8	6	4	2	1	2	1939
108	88	67	50	38	29	23	17	14	11	8	7	4	2	1	2	1940
107	80	60	46	36	28	22	18	15	12	8	6	4	2	2	2	1941
96	72	57	43	34	28	23	20	16	12	8	6	4	2	1	2	1942
89	68	54	43	35	30	25	21	15	11	8	6	4	2	1	2	1943
85	66	53	43	37	32	27	21	15	11	8	6	3	2	1	2	1944
83	66	56	47	42	34	26	21	16	12	9	6	4	2	1	2	1945
85	69	60	54	44	34	28	22	17	13	9	6	4	2	1	1	1946
83	73	64	53	41	34	27	22	16	12	9	6	4	2	1	1	1947
92	82	69	56	45	36	29	23	18	13	9	6	4	3	1	2	1948
99	85	69	55	46	37	31	24	19	14	10	7	4	3	1	1	1949
103	85	68	56	47	39	31	26	20	15	11	7	5	3	2	2	1950
100	83	70	58	49	42	34	27	21	16	11	8	5	3	2	2	1951
100	86	72	62	51	44	35	28	22	17	12	8	5	3	2	2	1952
102	88	76	64	54	45	37	30	23	18	13	8	5	3	2	2	1953
103	90	77	67	57	47	39	30	24	18	12	9	6	3	2	2	1954
106	91	81	68	58	49	40	32	24	19	14	9	6	4	2	2	1955
106	94	82	68	61	50	41	33	25	20	14	10	6	4	2		1956
109	94	82	72	62	52	42	34	26	20	15	10	6	4			1957
108	96	86	73	63	52	44	35	27	21	15	10	6				1958
108	99	86	74	63	54	44	35	28	22	15	11					1959
113	98	88	75	66	55	46	38	29	22	16						1960
111	98	86	76	65	55	47	38	29	22							1961
110	98	89	76	67	58	48	38	30								1962
109	100	88	78	68	59	48	39									1963
109	98	90	80	70	59	50										1964
108	100	90	80	71	60											1965
108	99	92	81	70												1966
107	100	91	80													1967
108	100	91														1968
105	97															1969
103																1970
																1971
																1972
																1973
																1974
																1975
																1976
																1977
																1978
																1979
																1980
																1981
																1982
																1983
																1984
																1985

Table 10.2 Average number of liveborn children: age and year of birth of woman, 1920-1985

Year of birth of woman/female birth cohort	Age of woman - completed years														
	15	16	17	18	19	20	21	22	23	24	25	26	27	28	29
1920	0.00	0.00	0.01	0.04	0.08	0.13	0.22	0.32	0.44	0.57	0.69	0.85	1.01	1.15	1.27
1925	0.00	0.00	0.01	0.03	0.08	0.14	0.24	0.39	0.55	0.70	0.85	0.99	1.13	1.26	1.37
1926	0.00	0.00	0.01	0.04	0.08	0.15	0.28	0.42	0.57	0.72	0.87	1.01	1.16	1.29	1.41
1927	0.00	0.00	0.01	0.04	0.08	0.17	0.29	0.43	0.57	0.72	0.87	1.02	1.16	1.30	1.43
1928	0.00	0.00	0.02	0.04	0.09	0.18	0.30	0.44	0.58	0.74	0.89	1.04	1.18	1.33	1.46
1929	0.00	0.00	0.01	0.04	0.10	0.19	0.31	0.44	0.59	0.75	0.90	1.05	1.20	1.35	1.49
1930	0.00	0.00	0.01	0.04	0.10	0.19	0.31	0.45	0.60	0.76	0.93	1.09	1.25	1.41	1.55
1931	0.00	0.00	0.02	0.05	0.11	0.19	0.31	0.45	0.61	0.77	0.94	1.11	1.27	1.42	1.57
1932	0.00	0.00	0.02	0.05	0.11	0.19	0.32	0.46	0.61	0.78	0.96	1.13	1.29	1.45	1.59
1933	0.00	0.00	0.02	0.05	0.11	0.20	0.32	0.47	0.63	0.81	1.00	1.18	1.35	1.51	1.66
1934	0.00	0.00	0.02	0.05	0.11	0.20	0.33	0.49	0.66	0.85	1.04	1.23	1.41	1.58	1.73
1935	0.00	0.00	0.02	0.05	0.11	0.20	0.34	0.50	0.68	0.87	1.07	1.26	1.45	1.62	1.78
1936	0.00	0.00	0.02	0.05	0.12	0.22	0.36	0.53	0.71	0.90	1.10	1.29	1.48	1.65	1.80
1937	0.00	0.00	0.02	0.05	0.12	0.23	0.38	0.54	0.73	0.93	1.13	1.33	1.52	1.69	1.83
1938	0.00	0.00	0.02	0.06	0.13	0.25	0.40	0.57	0.76	0.97	1.18	1.38	1.56	1.72	1.86
1939	0.00	0.00	0.02	0.07	0.14	0.26	0.42	0.60	0.80	1.00	1.22	1.41	1.58	1.74	1.87
1940	0.00	0.01	0.03	0.07	0.16	0.28	0.44	0.63	0.83	1.05	1.26	1.45	1.61	1.77	1.89
1941	0.00	0.01	0.03	0.08	0.17	0.30	0.47	0.66	0.87	1.08	1.28	1.46	1.63	1.77	1.89
1942	0.00	0.01	0.03	0.08	0.18	0.31	0.48	0.67	0.87	1.07	1.27	1.44	1.60	1.74	1.86
1943	0.00	0.01	0.03	0.09	0.19	0.32	0.49	0.67	0.87	1.06	1.25	1.42	1.57	1.71	1.83
1944	0.00	0.01	0.04	0.10	0.20	0.34	0.50	0.69	0.87	1.06	1.24	1.41	1.56	1.69	1.80
1945	0.00	0.01	0.05	0.11	0.22	0.35	0.52	0.69	0.87	1.06	1.23	1.40	1.55	1.67	1.77
1946	0.00	0.01	0.05	0.12	0.22	0.36	0.52	0.69	0.86	1.04	1.22	1.38	1.52	1.64	1.74
1947	0.00	0.01	0.05	0.12	0.21	0.34	0.49	0.65	0.82	0.98	1.14	1.29	1.42	1.53	1.63
1948	0.00	0.02	0.05	0.12	0.22	0.35	0.50	0.66	0.82	0.98	1.14	1.28	1.41	1.52	1.62
1949	0.00	0.02	0.05	0.13	0.23	0.35	0.49	0.65	0.80	0.95	1.09	1.23	1.35	1.47	1.57
1950	0.00	0.02	0.06	0.13	0.23	0.36	0.50	0.64	0.78	0.92	1.06	1.19	1.31	1.43	1.54
1951	0.00	0.02	0.06	0.14	0.24	0.36	0.49	0.62	0.76	0.89	1.02	1.14	1.27	1.40	1.51
1952	0.00	0.02	0.06	0.14	0.25	0.36	0.48	0.61	0.73	0.86	0.99	1.12	1.26	1.39	1.50
1953	0.00	0.02	0.07	0.14	0.24	0.35	0.46	0.58	0.70	0.82	0.96	1.10	1.24	1.36	1.47
1954	0.00	0.02	0.07	0.14	0.23	0.33	0.43	0.55	0.66	0.79	0.93	1.07	1.20	1.32	1.44
1955	0.00	0.02	0.07	0.14	0.22	0.31	0.41	0.52	0.64	0.77	0.92	1.05	1.18	1.30	1.42
1956	0.00	0.02	0.07	0.13	0.20	0.29	0.38	0.50	0.62	0.76	0.90	1.03	1.16	1.28	1.40
1957	0.00	0.02	0.06	0.12	0.19	0.27	0.37	0.48	0.61	0.74	0.88	1.01	1.14	1.27	1.38
1958	0.00	0.02	0.06	0.11	0.17	0.25	0.35	0.47	0.58	0.71	0.84	0.98	1.11	1.23	1.35
1959	0.00	0.02	0.05	0.09	0.16	0.24	0.34	0.45	0.56	0.69	0.82	0.95	1.08	1.20	1.32
1960	0.00	0.02	0.04	0.09	0.15	0.24	0.33	0.44	0.55	0.68	0.81	0.93	1.06	1.19	1.30
1961	0.00	0.01	0.04	0.09	0.15	0.23	0.32	0.42	0.53	0.65	0.78	0.91	1.03	1.16	1.28
1962	0.00	0.01	0.04	0.09	0.15	0.22	0.31	0.41	0.52	0.63	0.76	0.88	1.01	1.13	1.25
1963	0.00	0.01	0.04	0.08	0.14	0.21	0.29	0.39	0.50	0.61	0.73	0.85	0.98	1.10	1.22
1964	0.00	0.01	0.04	0.08	0.13	0.20	0.28	0.38	0.48	0.60	0.71	0.84	0.96	1.08	1.19
1965	0.00	0.01	0.04	0.08	0.13	0.20	0.28	0.37	0.48	0.59	0.71	0.83	0.95	1.06	1.18
1966	0.00	0.01	0.04	0.08	0.13	0.20	0.29	0.38	0.48	0.59	0.71	0.82	0.94	1.06	1.17
1967	0.00	0.01	0.04	0.08	0.14	0.21	0.30	0.39	0.49	0.59	0.71	0.82	0.94	1.05	1.16
1968	0.00	0.01	0.04	0.09	0.15	0.22	0.30	0.40	0.49	0.60	0.71	0.82	0.93	1.04	1.15
1969	0.00	0.01	0.04	0.09	0.15	0.22	0.30	0.39	0.49	0.59	0.69	0.80	0.91	1.02	1.12
1970	0.00	0.01	0.04	0.09	0.15	0.22	0.30	0.39	0.48	0.58	0.68	0.78	0.89	0.99	1.10
1971	0.00	0.01	0.04	0.09	0.15	0.22	0.30	0.38	0.47	0.56	0.65	0.75	0.86	0.96	1.06
1972	0.00	0.02	0.05	0.09	0.15	0.22	0.29	0.37	0.45	0.54	0.64	0.73	0.84	0.94	
1973	0.00	0.02	0.05	0.09	0.15	0.22	0.29	0.36	0.45	0.53	0.62	0.72	0.81		
1974	0.00	0.02	0.05	0.09	0.15	0.22	0.29	0.36	0.44	0.53	0.62	0.71			
1975	0.00	0.02	0.05	0.09	0.15	0.21	0.28	0.35	0.43	0.51	0.60				
1976	0.00	0.02	0.05	0.09	0.15	0.21	0.28	0.36	0.44	0.52					
1977	0.00	0.02	0.05	0.09	0.15	0.22	0.29	0.36	0.44						
1978	0.00	0.02	0.05	0.09	0.15	0.21	0.28	0.35							
1979	0.00	0.02	0.05	0.09	0.15	0.22	0.28								
1980	0.00	0.02	0.05	0.09	0.15	0.22									
1981	0.00	0.02	0.05	0.10	0.15										
1982	0.00	0.02	0.05	0.09											
1983	0.00	0.02	0.05												
1984	0.00	0.02													
1985	0.00														

* Includes births at ages 45 and over achieved up to the end of 2000 by women born in 1955 and earlier years

England and Wales

30	31	32	33	34	35	36	37	38	39	40	41	42	43	44	45*	Year of birth of woman/female birth cohort
1.38	1.47	1.56	1.64	1.70	1.76	1.81	1.86	1.90	1.93	1.95	1.97	1.98	1.99	2.00	2.00	1920
1.48	1.58	1.67	1.75	1.82	1.88	1.94	1.99	2.03	2.06	2.08	2.10	2.11	2.11	2.12	2.12	1925
1.52	1.62	1.72	1.80	1.87	1.94	2.00	2.05	2.09	2.12	2.14	2.16	2.17	2.17	2.18	2.18	1926
1.55	1.65	1.74	1.83	1.91	1.97	2.03	2.08	2.12	2.15	2.17	2.18	2.19	2.19	2.20	2.20	1927
1.58	1.69	1.79	1.88	1.95	2.02	2.08	2.13	2.16	2.19	2.21	2.22	2.23	2.24	2.24	2.24	1928
1.61	1.72	1.82	1.91	1.99	2.05	2.11	2.15	2.19	2.21	2.23	2.24	2.25	2.25	2.26	2.26	1929
1.68	1.80	1.91	2.00	2.08	2.15	2.20	2.25	2.28	2.30	2.32	2.33	2.34	2.34	2.34	2.35	1930
1.70	1.82	1.93	2.02	2.10	2.16	2.21	2.25	2.28	2.30	2.32	2.33	2.33	2.34	2.34	2.34	1931
1.73	1.84	1.95	2.04	2.11	2.17	2.22	2.26	2.28	2.30	2.32	2.33	2.33	2.33	2.33	2.34	1932
1.80	1.92	2.02	2.11	2.18	2.23	2.28	2.31	2.34	2.36	2.37	2.37	2.38	2.38	2.38	2.38	1933
1.88	1.99	2.08	2.16	2.23	2.28	2.33	2.36	2.38	2.40	2.41	2.41	2.42	2.42	2.42	2.42	1934
1.91	2.01	2.11	2.18	2.24	2.29	2.33	2.36	2.38	2.39	2.40	2.41	2.41	2.41	2.41	2.42	1935
1.93	2.03	2.12	2.19	2.25	2.29	2.33	2.35	2.37	2.38	2.39	2.39	2.40	2.40	2.40	2.40	1936
1.95	2.05	2.13	2.19	2.25	2.29	2.32	2.34	2.35	2.37	2.37	2.38	2.38	2.38	2.39	2.39	1937
1.98	2.07	2.15	2.21	2.26	2.29	2.32	2.34	2.35	2.36	2.37	2.38	2.38	2.38	2.38	2.39	1938
1.98	2.07	2.15	2.20	2.24	2.27	2.30	2.32	2.33	2.34	2.35	2.35	2.36	2.36	2.36	2.36	1939
2.00	2.09	2.16	2.21	2.24	2.27	2.30	2.31	2.33	2.34	2.35	2.35	2.36	2.36	2.36	2.36	1940
2.00	2.08	2.14	2.19	2.22	2.25	2.27	2.29	2.31	2.32	2.32	2.33	2.33	2.34	2.34	2.34	1941
1.96	2.03	2.09	2.13	2.16	2.19	2.21	2.23	2.25	2.26	2.27	2.28	2.28	2.28	2.28	2.29	1942
1.91	1.98	2.04	2.08	2.12	2.15	2.17	2.19	2.21	2.22	2.23	2.23	2.24	2.24	2.24	2.24	1943
1.88	1.95	2.00	2.04	2.08	2.11	2.14	2.16	2.18	2.19	2.20	2.20	2.20	2.21	2.21	2.21	1944
1.85	1.92	1.97	2.02	2.06	2.10	2.12	2.14	2.16	2.17	2.18	2.19	2.19	2.19	2.19	2.19	1945
1.82	1.89	1.95	2.00	2.05	2.08	2.11	2.13	2.15	2.16	2.17	2.18	2.18	2.18	2.18	2.19	1946
1.71	1.78	1.85	1.90	1.94	1.98	2.00	2.02	2.04	2.05	2.06	2.07	2.07	2.07	2.07	2.08	1947
1.71	1.79	1.86	1.92	1.96	2.00	2.03	2.05	2.07	2.08	2.09	2.10	2.10	2.11	2.11	2.11	1948
1.67	1.76	1.82	1.88	1.92	1.96	1.99	2.02	2.03	2.05	2.06	2.07	2.07	2.07	2.07	2.08	1949
1.65	1.73	1.80	1.86	1.90	1.94	1.98	2.00	2.02	2.04	2.05	2.05	2.06	2.06	2.06	2.06	1950
1.61	1.69	1.76	1.82	1.87	1.91	1.95	1.97	2.00	2.01	2.02	2.03	2.04	2.04	2.04	2.04	1951
1.60	1.69	1.76	1.82	1.87	1.91	1.95	1.98	2.00	2.02	2.03	2.04	2.04	2.04	2.05	2.05	1952
1.58	1.67	1.74	1.81	1.86	1.90	1.94	1.97	1.99	2.01	2.02	2.03	2.04	2.04	2.04	2.04	1953
1.54	1.63	1.71	1.77	1.83	1.88	1.92	1.95	1.97	1.99	2.00	2.01	2.01	2.02	2.02	2.02	1954
1.52	1.62	1.70	1.76	1.82	1.87	1.91	1.94	1.97	1.99	2.00	2.01	2.02	2.02	2.02	2.02	1955
1.50	1.60	1.68	1.75	1.81	1.86	1.90	1.93	1.96	1.98	1.99	2.00	2.01	2.01	2.01		1956
1.49	1.58	1.67	1.74	1.80	1.85	1.89	1.93	1.95	1.97	1.99	2.00	2.00	2.01			1957
1.46	1.55	1.64	1.71	1.77	1.83	1.87	1.90	1.93	1.95	1.97	1.98	1.98				1958
1.43	1.53	1.61	1.69	1.75	1.81	1.85	1.89	1.91	1.94	1.95	1.96					1959
1.42	1.52	1.60	1.68	1.74	1.80	1.85	1.88	1.91	1.93	1.95						1960
1.39	1.48	1.57	1.65	1.71	1.77	1.81	1.85	1.88	1.90							1961
1.36	1.45	1.54	1.62	1.69	1.74	1.79	1.83	1.86								1962
1.33	1.43	1.52	1.60	1.66	1.72	1.77	1.81									1963
1.30	1.40	1.49	1.57	1.64	1.70	1.75										1964
1.29	1.39	1.48	1.56	1.63	1.69											1965
1.28	1.38	1.47	1.55	1.62												1966
1.27	1.37	1.46	1.54													1967
1.26	1.36	1.45														1968
1.23	1.33															1969
1.20																1970
																1971
																1972
																1973
																1974
																1975
																1976
																1977
																1978
																1979
																1980
																1981
																1982
																1983
																1984
																1985

**Table 10.3 Estimated average number of first liveborn children*:
age and year of birth of woman, 1920-1985**

Year of birth of woman/female birth cohort	Age of woman - completed years														
	15	16	17	18	19	20	21	22	23	24	25	26	27	28	29
1920	0.00	0.00	0.01	0.03	0.07	0.11	0.18	0.25	0.33	0.40	0.46	0.53	0.60	0.64	0.68
1925	0.00	0.00	0.01	0.03	0.07	0.13	0.21	0.31	0.41	0.49	0.55	0.60	0.65	0.68	0.72
1926	0.00	0.00	0.01	0.03	0.07	0.13	0.23	0.33	0.41	0.48	0.55	0.60	0.65	0.69	0.72
1927	0.00	0.00	0.01	0.03	0.08	0.15	0.24	0.33	0.41	0.48	0.55	0.60	0.65	0.69	0.72
1928	0.00	0.00	0.01	0.04	0.08	0.16	0.25	0.33	0.41	0.49	0.55	0.61	0.66	0.70	0.73
1929	0.00	0.00	0.01	0.04	0.09	0.16	0.24	0.33	0.41	0.49	0.55	0.61	0.66	0.70	0.74
1930	0.00	0.00	0.01	0.04	0.09	0.16	0.24	0.33	0.42	0.49	0.56	0.62	0.68	0.72	0.75
1931	0.00	0.00	0.02	0.04	0.09	0.16	0.24	0.33	0.42	0.50	0.57	0.63	0.68	0.72	0.76
1932	0.00	0.00	0.02	0.05	0.09	0.16	0.24	0.33	0.42	0.50	0.57	0.64	0.68	0.73	0.76
1933	0.00	0.00	0.02	0.04	0.09	0.16	0.25	0.34	0.43	0.52	0.59	0.65	0.70	0.74	0.78
1934	0.00	0.00	0.02	0.04	0.10	0.17	0.25	0.35	0.45	0.53	0.61	0.67	0.72	0.76	0.79
1935	0.00	0.00	0.02	0.04	0.10	0.17	0.26	0.36	0.46	0.54	0.61	0.68	0.73	0.77	0.80
1936	0.00	0.00	0.02	0.05	0.10	0.18	0.27	0.37	0.47	0.55	0.62	0.68	0.73	0.77	0.80
1937	0.00	0.00	0.02	0.05	0.10	0.19	0.28	0.38	0.47	0.55	0.63	0.69	0.74	0.77	0.80
1938	0.00	0.00	0.02	0.05	0.11	0.20	0.29	0.39	0.49	0.57	0.64	0.70	0.75	0.79	0.81
1939	0.00	0.00	0.02	0.06	0.12	0.21	0.30	0.40	0.50	0.58	0.65	0.71	0.76	0.79	0.82
1940	0.00	0.01	0.02	0.06	0.13	0.22	0.32	0.42	0.51	0.59	0.66	0.72	0.76	0.80	0.82
1941	0.00	0.01	0.03	0.07	0.14	0.23	0.33	0.43	0.53	0.61	0.68	0.73	0.77	0.80	0.83
1942	0.00	0.01	0.03	0.07	0.14	0.23	0.33	0.43	0.52	0.60	0.67	0.72	0.76	0.79	0.82
1943	0.00	0.01	0.03	0.08	0.15	0.24	0.33	0.43	0.52	0.60	0.66	0.72	0.76	0.79	0.81
1944	0.00	0.01	0.04	0.09	0.16	0.25	0.34	0.44	0.52	0.60	0.66	0.72	0.76	0.79	0.82
1945	0.00	0.01	0.04	0.10	0.17	0.26	0.35	0.44	0.53	0.60	0.66	0.72	0.76	0.79	0.82
1946	0.00	0.01	0.05	0.10	0.18	0.26	0.35	0.44	0.52	0.59	0.66	0.71	0.76	0.79	0.82
1947	0.00	0.01	0.05	0.10	0.17	0.25	0.34	0.42	0.49	0.56	0.63	0.68	0.72	0.76	0.78
1948	0.00	0.02	0.05	0.10	0.18	0.26	0.34	0.42	0.50	0.56	0.62	0.68	0.72	0.76	0.79
1949	0.00	0.02	0.05	0.11	0.18	0.26	0.34	0.42	0.48	0.55	0.60	0.66	0.70	0.74	0.77
1950	0.00	0.02	0.05	0.11	0.19	0.26	0.34	0.41	0.47	0.53	0.59	0.64	0.68	0.72	0.76
1951	0.00	0.02	0.06	0.12	0.19	0.27	0.34	0.40	0.46	0.52	0.57	0.62	0.66	0.71	0.74
1952	0.00	0.02	0.06	0.12	0.20	0.26	0.33	0.39	0.45	0.50	0.55	0.61	0.66	0.70	0.73
1953	0.00	0.02	0.06	0.12	0.19	0.26	0.32	0.38	0.43	0.48	0.54	0.60	0.65	0.69	0.72
1954	0.00	0.02	0.06	0.12	0.18	0.24	0.30	0.35	0.40	0.46	0.52	0.58	0.62	0.66	0.70
1955	0.00	0.02	0.06	0.12	0.18	0.23	0.28	0.34	0.39	0.45	0.51	0.57	0.61	0.65	0.69
1956	0.00	0.02	0.06	0.11	0.16	0.21	0.27	0.32	0.38	0.44	0.50	0.55	0.60	0.64	0.68
1957	0.00	0.02	0.06	0.11	0.15	0.20	0.25	0.31	0.37	0.43	0.49	0.54	0.59	0.63	0.67
1958	0.00	0.02	0.05	0.09	0.14	0.19	0.24	0.30	0.36	0.41	0.47	0.52	0.57	0.61	0.65
1959	0.00	0.02	0.04	0.08	0.13	0.18	0.24	0.29	0.34	0.40	0.45	0.50	0.55	0.59	0.63
1960	0.00	0.01	0.04	0.08	0.13	0.18	0.23	0.28	0.34	0.39	0.45	0.49	0.54	0.59	0.62
1961	0.00	0.01	0.04	0.08	0.13	0.18	0.23	0.28	0.33	0.38	0.43	0.48	0.53	0.57	0.61
1962	0.00	0.01	0.04	0.08	0.12	0.17	0.22	0.27	0.32	0.37	0.42	0.47	0.52	0.56	0.60
1963	0.00	0.01	0.04	0.07	0.12	0.16	0.21	0.25	0.30	0.36	0.41	0.46	0.51	0.55	0.59
1964	0.00	0.01	0.03	0.07	0.11	0.15	0.20	0.25	0.30	0.35	0.40	0.45	0.50	0.54	0.58
1965	0.00	0.01	0.03	0.07	0.11	0.15	0.20	0.24	0.29	0.34	0.39	0.44	0.49	0.53	0.57
1966	0.00	0.01	0.03	0.07	0.11	0.15	0.20	0.24	0.29	0.34	0.39	0.44	0.49	0.53	0.57
1967	0.00	0.01	0.04	0.07	0.11	0.16	0.21	0.25	0.30	0.34	0.39	0.44	0.48	0.52	0.56
1968	0.00	0.01	0.04	0.08	0.12	0.17	0.21	0.26	0.30	0.35	0.39	0.44	0.48	0.53	0.57
1969	0.00	0.01	0.04	0.08	0.12	0.17	0.22	0.26	0.30	0.34	0.39	0.43	0.48	0.52	0.56
1970	0.00	0.01	0.04	0.08	0.13	0.17	0.22	0.26	0.30	0.34	0.38	0.43	0.47	0.51	0.55
1971	0.00	0.01	0.04	0.08	0.13	0.17	0.22	0.25	0.29	0.33	0.37	0.42	0.46	0.50	0.54
1972	0.00	0.02	0.04	0.08	0.13	0.17	0.22	0.25	0.29	0.32	0.37	0.41	0.45	0.49	
1973	0.00	0.02	0.04	0.08	0.13	0.17	0.21	0.24	0.28	0.32	0.36	0.40	0.44		
1974	0.00	0.02	0.05	0.08	0.13	0.17	0.21	0.24	0.28	0.31	0.36	0.39			
1975	0.00	0.02	0.04	0.08	0.12	0.17	0.21	0.24	0.27	0.31	0.35				
1976	0.00	0.02	0.04	0.08	0.12	0.17	0.21	0.24	0.28	0.31					
1977	0.00	0.02	0.04	0.08	0.13	0.17	0.21	0.25	0.28						
1978	0.00	0.02	0.04	0.08	0.13	0.17	0.21	0.24							
1979	0.00	0.02	0.05	0.08	0.13	0.17	0.21								
1980	0.00	0.02	0.05	0.09	0.13	0.17									
1981	0.00	0.02	0.05	0.09	0.13										
1982	0.00	0.02	0.05	0.08											
1983	0.00	0.02	0.04												
1984	0.00	0.02													
1985	0.00														

* See Section 2.15.

† Includes births at ages 45 and over achieved up to the end of 2000 by women born in 1955 and earlier years

England and Wales

30	31	32	33	34	35	36	37	38	39	40	41	42	43	44	45†	Year of birth of woman/female birth cohort
0.70	0.72	0.74	0.75	0.76	0.77	0.78	0.78	0.78	0.79	0.79	0.79	0.79	0.79	0.79	0.79	1920
0.74	0.76	0.78	0.79	0.81	0.81	0.82	0.82	0.83	0.83	0.83	0.83	0.84	0.84	0.84	0.84	1925
0.75	0.77	0.79	0.80	0.81	0.82	0.83	0.83	0.83	0.84	0.84	0.84	0.84	0.84	0.84	0.84	1926
0.75	0.78	0.79	0.81	0.82	0.82	0.83	0.83	0.84	0.84	0.84	0.84	0.84	0.84	0.84	0.84	1927
0.76	0.79	0.80	0.82	0.83	0.83	0.84	0.84	0.85	0.85	0.85	0.85	0.85	0.85	0.85	0.85	1928
0.77	0.79	0.81	0.82	0.83	0.83	0.84	0.84	0.85	0.85	0.85	0.85	0.85	0.85	0.85	0.85	1929
0.78	0.81	0.82	0.83	0.84	0.85	0.86	0.86	0.86	0.87	0.87	0.87	0.87	0.87	0.87	0.87	1930
0.78	0.80	0.82	0.83	0.84	0.85	0.85	0.86	0.86	0.86	0.86	0.86	0.86	0.86	0.87	0.87	1931
0.79	0.81	0.82	0.83	0.84	0.85	0.85	0.86	0.86	0.86	0.86	0.86	0.87	0.87	0.87	0.87	1932
0.80	0.82	0.84	0.85	0.86	0.86	0.87	0.87	0.87	0.88	0.88	0.88	0.88	0.88	0.88	0.88	1933
0.82	0.84	0.85	0.86	0.87	0.88	0.88	0.88	0.89	0.89	0.89	0.89	0.89	0.89	0.89	0.89	1934
0.82	0.84	0.85	0.86	0.87	0.88	0.88	0.88	0.88	0.89	0.89	0.89	0.89	0.89	0.89	0.89	1935
0.82	0.84	0.85	0.86	0.87	0.87	0.88	0.88	0.88	0.88	0.89	0.89	0.89	0.89	0.89	0.89	1936
0.82	0.84	0.85	0.86	0.87	0.87	0.87	0.88	0.88	0.88	0.88	0.88	0.88	0.88	0.88	0.88	1937
0.83	0.85	0.86	0.87	0.87	0.88	0.88	0.88	0.89	0.89	0.89	0.89	0.89	0.89	0.89	0.89	1938
0.83	0.85	0.86	0.87	0.87	0.88	0.88	0.88	0.89	0.89	0.89	0.89	0.89	0.89	0.89	0.89	1939
0.84	0.85	0.86	0.87	0.88	0.88	0.88	0.89	0.89	0.89	0.89	0.89	0.89	0.89	0.89	0.89	1940
0.84	0.86	0.87	0.88	0.88	0.89	0.89	0.89	0.89	0.90	0.90	0.90	0.90	0.90	0.90	0.90	1941
0.84	0.85	0.86	0.87	0.88	0.88	0.88	0.89	0.89	0.89	0.89	0.89	0.89	0.89	0.89	0.89	1942
0.83	0.85	0.86	0.87	0.87	0.88	0.88	0.88	0.89	0.89	0.89	0.89	0.89	0.89	0.89	0.89	1943
0.84	0.85	0.86	0.87	0.88	0.88	0.89	0.89	0.89	0.89	0.90	0.90	0.90	0.90	0.90	0.90	1944
0.84	0.85	0.87	0.87	0.88	0.89	0.89	0.89	0.90	0.90	0.90	0.90	0.90	0.90	0.90	0.90	1945
0.84	0.86	0.87	0.88	0.89	0.89	0.90	0.90	0.90	0.90	0.91	0.91	0.91	0.91	0.91	0.91	1946
0.81	0.82	0.84	0.85	0.85	0.86	0.86	0.87	0.87	0.87	0.87	0.87	0.87	0.88	0.88	0.88	1947
0.81	0.83	0.84	0.85	0.86	0.87	0.87	0.87	0.88	0.88	0.88	0.88	0.88	0.88	0.88	0.88	1948
0.79	0.81	0.83	0.84	0.84	0.85	0.86	0.86	0.86	0.87	0.87	0.87	0.87	0.87	0.87	0.87	1949
0.78	0.80	0.82	0.83	0.83	0.84	0.85	0.85	0.85	0.86	0.86	0.86	0.86	0.86	0.86	0.86	1950
0.77	0.78	0.80	0.81	0.82	0.83	0.83	0.84	0.84	0.84	0.84	0.84	0.85	0.85	0.85	0.85	1951
0.76	0.78	0.79	0.80	0.81	0.82	0.83	0.83	0.83	0.84	0.84	0.84	0.84	0.84	0.84	0.84	1952
0.75	0.77	0.78	0.80	0.81	0.82	0.82	0.83	0.83	0.84	0.84	0.84	0.84	0.84	0.84	0.84	1953
0.73	0.75	0.77	0.78	0.79	0.80	0.81	0.82	0.82	0.82	0.83	0.83	0.83	0.83	0.83	0.83	1954
0.72	0.74	0.76	0.78	0.79	0.80	0.81	0.82	0.82	0.83	0.83	0.83	0.83	0.83	0.83	0.83	1955
0.71	0.73	0.75	0.77	0.78	0.79	0.80	0.81	0.82	0.82	0.83	0.83	0.83	0.83	0.83		1956
0.70	0.72	0.75	0.77	0.78	0.79	0.80	0.81	0.82	0.82	0.83	0.83	0.83	0.83			1957
0.68	0.71	0.73	0.75	0.77	0.78	0.79	0.80	0.81	0.81	0.82	0.82					1958
0.67	0.70	0.72	0.74	0.76	0.77	0.78	0.79	0.80	0.80	0.81						1959
0.66	0.69	0.71	0.74	0.75	0.76	0.78	0.78	0.79	0.80	0.80						1960
0.65	0.68	0.70	0.72	0.74	0.75	0.76	0.77	0.78	0.78							1961
0.63	0.67	0.69	0.72	0.73	0.75	0.76	0.76	0.77								1962
0.62	0.66	0.68	0.71	0.73	0.74	0.75	0.76									1963
0.61	0.65	0.68	0.70	0.72	0.73	0.75										1964
0.61	0.64	0.67	0.70	0.72	0.73											1965
0.60	0.64	0.67	0.69	0.72												1966
0.60	0.63	0.67	0.69													1967
0.60	0.64	0.67														1968
0.59	0.63															1969
0.58																1970
																1971
																1972
																1973
																1974
																1975
																1976
																1977
																1978
																1979
																1980
																1981
																1982
																1983
																1984
																1985

Table 10.4 Components of average family size: occurrence within/outside marriage, birth order, mother's year of birth, and age of mother at birth, 1920-1981   **England and Wales**

Mother's year of birth	All live births	Outside marriage	Within marriage Birth order					
			All	First	Second	Third	Fourth	Fifth and later
All ages of mother at birth								
1920	**2.00**	0.13	1.87	0.77	0.55	0.28	0.13	0.15
1925	**2.12**	0.12	2.00	0.80	0.58	0.30	0.15	0.17
1926	**2.18**	0.12	2.05	0.80	0.60	0.32	0.16	0.17
1927	**2.20**	0.12	2.08	0.81	0.61	0.32	0.16	0.18
1928	**2.24**	0.12	2.13	0.82	0.62	0.33	0.17	0.18
1929	**2.26**	0.11	2.14	0.82	0.63	0.34	0.17	0.18
1930	**2.35**	0.12	2.23	0.84	0.66	0.36	0.18	0.19
1931	**2.34**	0.12	2.22	0.84	0.66	0.36	0.18	0.18
1932	**2.34**	0.12	2.22	0.84	0.66	0.36	0.18	0.18
1933	**2.39**	0.12	2.26	0.85	0.69	0.37	0.18	0.17
1934	**2.42**	0.13	2.30	0.86	0.70	0.38	0.18	0.17
1935	**2.42**	0.13	2.29	0.86	0.71	0.38	0.18	0.16
1936	**2.40**	0.13	2.27	0.86	0.71	0.38	0.17	0.15
1937	**2.39**	0.14	2.25	0.85	0.71	0.38	0.17	0.13
1938	**2.39**	0.14	2.24	0.86	0.72	0.38	0.17	0.12
1939	**2.36**	0.15	2.21	0.86	0.72	0.37	0.16	0.11
1940	**2.36**	0.16	2.21	0.86	0.73	0.37	0.15	0.11
1941	**2.34**	0.16	2.18	0.86	0.73	0.36	0.14	0.09
1942	**2.29**	0.16	2.12	0.85	0.72	0.34	0.13	0.08
1943	**2.24**	0.16	2.08	0.85	0.72	0.32	0.12	0.07
1944	**2.21**	0.16	2.04	0.85	0.72	0.31	0.11	0.06
1945	**2.19**	0.17	2.02	0.85	0.72	0.30	0.10	0.05
1946	**2.19**	0.18	2.01	0.85	0.72	0.29	0.09	0.05
1947	**2.08**	0.17	1.91	0.82	0.69	0.27	0.08	0.04
1948	**2.11**	0.18	1.93	0.83	0.71	0.27	0.08	0.04
1949	**2.08**	0.19	1.89	0.81	0.69	0.26	0.08	0.04
1950	**2.07**	0.20	1.87	0.80	0.68	0.26	0.08	0.04
1951	**2.04**	0.20	1.84	0.79	0.67	0.25	0.08	0.04
1952	**2.05**	0.21	1.84	0.79	0.67	0.25	0.08	0.05
1953	**2.05**	0.22	1.82	0.78	0.66	0.25	0.08	0.05
1954	**2.02**	0.23	1.79	0.76	0.65	0.25	0.08	0.05
1955	**2.02**	0.25	1.77	0.76	0.64	0.25	0.08	0.05
Under 20								
1920	**0.08**	0.01	0.06	0.06	0.01	0.00		
1925	**0.08**	0.02	0.06	0.05	0.00	0.00		
1926	**0.08**	0.02	0.06	0.05	0.00	0.00		
1927	**0.08**	0.02	0.06	0.05	0.00	0.00		
1928	**0.09**	0.02	0.07	0.06	0.01	0.00		
1929	**0.10**	0.02	0.08	0.07	0.01	0.00		
1930	**0.10**	0.02	0.09	0.08	0.01	0.00		
1931	**0.11**	0.02	0.09	0.08	0.01	0.00		
1932	**0.11**	0.02	0.09	0.08	0.01	0.00		
1933	**0.11**	0.02	0.09	0.08	0.01	0.00		
1934	**0.11**	0.02	0.09	0.08	0.01	0.00		
1935	**0.11**	0.02	0.09	0.08	0.01	0.00		
1936	**0.12**	0.02	0.10	0.08	0.01	0.00		
1937	**0.12**	0.02	0.10	0.09	0.01	0.00		
1938	**0.13**	0.02	0.11	0.10	0.01	0.00		
1939	**0.14**	0.02	0.12	0.10	0.02	0.00		
1940	**0.16**	0.03	0.13	0.11	0.02	0.00		
1941	**0.17**	0.03	0.14	0.12	0.02	0.00		
1942	**0.18**	0.03	0.14	0.12	0.02	0.00		
1943	**0.19**	0.03	0.15	0.13	0.02	0.00		
1944	**0.20**	0.04	0.16	0.13	0.03	0.00		
1945	**0.22**	0.04	0.17	0.14	0.03	0.00		
1946	**0.22**	0.05	0.17	0.14	0.03	0.00		
1947	**0.22**	0.05	0.17	0.13	0.03	0.00		
1948	**0.22**	0.05	0.17	0.13	0.03	0.00		
1949	**0.23**	0.06	0.17	0.14	0.03	0.00		
1950	**0.23**	0.06	0.17	0.14	0.03	0.00		
1951	**0.24**	0.06	0.18	0.14	0.03	0.00		
1952	**0.25**	0.06	0.18	0.15	0.03	0.00		
1953	**0.24**	0.06	0.18	0.14	0.03	0.00		
1954	**0.23**	0.06	0.17	0.14	0.03	0.00		
1955	**0.22**	0.06	0.16	0.13	0.03	0.00		
1956	**0.20**	0.06	0.14	0.12	0.03	0.00		
1957	**0.19**	0.06	0.13	0.10	0.02	0.00		
1958	**0.17**	0.06	0.11	0.09	0.02	0.00		
1959	**0.16**	0.06	0.10	0.08	0.02	0.00		
1960	**0.15**	0.06	0.09	0.08	0.02	0.00		

Note: Average family sizes are obtained by summing rates for each single year of age.

Table 10.4 - *continued*

Mother's year of birth	All live births	Outside marriage	Within marriage					
			Birth order					
			All	First	Second	Third	Fourth	Fifth and later
Under 20 - *continued*								
1961	**0.16**	0.06	0.09	0.08	0.02	0.00		
1962	**0.15**	0.07	0.09	0.07	0.02	0.00		
1963	**0.14**	0.07	0.07	0.06	0.01	0.00		
1964	**0.13**	0.07	0.06	0.05	0.01	0.00		
1965	**0.13**	0.08	0.06	0.05	0.01	0.00		
1966	**0.13**	0.08	0.05	0.04	0.01	0.00		
1967	**0.14**	0.09	0.05	0.04	0.01	0.00		
1968	**0.15**	0.10	0.04	0.03	0.01	0.00		
1969	**0.15**	0.11	0.04	0.03	0.01	0.00		
1970	**0.15**	0.12	0.04	0.03	0.01	0.00		
1971	**0.15**	0.12	0.03	0.02	0.01	0.00		
1972	**0.15**	0.13	0.03	0.02	0.01	0.00		
1973	**0.15**	0.13	0.03	0.02	0.01	0.00		
1974	**0.15**	0.13	0.02	0.02	0.01	0.00		
1975	**0.15**	0.13	0.02	0.02	0.00	0.00		
1976	**0.15**	0.13	0.02	0.02	0.00	0.00		
1977	**0.15**	0.13	0.02	0.02	0.00	0.00		
1978	**0.15**	0.13	0.02	0.01	0.00	0.00		
1979	**0.15**	0.14	0.02	0.01	0.00	0.00		
1980	**0.15**	0.14	0.02	0.01	0.00	0.00		
1981	**0.15**	0.14	0.02	0.01	0.00	0.00		
20-24								
1920	**0.49**	0.04	0.45	0.31	0.11	0.03	0.01	0.00
1925	**0.63**	0.05	0.58	0.39	0.15	0.04	0.01	0.00
1926	**0.64**	0.04	0.60	0.39	0.16	0.04	0.01	0.00
1927	**0.64**	0.04	0.60	0.39	0.16	0.04	0.01	0.00
1928	**0.64**	0.03	0.61	0.38	0.17	0.05	0.01	0.00
1929	**0.64**	0.03	0.61	0.38	0.17	0.05	0.01	0.00
1930	**0.66**	0.03	0.63	0.38	0.18	0.05	0.01	0.00
1931	**0.66**	0.03	0.63	0.39	0.18	0.05	0.01	0.00
1932	**0.68**	0.03	0.64	0.39	0.18	0.05	0.01	0.00
1933	**0.71**	0.03	0.67	0.41	0.19	0.06	0.01	0.00
1934	**0.74**	0.04	0.70	0.42	0.20	0.06	0.02	0.00
1935	**0.76**	0.04	0.72	0.43	0.21	0.06	0.02	0.00
1936	**0.78**	0.04	0.74	0.43	0.22	0.07	0.02	0.01
1937	**0.80**	0.04	0.76	0.43	0.23	0.07	0.02	0.01
1938	**0.83**	0.05	0.79	0.44	0.24	0.08	0.02	0.01
1939	**0.86**	0.05	0.81	0.44	0.25	0.08	0.02	0.01
1940	**0.89**	0.06	0.83	0.44	0.27	0.09	0.03	0.01
1941	**0.91**	0.06	0.84	0.44	0.28	0.09	0.02	0.01
1942	**0.90**	0.07	0.83	0.44	0.27	0.09	0.02	0.01
1943	**0.87**	0.06	0.81	0.43	0.27	0.08	0.02	0.01
1944	**0.86**	0.07	0.79	0.42	0.27	0.08	0.02	0.01
1945	**0.84**	0.07	0.77	0.41	0.27	0.08	0.02	0.01
1946	**0.82**	0.07	0.76	0.40	0.26	0.08	0.02	0.00
1947	**0.77**	0.06	0.71	0.38	0.24	0.07	0.02	0.00
1948	**0.76**	0.06	0.70	0.37	0.24	0.07	0.02	0.00
1949	**0.72**	0.06	0.66	0.35	0.23	0.06	0.01	0.00
1950	**0.69**	0.06	0.63	0.34	0.22	0.06	0.01	0.00
1951	**0.65**	0.05	0.59	0.31	0.21	0.05	0.01	0.00
1952	**0.62**	0.05	0.56	0.29	0.21	0.05	0.01	0.00
1953	**0.58**	0.05	0.53	0.28	0.20	0.04	0.01	0.00
1954	**0.56**	0.05	0.51	0.27	0.19	0.04	0.01	0.00
1955	**0.55**	0.05	0.50	0.27	0.18	0.04	0.01	0.00
1956	**0.55**	0.06	0.50	0.27	0.18	0.04	0.01	0.00
1957	**0.55**	0.06	0.49	0.26	0.17	0.04	0.01	0.00
1958	**0.54**	0.07	0.47	0.26	0.17	0.04	0.01	0.00
1959	**0.53**	0.08	0.45	0.25	0.16	0.04	0.01	0.00
1960	**0.52**	0.09	0.44	0.24	0.15	0.04	0.01	0.00
1961	**0.50**	0.09	0.41	0.22	0.14	0.04	0.01	0.00
1962	**0.48**	0.10	0.38	0.21	0.13	0.03	0.01	0.00
1963	**0.47**	0.11	0.35	0.19	0.12	0.03	0.01	0.00
1964	**0.46**	0.13	0.33	0.18	0.11	0.03	0.01	0.00
1965	**0.46**	0.14	0.31	0.17	0.10	0.03	0.01	0.00
1966	**0.46**	0.16	0.30	0.16	0.10	0.03	0.01	0.00
1967	**0.45**	0.18	0.28	0.15	0.09	0.03	0.01	0.00
1968	**0.45**	0.19	0.26	0.14	0.09	0.02	0.00	0.00
1969	**0.44**	0.20	0.24	0.13	0.08	0.02	0.00	0.00
1970	**0.42**	0.20	0.22	0.12	0.08	0.02	0.00	0.00

Table 10.4 - *continued*

Mother's year of birth	All live births	Outside marriage	Within marriage					
			Birth order					
			All	First	Second	Third	Fourth	Fifth and later
20-24 - *continued*								
1971	**0.40**	0.21	0.20	0.11	0.07	0.02	0.00	0.00
1972	**0.39**	0.21	0.18	0.10	0.06	0.02	0.00	0.00
1973	**0.38**	0.21	0.17	0.09	0.06	0.02	0.00	0.00
1974	**0.38**	0.22	0.16	0.08	0.06	0.02	0.00	0.00
1975	**0.37**	0.22	0.15	0.08	0.05	0.01	0.00	0.00
1976	**0.37**	0.23	0.14	0.08	0.05	0.01	0.00	0.00
25-29								
1920	**0.70**	0.04	0.66	0.28	0.24	0.10	0.03	0.02
1925	**0.67**	0.02	0.65	0.23	0.24	0.11	0.04	0.03
1926	**0.69**	0.02	0.67	0.24	0.24	0.11	0.05	0.03
1927	**0.70**	0.02	0.68	0.25	0.24	0.11	0.05	0.03
1928	**0.72**	0.02	0.70	0.25	0.25	0.12	0.05	0.03
1929	**0.74**	0.02	0.72	0.26	0.26	0.12	0.05	0.04
1930	**0.78**	0.02	0.76	0.26	0.27	0.13	0.05	0.04
1931	**0.80**	0.03	0.77	0.26	0.28	0.13	0.06	0.04
1932	**0.81**	0.03	0.79	0.26	0.28	0.14	0.06	0.04
1933	**0.85**	0.03	0.82	0.26	0.30	0.15	0.06	0.04
1934	**0.89**	0.03	0.85	0.26	0.31	0.16	0.07	0.05
1935	**0.90**	0.04	0.87	0.26	0.32	0.17	0.07	0.05
1936	**0.91**	0.04	0.87	0.25	0.32	0.17	0.07	0.05
1937	**0.90**	0.04	0.86	0.25	0.32	0.17	0.07	0.05
1938	**0.89**	0.04	0.85	0.24	0.32	0.17	0.07	0.05
1939	**0.87**	0.04	0.83	0.23	0.31	0.17	0.07	0.04
1940	**0.85**	0.04	0.80	0.23	0.31	0.16	0.07	0.04
1941	**0.81**	0.04	0.77	0.22	0.30	0.16	0.06	0.04
1942	**0.79**	0.04	0.75	0.22	0.30	0.15	0.06	0.03
1943	**0.76**	0.04	0.73	0.22	0.29	0.14	0.05	0.03
1944	**0.73**	0.03	0.70	0.22	0.29	0.13	0.04	0.02
1945	**0.71**	0.03	0.68	0.23	0.28	0.12	0.04	0.02
1946	**0.69**	0.03	0.66	0.23	0.28	0.11	0.03	0.01
1947	**0.64**	0.03	0.62	0.22	0.26	0.09	0.03	0.01
1948	**0.64**	0.03	0.61	0.23	0.26	0.09	0.02	0.01
1949	**0.62**	0.03	0.59	0.22	0.25	0.08	0.02	0.01
1950	**0.62**	0.03	0.59	0.23	0.25	0.08	0.02	0.01
1951	**0.63**	0.03	0.59	0.23	0.25	0.08	0.02	0.01
1952	**0.64**	0.04	0.60	0.23	0.25	0.09	0.03	0.01
1953	**0.65**	0.04	0.61	0.24	0.25	0.09	0.03	0.01
1954	**0.65**	0.04	0.61	0.24	0.24	0.09	0.03	0.01
1955	**0.65**	0.05	0.60	0.23	0.24	0.09	0.03	0.01
1956	**0.64**	0.05	0.59	0.23	0.24	0.09	0.03	0.01
1957	**0.64**	0.06	0.58	0.22	0.23	0.09	0.03	0.01
1958	**0.64**	0.07	0.57	0.23	0.22	0.08	0.03	0.01
1959	**0.63**	0.07	0.56	0.22	0.22	0.08	0.02	0.01
1960	**0.63**	0.08	0.55	0.22	0.21	0.08	0.02	0.01
1961	**0.62**	0.09	0.53	0.22	0.20	0.08	0.02	0.01
1962	**0.61**	0.10	0.51	0.22	0.19	0.07	0.02	0.01
1963	**0.61**	0.11	0.50	0.21	0.19	0.07	0.02	0.01
1964	**0.60**	0.12	0.48	0.21	0.18	0.06	0.02	0.01
1965	**0.59**	0.13	0.46	0.20	0.17	0.06	0.02	0.01
1966	**0.58**	0.14	0.44	0.19	0.16	0.06	0.02	0.01
1967	**0.56**	0.15	0.42	0.19	0.15	0.05	0.02	0.01
1968	**0.55**	0.15	0.40	0.18	0.15	0.05	0.02	0.01
1969	**0.54**	0.16	0.38	0.18	0.14	0.05	0.02	0.01
1970	**0.53**	0.16	0.36	0.17	0.13	0.05	0.01	0.01
1971	**0.51**	0.17	0.34	0.16	0.12	0.04	0.01	0.01
30-34								
1920	**0.43**	0.02	0.41	0.09	0.14	0.09	0.05	0.05
1925	**0.45**	0.02	0.43	0.09	0.14	0.09	0.05	0.06
1926	**0.46**	0.02	0.45	0.09	0.14	0.10	0.05	0.06
1927	**0.48**	0.02	0.46	0.09	0.14	0.10	0.06	0.06
1928	**0.49**	0.02	0.47	0.09	0.15	0.11	0.06	0.07
1929	**0.50**	0.02	0.48	0.09	0.15	0.11	0.06	0.07
1930	**0.53**	0.02	0.51	0.09	0.15	0.12	0.07	0.08
1931	**0.53**	0.02	0.50	0.09	0.15	0.12	0.07	0.08
1932	**0.52**	0.02	0.49	0.08	0.14	0.12	0.07	0.08
1933	**0.51**	0.03	0.49	0.08	0.14	0.12	0.07	0.07
1934	**0.50**	0.02	0.47	0.08	0.14	0.12	0.07	0.07
1935	**0.47**	0.02	0.44	0.07	0.13	0.11	0.06	0.06

Table 10.4 - *continued*

Mother's year of birth	**All live births**	Outside marriage	Within marriage					
			Birth order					
			All	First	Second	Third	Fourth	Fifth and later
30-34 - *continued*								
1936	**0.44**	0.02	0.42	0.07	0.13	0.11	0.06	0.06
1937	**0.42**	0.02	0.40	0.06	0.12	0.11	0.06	0.05
1938	**0.40**	0.02	0.38	0.06	0.12	0.10	0.05	0.05
1939	**0.37**	0.02	0.35	0.06	0.11	0.09	0.05	0.04
1940	**0.35**	0.02	0.33	0.06	0.11	0.09	0.04	0.03
1941	**0.33**	0.02	0.31	0.06	0.10	0.08	0.04	0.03
1942	**0.30**	0.02	0.29	0.06	0.10	0.07	0.03	0.02
1943	**0.29**	0.02	0.27	0.06	0.10	0.07	0.03	0.02
1944	**0.28**	0.02	0.27	0.06	0.11	0.06	0.02	0.02
1945	**0.29**	0.02	0.28	0.06	0.11	0.07	0.02	0.01
1946	**0.31**	0.02	0.29	0.07	0.12	0.07	0.02	0.01
1947	**0.31**	0.02	0.30	0.07	0.12	0.07	0.02	0.01
1948	**0.34**	0.02	0.32	0.08	0.13	0.08	0.03	0.01
1949	**0.35**	0.02	0.33	0.08	0.13	0.08	0.03	0.01
1950	**0.36**	0.02	0.34	0.08	0.14	0.08	0.03	0.01
1951	**0.36**	0.03	0.33	0.08	0.13	0.08	0.03	0.02
1952	**0.37**	0.03	0.34	0.08	0.14	0.08	0.03	0.02
1953	**0.38**	0.03	0.35	0.09	0.14	0.08	0.03	0.02
1954	**0.39**	0.04	0.36	0.09	0.14	0.08	0.03	0.02
1955	**0.40**	0.04	0.36	0.10	0.14	0.08	0.03	0.02
1956	**0.41**	0.05	0.36	0.10	0.14	0.08	0.03	0.02
1957	**0.42**	0.06	0.36	0.10	0.14	0.08	0.03	0.02
1958	**0.43**	0.06	0.37	0.10	0.14	0.07	0.03	0.02
1959	**0.43**	0.07	0.36	0.11	0.14	0.07	0.03	0.01
1960	**0.44**	0.07	0.37	0.11	0.15	0.07	0.02	0.01
1961	**0.44**	0.08	0.36	0.11	0.14	0.07	0.02	0.01
1962	**0.44**	0.08	0.36	0.11	0.14	0.07	0.02	0.01
1963	**0.44**	0.09	0.35	0.11	0.15	0.06	0.02	0.01
1964	**0.45**	0.09	0.35	0.11	0.14	0.06	0.02	0.01
1965	**0.45**	0.10	0.35	0.12	0.14	0.06	0.02	0.01
1966	**0.45**	0.10	0.35	0.12	0.14	0.06	0.02	0.01
35 and over								
1920	**0.30**	0.02	0.28	0.03	0.06	0.06	0.05	0.08
1925	**0.30**	0.02	0.28	0.03	0.06	0.06	0.05	0.08
1926	**0.30**	0.02	0.29	0.03	0.06	0.06	0.05	0.09
1927	**0.29**	0.02	0.28	0.03	0.05	0.06	0.05	0.08
1928	**0.29**	0.02	0.27	0.03	0.05	0.06	0.05	0.08
1929	**0.27**	0.02	0.25	0.03	0.05	0.06	0.04	0.07
1930	**0.26**	0.02	0.25	0.03	0.05	0.06	0.04	0.07
1931	**0.24**	0.02	0.23	0.03	0.04	0.05	0.04	0.06
1932	**0.22**	0.02	0.21	0.02	0.04	0.05	0.04	0.06
1933	**0.21**	0.01	0.19	0.02	0.04	0.05	0.03	0.05
1934	**0.19**	0.01	0.18	0.02	0.04	0.04	0.03	0.05
1935	**0.17**	0.01	0.16	0.02	0.03	0.04	0.03	0.04
1936	**0.16**	0.01	0.14	0.02	0.03	0.03	0.02	0.03
1937	**0.14**	0.01	0.13	0.02	0.03	0.03	0.02	0.03
1938	**0.13**	0.01	0.12	0.02	0.03	0.03	0.02	0.03
1939	**0.12**	0.01	0.11	0.02	0.03	0.03	0.02	0.02
1940	**0.12**	0.01	0.11	0.02	0.03	0.03	0.02	0.02
1941	**0.12**	0.01	0.11	0.02	0.03	0.03	0.02	0.02
1942	**0.12**	0.01	0.11	0.02	0.03	0.03	0.02	0.02
1943	**0.12**	0.01	0.11	0.02	0.03	0.03	0.02	0.02
1944	**0.13**	0.01	0.12	0.02	0.03	0.03	0.02	0.02
1945	**0.13**	0.01	0.12	0.02	0.03	0.03	0.02	0.02
1946	**0.14**	0.02	0.12	0.02	0.03	0.03	0.02	0.02
1947	**0.14**	0.02	0.12	0.02	0.03	0.03	0.02	0.01
1948	**0.14**	0.02	0.13	0.02	0.04	0.03	0.02	0.01
1949	**0.15**	0.02	0.13	0.02	0.04	0.03	0.02	0.02
1950	**0.16**	0.02	0.14	0.03	0.04	0.04	0.02	0.02
1951	**0.17**	0.03	0.14	0.03	0.04	0.04	0.02	0.02
1952	**0.18**	0.03	0.15	0.03	0.05	0.04	0.02	0.02
1953	**0.19**	0.03	0.15	0.03	0.05	0.04	0.02	0.02
1954	**0.19**	0.04	0.15	0.03	0.05	0.04	0.02	0.02
1955	**0.20**	0.04	0.16	0.04	0.05	0.04	0.02	0.02

Table 10.5 Estimated distribution of women of childbearing age by number of liveborn children (percentages): year of birth and age, 1920-1980

England and Wales

Year of birth of woman	Age of woman (completed years)	Number of liveborn children†				
		0 (Childless women)	1	2	3	4 or more
1920	20	89	10	2	0	0
1925		87	11	2	0	0
1930		84	13	3	0	0
1935		83	14	3	0	0
1940		78	16	4	1	0
1945		74	18	6	1	0
1950		74	18	7	1	0
1955		77	16	6	1	0
1960		82	13	4	1	0
1965		85	11	3	1	0
1970		83	13	3	1	0
1975		83	13	3	1	0
1980		83	14	3	1	0
1920	25	54	29	13	3	1
1925		45	32	17	5	1
1930		44	31	18	6	2
1935		38	30	22	7	3
1940		33	28	25	9	5
1945		34	26	27	9	4
1950		41	24	25	7	2
1955		49	22	22	6	2
1960		55	19	18	6	2
1965		61	17	16	5	2
1970		62	17	16	5	1
1975		65	16	14	4	1
1920	30	30	28	26	10	6
1925		26	29	27	11	7
1930		22	26	30	13	9
1935		18	21	33	16	12
1940		16	17	36	18	12
1945		16	19	41	17	8
1950		22	19	39	14	5
1955		28	18	35	13	5
1960		34	17	29	14	6
1965		39	18	25	13	5
1970		41	20	22	12	5
1920	35	23	23	28	14	11
1925		19	25	30	15	12
1930		15	20	31	18	16
1935		12	16	33	20	18
1940		12	14	37	22	16
1945		11	14	44	20	11
1950		16	14	43	19	9
1955		20	14	39	19	9
1960		23	14	34	20	9
1965		27	16	30	20	8
1920	40	21	22	27	16	14
1925		17	23	29	17	15
1930		13	19	30	19	19
1935		11	15	33	21	19
1940		11	13	37	22	17
1945		10	14	43	21	12
1950		14	12	43	20	10
1955		17	12	40	20	10
1960		20	12	35	22	11
1920	45*	21	21	27	16	15
1925		16	23	28	17	16
1930		13	19	30	19	20
1935		11	15	33	21	20
1940		11	13	37	22	18
1945		10	13	43	21	12
1950		14	12	43	20	10
1955		17	12	41	20	10

*   Includes birth at ages of over 45
†   Estimates including births within and outside marriage - see Section 2.15

Table 11.1 Live births within marriage: estimated distribution by social class of father as defined by occupation, by number of previous liveborn children and age of mother, 1990-2000

England and Wales

thousands

Year	Number of previous liveborn children					Year	Number of previous liveborn children				
	Total	0	1	2	3 or more		Total	0	1	2	3 or more

Social classes I and II — **All ages of mother at birth** | **Social class IIIN** — **All ages of mother at birth**

Year	Total	0	1	2	3 or more	Year	Total	0	1	2	3 or more
1990	177.4	73.9	66.8	26.5	10.2	1990	53.2	23.8	19.5	6.8	3.1
1991	173.3	72.8	64.4	26.2	9.9	1991	50.7	22.0	19.5	6.3	2.8
1992	170.5	73.1	62.9	24.6	9.8	1992	49.4	21.4	18.5	7.0	2.5
1993	165.8	70.0	62.9	23.6	9.3	1993	50.6	21.5	19.1	6.9	3.1
1994	166.1	70.0	61.9	24.3	9.9	1994	50.5	22.1	18.7	7.0	2.7
1995	161.6	67.6	61.7	23.3	9.0	1995	48.2	20.9	18.0	6.5	2.7
1996	161.5	67.6	61.8	23.3	8.8	1996	47.6	20.4	18.2	6.2	2.8
1997	162.5	67.7	62.5	23.2	9.2	1997	44.0	19.1	16.7	5.7	2.5
1998	162.8	68.9	62.3	23.0	8.6	1998	42.5	18.5	16.0	5.5	2.5
1999	163.6	70.1	61.9	22.9	8.6	1999	39.8	17.3	14.9	5.0	2.5
2000	161.5	68.5	62.1	22.5	8.4	2000	37.8	17.1	13.6	4.7	2.5

Under 20 | **Under 20**

Year	Total	0	1	2	3 or more	Year	Total	0	1	2	3 or more
1990	1.3	1.1	0.2	0.0		1990	0.9	0.7	0.1	0.0	
1991	1.0	0.8	0.2	0.0		1991	0.8	0.7	0.2	0.0	
1992	1.0	0.8	0.2	0.0		1992	0.7	0.6	0.1	0.0	
1993	1.0	0.8	0.2	0.0		1993	0.6	0.5	0.1	0.0	
1994	0.9	0.8	0.1	-		1994	0.7	0.5	0.1	0.0	
1995	1.0	0.8	0.2	0.0		1995	0.5	0.4	0.1	0.0	
1996	0.8	0.7	0.0	-		1996	0.5	0.4	0.1	-	
1997	0.8	0.8	0.1	0.0		1997	0.6	0.5	0.1	-	
1998	0.6	0.5	0.1	0.0		1998	0.5	0.5	0.1	-	
1999	1.0	0.9	0.1	0.0		1999	0.6	0.5	0.1	0.0	
2000	0.7	0.7	0.0	0.0		2000	0.5	0.5	0.1	-	

20-24 | **20-24**

Year	Total	0	1	2	3 or more	Year	Total	0	1	2	3 or more
1990	20.3	12.9	6.3	1.0	0.2	1990	9.7	6.1	2.9	0.7	0.1
1991	18.8	11.8	5.8	1.1	0.1	1991	8.7	5.2	2.8	0.6	0.1
1992	16.8	10.7	4.9	1.0	0.2	1992	8.3	4.9	2.6	0.8	0.1
1993	15.1	9.6	4.3	1.0	0.2	1993	7.8	4.5	2.7	0.5	0.1
1994	13.3	8.4	3.8	1.0	0.2	1994	7.0	4.2	2.2	0.4	0.1
1995	12.2	7.9	3.4	0.8	0.2	1995	6.1	3.5	2.0	0.5	0.1
1996	10.9	6.8	3.2	0.7	0.2	1996	6.2	3.9	1.8	0.5	0.1
1997	10.3	6.4	3.1	0.7	0.1	1997	5.1	3.2	1.4	0.4	0.1
1998	10.2	6.5	2.9	0.7	0.1	1998	5.0	3.1	1.4	0.4	0.0
1999	9.8	6.1	3.0	0.7	0.1	1999	4.5	2.6	1.5	0.4	0.1
2000	9.5	5.9	2.9	0.5	0.1	2000	4.1	2.5	1.3	0.3	0.1

25-29 | **25-29**

Year	Total	0	1	2	3 or more	Year	Total	0	1	2	3 or more
1990	68.5	33.9	25.5	7.2	1.8	1990	22.6	11.0	8.5	2.2	0.8
1991	64.3	32.1	23.9	6.5	1.7	1991	21.3	10.4	8.1	2.1	0.7
1992	63.1	32.9	22.5	6.2	1.5	1992	19.5	9.6	7.2	2.0	0.6
1993	59.1	30.3	21.8	5.6	1.4	1993	20.3	9.7	7.4	2.3	0.9
1994	55.0	29.2	18.7	5.5	1.6	1994	20.0	10.3	7.1	2.1	0.5
1995	52.2	27.1	19.1	4.7	1.4	1995	18.4	9.5	6.4	1.7	0.7
1996	50.0	26.3	17.4	5.0	1.2	1996	17.4	8.8	6.2	1.7	0.6
1997	48.5	26.0	16.6	4.6	1.3	1997	15.8	8.0	5.7	1.6	0.6
1998	46.2	25.2	16.0	4.0	1.0	1998	14.2	7.3	4.9	1.4	0.6
1999	44.7	24.8	14.9	3.8	1.1	1999	12.6	6.4	4.3	1.3	0.6
2000	42.3	23.6	13.9	3.7	1.1	2000	11.9	6.3	3.9	1.3	0.4

30 and over | **30 and over**

Year	Total	0	1	2	3 or more	Year	Total	0	1	2	3 or more
1990	87.3	26.1	34.8	18.3	8.2	1990	20.0	5.9	8.0	3.9	2.2
1991	89.2	28.0	34.6	18.6	8.0	1991	19.8	5.7	8.5	3.6	2.0
1992	89.5	28.6	35.3	17.5	8.1	1992	21.0	6.3	8.6	4.2	1.8
1993	90.6	29.3	36.7	17.0	7.6	1993	21.8	6.8	8.9	4.0	2.1
1994	96.9	31.7	39.3	17.8	8.1	1994	22.8	7.0	9.2	4.5	2.1
1995	96.2	31.9	39.1	17.8	7.4	1995	23.2	7.5	9.5	4.3	1.9
1996	99.9	33.7	41.1	17.7	7.4	1996	23.5	7.3	10.1	4.0	2.1
1997	102.9	34.6	42.7	17.9	7.7	1997	22.5	7.5	9.4	3.8	1.8
1998	105.9	36.8	43.3	18.3	7.5	1998	22.7	7.6	9.5	3.7	1.9
1999	108.1	38.4	43.8	18.5	7.4	1999	22.1	7.8	9.1	3.3	1.9
2000	109.0	38.4	45.2	18.2	7.2	2000	21.2	7.9	8.3	3.1	2.0

Notes:
1. For a description of social classes and the sample used in calculation - see Section 3.10.
2. Table includes 1990 data based on the 1980 *Classification of Occupations* and for 1991-2000 on the *Standard Occupational Classification.*

Table 11.1 - *continued*   *thousands*

Social class IIIM

All ages of mother at birth

Year	Total	0	1	2	3 or more
1990	**168.8**	63.3	62.1	28.4	15.0
1991	**162.0**	61.3	58.5	27.1	15.1
1992	**153.6**	56.1	56.9	26.1	14.4
1993	**139.0**	49.6	51.7	24.1	13.6
1994	**134.9**	48.1	51.7	22.0	13.0
1995	**124.7**	45.2	46.3	20.9	12.3
1996	**117.8**	42.6	43.0	20.3	12.0
1997	**112.0**	39.3	41.0	19.5	12.2
1998	**105.5**	37.7	39.1	17.9	10.7
1999	**97.6**	35.9	35.7	15.9	10.1
2000	**91.6**	32.9	33.7	15.2	9.7

Under 20

Year	Total	0	1	2	3 or more
1990	**4.2**	3.1	1.0	0.1	
1991	**3.3**	2.5	0.8	0.1	
1992	**2.6**	1.9	0.6	0.1	
1993	**2.1**	1.5	0.6	0.0	
1994	**1.9**	1.4	0.5	0.0	
1995	**1.8**	1.3	0.4	0.1	
1996	**1.6**	1.2	0.4	0.0	
1997	**1.3**	1.0	0.3	0.0	
1998	**1.5**	1.2	0.3	0.0	
1999	**1.2**	0.9	0.3	0.0	
2000	**1.4**	1.0	0.4	0.0	

20-24

Year	Total	0	1	2	3 or more
1990	**42.7**	22.1	15.1	4.4	1.1
1991	**37.7**	19.3	13.3	4.1	1.0
1992	**33.0**	16.5	11.9	3.6	1.0
1993	**27.4**	13.6	9.9	3.1	0.7
1994	**24.7**	12.0	9.3	2.7	0.6
1995	**21.1**	10.4	7.8	2.4	0.6
1996	**18.6**	9.1	6.8	2.1	0.5
1997	**16.6**	8.0	6.0	2.0	0.5
1998	**14.5**	6.9	5.5	1.7	0.5
1999	**13.5**	6.8	4.7	1.6	0.5
2000	**12.1**	5.9	4.5	1.4	0.3

25-29

Year	Total	0	1	2	3 or more
1990	**72.0**	27.0	28.2	12.0	4.9
1991	**70.5**	27.6	26.9	11.2	4.8
1992	**65.9**	25.3	25.5	10.5	4.6
1993	**58.8**	22.9	22.6	9.1	4.1
1994	**56.3**	21.7	22.5	8.2	3.9
1995	**50.7**	20.6	18.7	7.8	3.5
1996	**46.3**	19.1	17.0	6.7	3.4
1997	**42.2**	16.9	15.7	6.4	3.1
1998	**39.6**	16.3	14.4	6.0	2.9
1999	**35.3**	14.9	12.8	5.2	2.3
2000	**32.0**	12.8	11.5	4.9	2.7

30 and over

Year	Total	0	1	2	3 or more
1990	**50.0**	11.2	17.8	11.9	9.0
1991	**50.5**	11.9	17.6	11.7	9.3
1992	**52.1**	12.4	19.0	11.9	8.9
1993	**50.7**	11.6	18.5	11.8	8.8
1994	**51.9**	13.0	19.4	11.0	8.5
1995	**51.1**	13.0	19.2	10.6	8.2
1996	**51.4**	13.2	18.7	11.4	8.1
1997	**52.0**	13.4	18.9	11.1	8.5
1998	**49.8**	13.4	19.0	10.2	7.3
1999	**47.6**	13.3	17.9	9.1	7.2
2000	**46.1**	13.2	17.3	8.9	6.7

Social classes IV and V

All ages of mother at birth

Year	Total	0	1	2	3 or more
1990	**85.3**	30.2	29.3	14.3	11.5
1991	**79.1**	28.0	27.9	13.4	9.9
1992	**77.1**	26.8	26.9	13.2	10.1
1993	**77.7**	27.0	27.5	13.9	9.2
1994	**75.6**	26.8	26.6	13.1	9.2
1995	**72.5**	25.1	25.5	12.8	9.1
1996	**70.1**	24.5	24.4	12.6	8.7
1997	**67.0**	23.4	23.9	11.7	8.1
1998	**65.7**	23.2	23.2	11.2	8.1
1999	**59.6**	21.8	21.2	9.6	7.1
2000	**56.7**	20.7	19.4	9.7	6.9

Under 20

Year	Total	0	1	2	3 or more
1990	**3.7**	2.7	0.9	0.1	
1991	**2.9**	2.1	0.7	0.1	
1992	**2.6**	1.9	0.6	0.0	
1993	**2.0**	1.5	0.5	0.0	
1994	**1.8**	1.4	0.4	0.0	
1995	**1.3**	1.0	0.4	0.0	
1996	**1.6**	1.2	0.3	0.0	
1997	**1.5**	1.2	0.3	0.0	
1998	**1.7**	1.3	0.4	0.0	
1999	**1.7**	1.2	0.4	0.0	
2000	**1.3**	1.0	0.3	0.0	

20-24

Year	Total	0	1	2	3 or more
1990	**27.4**	12.6	10.3	3.5	1.0
1991	**23.6**	11.1	8.6	3.0	0.9
1992	**21.2**	10.1	7.7	2.7	0.7
1993	**19.9**	8.9	7.7	2.6	0.6
1994	**18.1**	8.5	6.6	2.4	0.6
1995	**16.3**	7.5	5.8	2.3	0.7
1996	**14.0**	6.5	5.0	2.0	0.5
1997	**12.5**	5.7	4.5	1.8	0.5
1998	**12.1**	5.7	4.5	1.4	0.5
1999	**11.3**	5.7	4.2	1.2	0.3
2000	**10.4**	5.1	3.6	1.4	0.4

25-29

Year	Total	0	1	2	3 or more
1990	**33.3**	11.1	12.0	6.1	4.0
1991	**31.4**	10.7	11.8	5.7	3.3
1992	**31.4**	10.3	12.0	5.7	3.4
1993	**31.4**	11.2	11.5	5.7	3.1
1994	**31.0**	11.2	11.3	5.5	3.1
1995	**28.7**	10.5	10.2	5.1	2.8
1996	**27.8**	10.0	10.2	5.0	2.6
1997	**25.8**	9.7	9.4	4.3	2.5
1998	**24.1**	9.3	8.7	4.1	2.1
1999	**21.6**	8.5	7.7	3.4	2.0
2000	**19.2**	7.5	6.7	3.3	1.7

30 and over

Year	Total	0	1	2	3 or more
1990	**20.9**	3.8	6.0	4.6	6.5
1991	**21.2**	4.1	6.7	4.6	5.7
1992	**21.8**	4.5	6.6	4.7	6.0
1993	**24.4**	5.4	7.9	5.5	5.5
1994	**24.7**	5.7	8.3	5.3	5.4
1995	**26.2**	6.2	9.1	5.4	5.6
1996	**26.8**	6.8	8.9	5.6	5.5
1997	**27.1**	6.8	9.6	5.6	5.1
1998	**27.8**	6.8	9.6	5.7	5.6
1999	**25.0**	6.4	9.0	4.9	4.8
2000	**25.7**	7.1	8.7	5.0	4.8

Notes: 1. For a description of social classes and the sample used in calculation - see Section 3.10.
2. Table includes 1990 data based on the 1980 *Classification of Occupations* and for 1991-2000 on the *Standard Occupational Classification*.

Table 11.1 - *continued*

thousands

Year	Number of previous liveborn children					Year	Number of previous liveborn children				
	Total	0	1	2	3 or more		**Total**	0	1	2	3 or more
	Social class: non-manual						**Social class: manual**				
	All ages of mother at birth						**All ages of mother at birth**				
1990	**230.6**	97.7	86.3	33.3	13.3	1990	**254.1**	93.5	91.4	42.7	26.5
1991	**224.0**	94.8	84.0	32.5	12.8	1991	**241.1**	89.3	86.3	40.5	25.0
1992	**219.9**	94.5	81.4	31.6	12.4	1992	**230.6**	83.0	83.8	39.3	24.5
1993	**216.3**	91.5	82.0	30.5	12.3	1993	**216.7**	76.6	79.2	38.0	22.9
1994	**216.6**	92.1	80.6	31.3	12.7	1994	**210.5**	74.9	78.3	35.1	22.2
1995	**209.8**	88.5	79.7	29.8	11.7	1995	**197.2**	70.4	71.7	33.8	21.3
1996	**209.1**	88.0	80.0	29.5	11.6	1996	**188.0**	67.0	67.4	32.9	20.7
1997	**206.5**	86.9	79.2	28.9	11.7	1997	**179.0**	62.7	64.9	31.2	20.3
1998	**205.3**	87.4	78.3	28.5	11.1	1998	**171.2**	60.9	62.4	29.1	18.8
1999	**203.4**	87.4	76.8	28.0	11.2	1999	**157.2**	57.7	56.9	25.5	17.2
2000	**199.3**	85.6	75.7	27.1	10.9	2000	**148.3**	53.7	53.1	24.9	16.6
	Under 20						**Under 20**				
1990	**2.2**	1.8	0.3		0.1	1990	**7.9**	5.8	1.9	0.1	
1991	**1.8**	1.5	0.3		0.0	1991	**6.2**	4.6	1.5	0.1	
1992	**1.7**	1.4	0.3		0.0	1992	**5.2**	3.8	1.2	0.1	
1993	**1.6**	1.3	0.3		0.1	1993	**4.2**	3.0	1.1	0.1	
1994	**1.6**	1.3	0.3		0.0	1994	**3.7**	2.7	0.9	0.1	
1995	**1.5**	1.2	0.3		0.0	1995	**3.1**	2.3	0.8	0.1	
1996	**1.3**	1.1	0.1		0.0	1996	**3.2**	2.4	0.7	0.1	
1997	**1.5**	1.2	0.2		0.0	1997	**2.9**	2.2	0.6	0.1	
1998	**1.1**	0.9	0.2		0.0	1998	**3.2**	2.5	0.6	0.1	
1999	**1.5**	1.3	0.2		0.0	1999	**2.9**	2.1	0.7	0.1	
2000	**1.3**	1.1	0.1		0.0	2000	**2.7**	2.0	0.7	0.0	
	20-24						**20-24**				
1990	**30.1**	19.0	9.1	1.7	0.3	1990	**70.1**	34.6	25.4	7.9	2.1
1991	**27.6**	17.0	8.6	1.7	0.3	1991	**61.3**	30.4	21.8	7.1	1.9
1992	**25.1**	15.6	7.5	1.7	0.3	1992	**54.2**	26.6	19.6	6.3	1.7
1993	**22.9**	14.1	6.9	1.5	0.3	1993	**47.3**	22.5	17.6	5.8	1.3
1994	**20.3**	12.6	6.0	1.4	0.3	1994	**42.9**	20.5	16.0	5.1	1.3
1995	**18.3**	11.4	5.3	1.3	0.2	1995	**37.4**	17.9	13.6	4.7	1.2
1996	**17.1**	10.7	5.0	1.2	0.2	1996	**32.6**	15.6	11.8	4.2	1.0
1997	**15.4**	9.6	4.5	1.0	0.2	1997	**29.1**	13.7	10.6	3.8	1.0
1998	**15.1**	9.6	4.3	1.1	0.2	1998	**26.7**	12.6	10.0	3.1	0.9
1999	**14.3**	8.6	4.5	1.1	0.2	1999	**24.9**	12.5	8.8	2.8	0.8
2000	**13.6**	8.4	4.3	0.8	0.2	2000	**22.5**	11.0	8.1	2.7	0.7
	25-29						**25-29**				
1990	**91.1**	44.9	34.1	9.5	2.6	1990	**105.3**	38.1	40.2	18.1	8.9
1991	**85.6**	42.5	32.0	8.6	2.5	1991	**101.9**	38.3	38.7	16.9	8.0
1992	**82.6**	42.5	29.7	8.2	2.2	1992	**97.3**	35.6	37.5	16.2	8.0
1993	**79.4**	40.0	29.2	7.9	2.3	1993	**90.2**	34.1	34.1	14.8	7.2
1994	**75.0**	39.5	25.8	7.5	2.1	1994	**87.3**	32.9	33.8	13.7	7.0
1995	**70.6**	36.5	25.5	6.4	2.1	1995	**79.4**	31.1	28.9	13.0	6.3
1996	**67.4**	35.2	23.7	6.7	1.8	1996	**74.0**	29.1	27.3	11.7	6.0
1997	**64.3**	33.9	22.3	6.2	1.9	1997	**68.0**	26.6	25.1	10.7	5.6
1998	**60.4**	32.5	20.9	5.4	1.6	1998	**63.7**	25.5	23.1	10.0	5.0
1999	**57.3**	31.3	19.2	5.1	1.7	1999	**56.9**	23.4	20.5	8.6	4.4
2000	**54.2**	29.9	17.9	5.0	1.5	2000	**51.2**	20.3	18.2	8.2	4.4
	30 and over						**30 and over**				
1990	**107.3**	32.0	42.8	22.1	10.4	1990	**70.9**	15.0	23.8	16.5	15.6
1991	**109.0**	33.7	43.1	22.2	10.0	1991	**71.7**	16.0	24.3	16.3	15.1
1992	**110.5**	35.0	43.9	21.7	9.9	1992	**74.0**	16.9	25.5	16.7	14.9
1993	**112.5**	36.1	45.5	21.1	9.7	1993	**75.1**	17.0	26.4	17.3	14.3
1994	**119.7**	38.7	48.5	22.3	10.2	1994	**76.5**	18.7	27.6	16.2	14.0
1995	**119.5**	39.4	48.6	22.1	9.4	1995	**77.3**	19.2	28.4	16.0	13.8
1996	**123.4**	41.0	51.2	21.7	9.5	1996	**78.2**	20.0	27.6	16.9	13.6
1997	**125.4**	42.1	52.1	21.6	9.6	1997	**79.1**	20.3	28.6	16.7	13.6
1998	**128.6**	44.4	52.8	22.0	9.3	1998	**77.6**	20.2	28.6	15.9	12.9
1999	**130.2**	46.2	52.9	21.8	9.3	1999	**72.6**	19.7	26.9	14.0	12.0
2000	**130.2**	46.3	53.5	21.3	9.3	2000	**71.9**	20.3	26.1	13.9	11.5

Notes: 1.   For a description of social classes and the sample used in calculation - see Section 3.10.
2.   Table includes 1990 data based on the 1980 *Classification of Occupations* and for 1991-2000 on the *Standard Occupational Classification.*

Social class Series FM1 no. 29

Table 11.1 - *continued*   *thousands*

Year	Number of previous liveborn children					Year	Number of previous liveborn children				
	Total	0	1	2	3 or more		**Total**	0	1	2	3 or more
	Others						**All social classes**				
	All ages of mother at birth						**All ages of mother at birth**				
1990	**21.4**	9.2	7.6	3.0	1.6	1990	**506.1**	200.4	185.3	79.0	41.4
1991	**22.8**	9.6	8.0	3.1	2.0	1991	**487.9**	193.7	178.3	76.1	39.8
1992	**23.9**	9.8	8.7	3.3	2.0	1992	**474.4**	187.3	174.0	74.2	38.9
1993	**23.9**	10.0	8.3	3.3	2.3	1993	**456.9**	178.1	169.4	71.8	37.5
1994	**22.1**	9.1	7.4	3.4	2.2	1994	**449.2**	176.0	166.3	69.7	37.1
1995	**21.2**	9.2	6.6	3.1	2.2	1995	**428.2**	168.1	158.1	66.7	35.3
1996	**19.7**	8.0	6.4	2.9	2.5	1996	**416.8**	163.0	153.8	65.3	34.7
1997	**19.3**	7.5	6.4	3.2	2.3	1997	**404.9**	157.0	150.4	63.2	34.2
1998	**18.8**	7.4	6.2	2.8	2.4	1998	**395.3**	155.7	146.9	60.4	32.3
1999	**19.4**	8.3	5.8	2.9	2.4	1999	**380.0**	153.4	139.5	56.4	30.7
2000	**18.2**	7.3	5.9	2.9	2.2	2000	**365.8**	146.5	134.7	54.9	29.7
	Under 20						**Under 20**				
1990	**0.9**	0.7	0.2	0.0		1990	**11.0**	8.3	2.4	0.2	
1991	**0.9**	0.7	0.2	0.0		1991	**8.9**	6.7	2.0	0.2	
1992	**0.9**	0.7	0.2	0.0		1992	**7.8**	6.0	1.7	0.1	
1993	**1.1**	0.9	0.2	-		1993	**6.9**	5.2	1.5	0.2	
1994	**0.8**	0.7	0.1	0.0		1994	**6.1**	4.7	1.3	0.1	
1995	**1.0**	0.9	0.1	-		1995	**5.6**	4.3	1.2	0.1	
1996	**0.9**	0.7	0.2	0.0		1996	**5.4**	4.2	1.0	0.1	
1997	**0.9**	0.7	0.2	0.0		1997	**5.2**	4.1	1.0	0.1	
1998	**0.9**	0.7	0.2	-		1998	**5.3**	4.2	1.0	0.1	
1999	**0.9**	0.8	0.1	0.0		1999	**5.3**	4.3	0.9	0.1	
2000	**0.8**	0.7	0.1	0.0		2000	**4.7**	3.8	0.8	0.1	
	20-24						**20-24**				
1990	**6.0**	3.4	2.0	0.5	0.2	1990	**106.2**	57.0	36.5	10.1	2.5
1991	**6.8**	3.7	2.4	0.5	0.1	1991	**95.6**	51.2	32.8	9.4	2.3
1992	**6.9**	3.7	2.5	0.6	0.1	1992	**86.2**	45.9	29.6	8.6	2.1
1993	**6.8**	3.8	2.2	0.6	0.2	1993	**76.9**	40.4	26.8	7.9	1.8
1994	**6.0**	3.3	1.9	0.6	0.2	1994	**69.2**	36.4	23.9	7.1	1.8
1995	**5.4**	3.1	1.7	0.5	0.2	1995	**61.0**	32.3	20.6	6.5	1.6
1996	**5.0**	2.7	1.7	0.5	0.2	1996	**54.7**	28.9	18.5	5.8	1.5
1997	**4.6**	2.6	1.5	0.4	0.1	1997	**49.1**	25.9	16.6	5.3	1.4
1998	**3.9**	2.1	1.3	0.4	0.1	1998	**45.7**	24.3	15.5	4.7	1.2
1999	**4.0**	2.4	1.1	0.4	0.1	1999	**43.2**	23.5	14.4	4.2	1.1
2000	**4.2**	2.2	1.4	0.4	0.1	2000	**40.3**	21.6	13.7	3.9	1.0
	25-29						**25-29**				
1990	**8.4**	3.4	3.4	1.1	0.4	1990	**204.7**	86.4	77.7	28.7	11.9
1991	**8.8**	3.7	3.2	1.3	0.6	1991	**196.3**	84.5	73.9	26.8	11.1
1992	**9.0**	3.5	3.5	1.3	0.6	1992	**188.9**	81.7	70.7	25.7	10.7
1993	**8.9**	3.5	3.4	1.3	0.7	1993	**178.5**	77.6	66.7	24.0	10.1
1994	**8.2**	3.2	3.1	1.3	0.6	1994	**170.6**	75.7	62.7	22.6	9.7
1995	**7.9**	3.4	2.8	1.2	0.6	1995	**157.9**	71.0	57.3	20.5	9.0
1996	**7.4**	2.9	2.5	1.2	0.8	1996	**148.8**	67.2	53.4	19.6	8.6
1997	**7.1**	2.7	2.6	1.2	0.6	1997	**139.4**	63.1	50.0	18.1	8.1
1998	**6.6**	2.6	2.3	1.0	0.8	1998	**130.7**	60.6	46.4	16.4	7.4
1999	**6.6**	2.8	2.1	1.0	0.7	1999	**120.7**	57.4	41.8	14.7	6.8
2000	**6.2**	2.4	2.3	0.9	0.6	2000	**111.6**	52.7	38.4	14.1	6.4
	30 and over						**30 and over**				
1990	**6.1**	1.6	2.1	1.3	1.0	1990	**184.3**	48.6	68.7	40.0	26.9
1991	**6.4**	1.5	2.2	1.3	1.3	1991	**187.1**	51.3	69.6	39.8	26.4
1992	**7.1**	1.9	2.5	1.4	1.3	1992	**191.5**	53.8	72.0	39.7	26.0
1993	**7.1**	1.8	2.5	1.3	1.5	1993	**194.6**	54.9	74.4	39.7	25.6
1994	**7.0**	1.9	2.3	1.4	1.4	1994	**203.3**	59.3	78.4	39.9	25.6
1995	**6.9**	1.9	2.0	1.5	1.5	1995	**203.7**	60.4	79.0	39.6	24.6
1996	**6.5**	1.6	2.1	1.2	1.5	1996	**208.0**	62.7	80.8	39.8	24.7
1997	**6.7**	1.6	2.1	1.5	1.6	1997	**211.2**	63.9	82.8	39.8	24.7
1998	**7.4**	2.0	2.4	1.4	1.5	1998	**213.5**	66.6	83.9	39.3	23.8
1999	**7.9**	2.3	2.5	1.6	1.5	1999	**210.7**	68.3	82.4	37.4	22.7
2000	**7.1**	1.9	2.2	1.6	1.5	2000	**209.2**	68.5	81.7	36.8	22.3

Notes: 1. For a description of social classes and the sample used in calculation - see Section 3.10.
        2. Table includes 1990 data based on the 1980 *Classification of Occupations* and for 1991-2000 on the *Standard Occupational Classification.*

64

Table 11.2 Pre-maritally conceived first live births to married women (numbers and percentages): estimated distribution by social class of father as defined by occupation, and age of mother, 1990-2000   **England and Wales**

Year	All social classes (including 'others')	I and II	IIIN	IIIM	IV and V	Non-manual	Manual	All social classes (including 'others')	I and II	IIIN	IIIM	IV and V	Non-manual	Manual
	Number (thousands)							As a percentage of all first live births within marriage						
All ages of mother at birth														
1990	**27.1**	6.5	2.4	10.5	6.3	8.9	16.8	**13.5**	8.8	10.3	16.5	21.0	9.1	18.0
1991	**23.5**	6.1	2.1	8.8	5.1	8.2	13.9	**12.2**	8.4	9.5	14.3	18.1	8.6	15.5
1992	**21.7**	5.8	2.0	7.6	4.8	7.8	12.4	**11.6**	7.9	9.3	13.6	17.8	8.2	15.0
1993	**20.0**	6.0	2.1	6.1	4.1	8.1	10.2	**11.2**	8.6	9.8	12.3	15.0	8.9	13.3
1994	**18.6**	6.1	2.2	6.0	4.0	8.3	10.0	**10.6**	8.7	9.7	12.4	14.9	8.9	13.3
1995	**17.3**	5.7	1.8	5.3	3.1	7.4	8.4	**10.3**	8.4	8.5	11.7	12.5	8.4	12.0
1996	**17.3**	5.6	1.9	5.3	3.1	7.5	8.4	**10.6**	8.3	9.4	12.4	12.6	8.6	12.5
1997	**16.8**	5.9	1.9	4.8	3.1	7.8	7.9	**10.7**	8.7	9.8	12.2	13.1	8.9	12.6
1998	**16.6**	6.2	1.7	4.3	3.2	7.9	7.6	**10.6**	9.0	9.1	11.5	14.0	9.0	12.4
1999	**16.2**	5.6	1.9	4.3	3.2	7.5	7.5	**10.6**	7.9	11.0	12.0	14.6	8.5	13.0
2000	**14.4**	5.7	1.6	3.5	2.7	7.3	6.3	**9.8**	8.3	9.4	10.7	13.2	8.5	11.7
Under 20														
1990	**4.4**	0.5	0.3	1.9	1.5	0.8	3.4	**55.3**	42.5	42.8	62.7	55.4	42.6	59.3
1991	**3.3**	0.3	0.3	1.4	1.0	0.6	2.5	**48.6**	33.9	46.0	57.5	50.4	39.2	54.3
1992	**2.6**	0.3	0.2	1.0	0.8	0.5	1.8	**44.3**	36.1	39.7	50.8	43.6	37.7	47.2
1993	**2.2**	0.3	0.2	0.7	0.7	0.5	1.4	**41.9**	37.6	42.3	45.4	47.7	39.3	46.6
1994	**1.9**	0.2	0.1	0.7	0.6	0.3	1.3	**39.9**	29.7	19.6	50.0	45.5	25.6	47.7
1995	**1.6**	0.2	0.1	0.6	0.4	0.4	1.0	**37.3**	30.1	32.2	48.2	38.0	30.8	43.8
1996	**1.6**	0.2	0.2	0.6	0.5	0.4	1.0	**37.1**	29.3	38.3	47.0	39.7	32.7	43.4
1997	**1.5**	0.2	0.2	0.4	0.5	0.4	0.9	**36.5**	25.9	42.5	40.6	44.3	32.4	42.7
1998	**1.5**	0.2	0.2	0.4	0.4	0.3	0.9	**35.6**	32.2	32.9	37.6	32.3	32.6	34.8
1999	**1.5**	0.3	0.2	0.3	0.5	0.5	0.8	**33.9**	29.9	44.1	33.8	38.4	35.0	36.4
2000	**1.2**	0.2	0.1	0.4	0.4	0.3	0.8	**32.2**	27.6	25.8	40.4	39.4	26.9	39.9
20-24														
1990	**11.0**	1.9	1.0	4.5	3.0	2.9	7.5	**19.4**	14.7	16.7	20.5	23.7	15.3	21.7
1991	**9.3**	1.7	0.8	3.7	2.3	2.5	6.0	**18.1**	14.8	15.2	19.3	20.6	14.9	19.8
1992	**8.3**	1.5	0.7	3.3	2.1	2.2	5.4	**18.0**	14.1	13.9	19.8	21.2	14.0	20.3
1993	**7.2**	1.5	0.8	2.4	1.8	2.4	4.1	**17.9**	16.2	18.1	17.4	19.9	16.8	18.4
1994	**6.3**	1.3	0.8	2.4	1.6	2.0	3.9	**17.4**	15.0	17.6	19.4	18.2	15.9	18.9
1995	**5.8**	1.1	0.5	2.1	1.5	1.6	3.6	**17.9**	14.1	14.4	20.2	19.4	14.2	19.9
1996	**5.4**	1.2	0.7	1.8	1.1	1.8	2.9	**18.7**	17.2	16.9	20.2	16.5	17.1	18.6
1997	**4.9**	1.1	0.6	1.7	1.0	1.7	2.7	**19.0**	16.6	18.4	21.1	17.7	17.2	19.7
1998	**4.5**	1.1	0.5	1.4	1.2	1.5	2.5	**18.5**	16.5	15.0	19.6	20.7	16.0	20.1
1999	**4.3**	1.0	0.5	1.4	1.1	1.4	2.5	**18.5**	15.8	17.8	20.2	19.6	16.4	19.9
2000	**3.9**	1.0	0.5	1.0	1.0	1.5	2.1	**18.1**	16.9	19.1	17.1	20.5	17.5	18.7
25-29														
1990	**7.4**	2.4	0.7	2.6	1.3	3.1	4.0	**8.5**	6.9	6.5	9.8	12.1	6.8	10.5
1991	**6.8**	2.1	0.6	2.4	1.2	2.7	3.7	**8.0**	6.7	5.9	8.9	11.4	6.5	9.6
1992	**6.5**	2.2	0.6	2.1	1.3	2.8	3.4	**7.9**	6.7	6.4	8.3	12.2	6.6	9.4
1993	**6.2**	2.1	0.6	2.0	1.0	2.7	3.0	**8.0**	6.9	6.5	8.7	9.4	6.8	8.9
1994	**5.8**	2.2	0.7	1.9	1.3	2.9	3.2	**7.6**	7.3	7.0	8.6	11.1	7.2	9.4
1995	**5.4**	1.9	0.6	1.6	0.9	2.5	2.5	**7.6**	7.0	6.7	7.7	8.5	6.9	7.9
1996	**5.4**	1.8	0.6	1.7	0.9	2.5	2.5	**8.0**	7.0	7.2	8.7	8.7	7.0	8.7
1997	**5.3**	1.8	0.6	1.7	0.9	2.4	2.6	**8.4**	7.1	7.4	10.0	9.4	7.2	9.8
1998	**5.4**	2.1	0.6	1.4	1.0	2.7	2.5	**8.9**	8.4	7.8	8.7	11.2	8.3	9.6
1999	**5.2**	1.7	0.7	1.4	1.0	2.4	2.4	**9.0**	6.8	10.4	9.7	11.8	7.5	10.5
2000	**4.4**	1.7	0.4	1.1	0.8	2.2	1.9	**8.3**	7.3	6.7	8.9	10.6	7.2	9.6
30 and over														
1990	**4.3**	1.8	0.4	1.4	0.5	2.2	1.9	**8.6**	6.9	6.5	12.2	13.4	6.8	12.5
1991	**4.2**	1.9	0.4	1.2	0.5	2.3	1.7	**8.2**	6.9	6.7	9.9	12.9	6.8	10.7
1992	**4.3**	1.8	0.5	1.3	0.5	2.3	1.8	**8.0**	6.2	7.5	10.5	12.0	6.5	10.9
1993	**4.4**	2.1	0.5	1.1	0.5	2.5	1.6	**7.9**	7.1	6.7	9.2	9.6	7.0	9.3
1994	**4.6**	2.5	0.6	1.1	0.6	3.1	1.7	**7.8**	7.8	8.4	8.3	10.7	7.9	9.0
1995	**4.6**	2.4	0.5	1.0	0.4	2.9	1.4	**7.5**	7.6	6.7	7.8	6.7	7.4	7.4
1996	**4.9**	2.4	0.5	1.2	0.7	2.9	1.9	**7.9**	7.1	6.6	9.3	10.0	7.0	9.6
1997	**5.1**	2.8	0.5	1.0	0.6	3.3	1.6	**7.9**	8.1	6.5	7.7	9.0	7.8	8.1
1998	**5.2**	2.8	0.5	1.1	0.6	3.3	1.7	**7.8**	7.7	6.6	8.4	8.5	7.5	8.5
1999	**5.3**	2.7	0.6	1.2	0.6	3.3	1.8	**7.7**	7.0	7.2	9.0	9.1	7.0	9.0
2000	**5.0**	2.8	0.6	1.0	0.5	3.4	1.5	**7.2**	7.2	7.6	7.2	7.1	7.3	7.2

Notes: 1. For a description of social classes and the sample used in calculation - see Section 3.10.
2. Table include 1990 data based on the 1980 *Classification of Occupations* and for 1991-2000 on the *Standard Occupational Classification*

To link to Excel version of the table - click on
the red box surrounding the table title

Table 11.3 Median birth intervals: social class of father as defined by occupation (for interval to first birth), and mother's marriage order, 1990-2000

Great Britain, England and Wales

Year	Median intervals in months*							
	Marriage to first birth					First to second birth	Second to third birth	Third to fourth birth
	All social classes	I and II	IIIN	IIIM	IV and V			
	Women married once only (England and Wales)					All women (Great Britain)*		
1990	27	34	30	25	21	33	37	32
1991	28	33	32	26	21	34	39	33
1992	28	34	31	25	20	34	38	33
1993	29	34	32	27	24	34	39	34
1994	28	33	30	27	24	35	39	38
1995	29	33	30	27	25	35	39	36
1996	28	32	29	27	25	35	40	34
1997	28	31	28	27	24	36	42	33
1998	27	30	27	26	23			
1999	27	30	28	26	23			
2000	26	29	27	25	23			
	Remarried women (England and Wales)							
1990	16	15	16	15	12			
1991	17	17	18	13	17			
1992	17	18	18	17	15			
1993	16	16	19	16	14			
1994	18	18	18	17	15			
1995	18	18	18	17	21			
1996	17	18	18	13	16			
1997	18	18	22	17	14			
1998	17	17	19	17	17			
1999	17	17	19	16	15			
2000	18	20	16	17	16			

* See Section 3.11

To link to Excel version of the table - click on
the red box surrounding the table title

Table 11.4 Mean age of women at live births within marriage: social class of father as defined by occupation, and birth order, 1990-2000

England and Wale

Year	All social classes	I and II	IIIN	IIIM	IV and V	All social classes	I and II	IIIN	IIIM	IV and V
	All live births within marriage					Second live births within marriage				
1990	**28.6**	30.1	28.9	27.9	27.1	**28.7**	30.3	29.3	27.8	26.6
1991	**28.9**	30.3	29.0	28.1	27.4	**28.9**	30.6	29.4	28.1	27.2
1992	**29.1**	30.5	29.3	28.5	27.7	**29.2**	30.8	29.7	28.3	27.3
1993	**29.3**	30.6	29.4	28.7	28.0	**29.5**	31.0	29.6	28.7	27.8
1994	**29.6**	30.9	29.6	28.9	28.2	**29.7**	31.3	29.9	28.8	28.0
1995	**29.8**	31.1	29.9	29.1	28.6	**30.0**	31.4	30.2	29.1	28.4
1996	**30.1**	31.3	30.0	29.4	28.8	**30.3**	31.6	30.4	29.3	28.5
1997	**30.3**	31.5	30.1	29.7	29.0	**30.5**	31.9	30.7	29.6	29.0
1998	**30.5**	31.7	30.4	29.8	29.2	**30.7**	32.1	31.0	29.8	29.1
1999	**30.6**	31.8	30.6	30.0	29.1	**30.9**	32.2	31.1	30.1	29.1
2000	**30.8**	32.0	30.7	30.2	29.4	**31.1**	32.3	31.0	30.2	29.4
	First live births within marriage					Third live births within marriage				
1990	**27.2**	28.7	27.4	26.3	25.3	**30.3**	32.1	30.7	29.5	28.4
1991	**27.5**	29.0	27.6	26.7	25.7	**30.4**	32.1	30.9	29.4	28.4
1992	**27.8**	29.2	28.0	27.1	26.1	**30.5**	32.4	31.0	29.8	28.9
1993	**28.0**	29.3	28.2	27.3	26.5	**30.7**	32.4	31.2	30.0	29.0
1994	**28.3**	29.6	28.3	27.6	26.8	**30.9**	32.6	31.4	30.1	29.1
1995	**28.5**	29.9	28.6	27.9	27.2	**31.1**	32.9	31.7	30.1	29.3
1996	**28.8**	30.1	28.6	28.1	27.5	**31.3**	32.9	31.6	30.7	29.6
1997	**29.0**	30.2	28.8	28.4	27.6	**31.5**	33.0	31.7	30.8	29.8
1998	**29.2**	30.5	29.1	28.6	27.6	**31.8**	33.4	31.7	30.9	30.2
1999	**29.3**	30.6	29.4	28.7	27.5	**32.0**	33.5	31.8	30.9	30.2
2000	**29.6**	30.7	29.6	28.9	27.9	**32.1**	33.6	32.2	31.3	30.5

Notes: 1. For a description of social classes and the sample used in calculation - see Section 3.10
2. Table includes 1990 data based on the 1980 *Classification of Occupations* and for 1991-2000 on the *Standard Occupational Classification*.
3. The mean ages presented in this table do not take account of the changing population distribution of women.

Table 11.5   Jointly registered live births outside marriage: social class of father as   **England and Wales**
defined by occupation, and age of mother, 1990-2000   *thousands*

Year	Age of mother	All social classes (including 'others')	Social class of father					
			I and II	IIIN	IIIM	IV and V	Non-manual	Manual
1990	**All ages**	**145.5**	23.1	9.5	62.7	44.6	32.6	107.3
1991		**157.2**	26.4	10.9	66.8	46.4	37.2	113.2
1992		**165.2**	28.5	11.6	69.7	46.7	40.1	116.4
1993		**166.3**	28.9	12.0	66.3	49.2	40.9	115.5
1994		**166.5**	29.5	12.3	65.7	48.0	41.8	113.7
1995		**172.0**	31.6	13.0	67.9	49.3	44.6	117.3
1996		**181.6**	33.9	13.8	70.7	52.4	47.8	123.2
1997		**187.6**	37.7	14.2	69.8	55.0	52.0	124.8
1998		**190.7**	40.2	14.6	70.2	55.2	54.8	125.3
1999		**193.7**	43.7	15.3	69.9	53.5	59.0	123.4
2000		**192.8**	44.3	15.0	68.3	53.8	59.3	122.1
1990	Under 20	**28.9**	1.8	1.6	12.2	11.6	3.4	22.4
1991		**28.2**	2.2	1.7	11.5	10.7	3.8	22.2
1992		**27.2**	1.8	1.7	11.0	10.1	3.5	21.1
1993		**25.7**	1.9	1.6	10.1	9.2	3.5	19.3
1994		**23.9**	1.5	1.5	8.8	8.8	3.0	17.6
1995		**24.4**	1.7	1.7	8.9	9.1	3.3	18.0
1996		**26.4**	1.9	1.7	9.3	10.1	3.6	19.4
1997		**27.9**	2.0	1.9	9.4	10.9	3.9	20.3
1998		**29.2**	2.3	2.0	9.5	11.7	4.4	21.2
1999		**29.8**	2.4	2.1	10.0	11.2	4.5	21.2
2000		**28.6**	2.4	2.1	9.6	10.7	4.5	20.3
1990	20-24	**53.7**	6.4	3.2	24.3	17.9	9.6	42.2
1991		**58.1**	7.1	3.7	25.4	19.3	10.8	44.8
1992		**59.2**	7.4	3.9	26.2	18.7	11.3	44.8
1993		**57.5**	7.1	4.0	23.7	19.3	11.0	43.0
1994		**54.6**	6.3	4.0	22.6	17.9	10.2	40.5
1995		**54.1**	6.6	4.1	22.9	17.4	10.7	40.3
1996		**54.8**	6.8	4.2	22.7	17.9	11.0	40.6
1997		**53.9**	7.7	4.1	20.4	18.4	11.7	38.7
1998		**53.0**	7.9	3.8	20.6	17.6	11.7	38.2
1999		**53.1**	8.6	3.8	19.9	17.3	12.4	37.2
2000		**53.6**	8.5	3.9	20.1	17.4	12.4	37.5
1990	25-29	**36.4**	6.9	2.5	16.1	9.7	9.4	25.8
1991		**41.1**	8.0	3.2	18.0	10.4	11.3	28.5
1992		**44.3**	9.2	3.1	18.9	11.2	12.3	30.2
1993		**46.1**	8.9	3.4	18.9	12.9	12.4	31.8
1994		**47.1**	9.4	3.4	19.3	13.0	12.8	32.3
1995		**48.7**	9.7	3.5	19.7	13.5	13.1	33.2
1996		**51.0**	10.0	3.8	21.0	13.6	13.8	34.6
1997		**52.4**	11.3	4.1	20.7	14.3	15.4	35.0
1998		**51.7**	11.3	4.1	20.4	14.2	15.3	34.6
1999		**51.3**	12.4	4.4	19.7	12.8	16.8	32.5
2000		**49.9**	12.1	3.7	18.8	13.3	15.8	32.1
1990	30 and over	**26.5**	8.0	2.2	10.0	5.4	10.2	15.5
1991		**29.8**	9.1	2.2	11.9	5.9	11.3	17.8
1992		**34.6**	10.2	2.8	13.7	6.6	13.0	20.3
1993		**37.0**	11.1	3.0	13.6	7.8	14.0	21.4
1994		**40.9**	12.3	3.4	15.1	8.3	15.7	23.3
1995		**44.8**	13.6	3.8	16.4	9.4	17.4	25.8
1996		**49.5**	15.2	4.2	17.7	10.8	19.4	28.6
1997		**53.4**	16.8	4.1	19.4	11.4	20.9	30.8
1998		**56.8**	18.7	4.8	19.6	11.7	23.4	31.3
1999		**59.5**	20.3	5.0	20.3	12.2	25.3	32.5
2000		**60.7**	21.3	5.3	19.8	12.4	26.6	32.2

Notes: 1. For a description of social classes and the sample used in calculation - see Section 3.10.
        2. Table includes 1990 data based on the 1980 *Classification of Occupations* and for 1991-2000 on the *Standard Occupational Classification*.

Table 12.1 Conceptions (numbers and percentages and rates): occurrence within/outside marriage and outcome, and age at conception, 1989-1999

England and Wal
Resider

Age of woman at conception and year of conception	Number of conceptions (thousands)			Percentage of all conceptions				Conception rates per 1,000 women in age-group		
	Total con-ceptions	Conceptions leading to maternities	Conceptions terminated by abortion	Outcome		Occurrence		Total con-ceptions	Conceptions leading to maternities	Conceptions terminated b abortion
				Leading to maternities	Terminated by abortion	Within marriage	Outside marriage			
All ages*										
1989	**864.7**	693.5	171.2	80.2	19.8	57.7	42.3	**78.5**	63.0	15.5
1990	**871.5**	697.7	173.8	80.1	19.9	56.7	43.3	**79.2**	63.4	15.8
1991	**853.7**	688.4	165.2	80.6	19.4	56.2	43.8	**77.7**	62.7	15.0
1992	**828.0**	667.9	160.1	80.7	19.3	55.6	44.4	**76.3**	61.5	14.8
1993	**819.0**	662.0	156.9	80.8	19.2	55.5	44.5	**76.1**	61.5	14.6
1994	**801.6**	645.5	156.0	80.5	19.5	54.4	45.6	**74.7**	60.1	14.5
1995	**790.3**	634.4	155.8	80.3	19.7	52.9	47.1	**73.7**	59.1	14.5
1996	**816.9**	647.2	169.7	79.2	20.8	51.0	49.0	**76.1**	60.3	15.8
1997	**800.4**	629.9	170.5	78.7	21.3	50.2	49.8	**74.4**	58.6	15.9
1998	**797.0**	619.6	177.4	77.7	22.3	48.8	51.2	**74.0**	57.5	16.5
1999	**774.0**	599.4	174.6	77.4	22.6	48.3	51.7	**71.7**	55.5	16.2
Under 16†										
1989	**8.0**	3.8	4.1	48.0	52.0	0.4	99.6	**8.9**	4.3	4.6
1990	**8.1**	4.0	4.1	49.2	50.8	0.0	99.6	**9.5**	4.7	4.8
1991	**7.5**	3.7	3.8	48.9	51.1	0.3	99.7	**8.9**	4.3	4.6
1992	**7.2**	3.7	3.5	51.4	48.6	0.6	99.4	**8.4**	4.3	4.1
1993	**7.3**	3.6	3.6	50.2	49.8	0.5	99.5	**8.1**	4.1	4.0
1994	**7.8**	3.9	3.9	49.7	50.3	0.4	99.6	**8.3**	4.1	4.2
1995	**8.1**	4.2	3.8	52.4	47.6	0.3	99.7	**8.6**	4.5	4.1
1996	**8.9**	4.5	4.4	50.8	49.2	0.2	99.8	**9.5**	4.8	4.7
1997	**8.3**	4.2	4.1	50.3	49.7	0.3	99.7	**8.9**	4.5	4.4
1998	**8.5**	4.0	4.4	47.6	52.4	0.3	99.7	**9.0**	4.3	4.7
1999	**7.9**	3.8	4.2	47.4	52.6	0.5	99.5	**8.3**	3.9	4.4
Under 18≠										
1989	**46.5**	27.2	19.3	58.4	41.6	3.0	97.0	**46.9**	27.4	19.5
1990	**44.8**	26.4	18.4	58.9	41.1	2.8	97.2	**47.7**	28.1	19.6
1991	**40.1**	24.1	16.0	60.1	39.9	3.0	97.0	**44.6**	26.8	17.8
1992	**37.6**	22.9	14.7	60.9	39.1	2.8	97.2	**43.6**	26.5	17.0
1993	**35.8**	21.8	14.0	60.8	39.2	3.0	97.0	**42.5**	25.9	16.7
1994	**36.1**	21.7	14.3	60.2	39.8	3.0	97.0	**42.0**	25.3	16.7
1995	**37.9**	23.2	14.7	61.3	38.7	2.6	97.4	**42.0**	25.7	16.3
1996	**43.5**	26.1	17.4	60.0	40.0	2.3	97.7	**46.4**	27.8	18.6
1997	**43.4**	25.8	17.6	59.4	40.6	2.4	97.6	**45.9**	27.3	18.6
1998	**44.1**	25.6	18.5	58.0	42.0	2.3	97.7	**47.0**	27.3	19.7
1999	**42.0**	23.9	18.1	57.0	43.0	2.2	97.8	**45.0**	25.7	19.4
Under 20**										
1989	**115.7**	74.5	41.2	64.4	35.6	10.4	89.6	**66.8**	43.0	23.8
1990	**113.3**	72.8	40.5	64.3	35.7	9.6	90.4	**68.0**	43.7	24.3
1991	**101.6**	66.6	35.0	65.5	34.5	9.4	90.6	**64.1**	42.0	22.1
1992	**93.4**	61.8	31.6	66.1	33.9	9.1	90.9	**61.9**	41.0	21.0
1993	**87.2**	57.3	29.9	65.7	34.3	8.9	91.1	**59.9**	39.4	20.5
1994	**85.4**	55.7	29.6	65.3	34.7	8.2	91.8	**58.9**	38.4	20.4
1995	**86.6**	56.6	29.9	65.4	34.6	7.6	92.4	**58.9**	38.6	20.4
1996	**94.9**	60.5	34.4	63.8	36.2	6.8	93.2	**63.3**	40.4	23.0
1997	**96.0**	60.7	35.3	63.2	36.8	6.7	93.3	**62.6**	39.6	23.0
1998	**101.6**	63.2	38.4	62.2	37.8	6.6	93.4	**64.9**	40.4	24.5
1999	**98.8**	60.7	38.1	61.4	38.6	6.5	93.5	**62.9**	38.6	24.3

*   Rates per 1,000 women aged 15-44
†   Rates per 1,000 women aged 13-15
≠   Rates per 1,000 women aged 15-17
** Rates per 1,000 women aged 15-19

Table 12.1 - *continued*

Age of woman at conception and year of conception	Number of conceptions (thousands)			Percentage of all conceptions				Conception rates per 1,000 women in age-group		
	Total conceptions	Conceptions leading to maternities	Conceptions terminated by abortion	Outcome		Occurrence		Total conceptions	Conceptions leading to maternities	Conceptions terminated by abortion
				Leading to maternities	Terminated by abortion	Within marriage	Outside marriage			
20-24										
1989	**250.8**	196.1	54.7	78.2	21.8	47.2	52.8	**124.2**	97.1	27.1
1990	**244.5**	190.0	54.5	77.7	22.3	45.1	54.9	**124.0**	96.4	27.6
1991	**233.3**	181.5	51.8	77.8	22.2	42.9	57.1	**120.2**	93.5	26.7
1992	**215.9**	167.8	48.2	77.7	22.3	41.1	58.9	**114.0**	88.6	25.4
1993	**203.6**	157.2	46.4	77.2	22.8	39.9	60.1	**110.8**	85.5	25.2
1994	**190.4**	145.8	44.6	76.6	23.4	37.7	62.3	**107.8**	82.5	25.2
1995	**181.1**	137.4	43.8	75.8	24.2	35.3	64.7	**106.3**	80.6	25.7
1996	**179.8**	133.5	46.3	74.3	25.7	32.5	67.5	**110.9**	82.3	28.5
1997	**167.3**	122.6	44.6	73.3	26.7	31.3	68.7	**108.0**	79.2	28.8
1998	**163.3**	117.8	45.4	72.2	27.8	29.9	70.1	**108.5**	78.3	30.2
1999	**157.6**	112.6	45.0	71.5	28.5	28.9	71.1	**104.9**	74.9	29.9
25-29										
1989	**278.6**	242.1	36.5	86.9	13.1	72.3	27.7	**138.1**	120.0	18.1
1990	**284.2**	245.9	38.4	86.5	13.5	70.6	29.4	**138.0**	119.4	18.6
1991	**281.5**	243.8	37.8	86.6	13.4	69.1	30.9	**135.1**	117.0	18.1
1992	**274.9**	236.6	38.3	86.1	13.9	67.3	32.7	**131.7**	113.4	18.3
1993	**271.7**	234.0	37.7	86.1	13.9	66.3	33.7	**131.4**	113.1	18.2
1994	**261.8**	224.3	37.5	85.7	14.3	64.6	35.4	**128.1**	109.8	18.4
1995	**250.3**	213.2	37.1	85.2	14.8	62.6	37.4	**125.0**	106.5	18.5
1996	**252.6**	213.1	39.5	84.4	15.6	60.4	39.6	**127.9**	107.9	20.0
1997	**242.6**	202.8	39.8	83.6	16.4	58.9	41.1	**125.4**	104.8	20.6
1998	**232.4**	192.6	39.8	82.9	17.1	57.3	42.7	**123.0**	101.9	21.1
1999	**218.5**	180.2	38.3	82.5	17.5	56.5	43.5	**119.2**	98.3	20.9
30-34										
1989	**153.7**	132.7	21.1	86.3	13.7	77.5	22.5	**88.0**	75.9	12.1
1990	**161.4**	139.1	22.3	86.2	13.8	76.6	23.4	**89.7**	77.3	12.4
1991	**167.5**	144.6	22.9	86.3	13.7	75.4	24.6	**90.1**	77.8	12.3
1992	**172.0**	148.2	23.8	86.1	13.9	74.2	25.8	**89.9**	77.4	12.5
1993	**180.9**	156.6	24.4	86.5	13.5	73.3	26.7	**92.0**	79.6	12.4
1994	**185.0**	159.9	25.1	86.4	13.6	72.1	27.9	**91.3**	79.0	12.4
1995	**190.3**	164.5	25.8	86.4	13.6	70.9	29.1	**91.7**	79.3	12.4
1996	**200.0**	171.8	28.2	85.9	14.1	69.6	30.4	**95.1**	81.7	13.4
1997	**200.9**	172.3	28.6	85.8	14.2	68.9	31.1	**95.2**	81.6	13.5
1998	**201.4**	171.4	30.0	85.1	14.9	67.7	32.3	**96.0**	81.7	14.3
1999	**197.1**	168.0	29.1	85.3	14.7	67.2	32.8	**94.9**	80.9	14.0
35-39										
1989	**54.1**	41.5	12.6	76.8	23.2	73.9	26.1	**32.2**	24.7	7.5
1990	**56.0**	43.1	13.0	76.9	23.1	72.7	25.5	**33.6**	25.8	7.8
1991	**57.6**	44.9	12.7	78.0	22.0	72.2	27.8	**34.4**	26.9	7.6
1992	**59.6**	46.4	13.2	77.8	22.2	71.2	28.8	**35.1**	27.4	7.8
1993	**63.0**	49.4	13.6	78.5	21.5	70.6	29.4	**36.5**	28.7	7.9
1994	**66.2**	52.2	14.0	78.9	21.1	69.5	30.5	**37.5**	29.6	7.9
1995	**68.7**	54.5	14.2	79.3	20.7	68.2	31.8	**37.9**	30.1	7.8
1996	**75.5**	59.5	16.0	78.8	21.2	67.2	32.8	**40.4**	31.8	8.6
1997	**78.9**	62.3	16.6	79.0	21.0	66.3	33.7	**41.0**	32.3	8.6
1998	**82.9**	65.0	17.8	78.5	21.5	65.3	34.7	**41.8**	32.8	9.0
1999	**86.0**	67.7	18.2	78.8	21.2	64.9	35.1	**42.1**	33.2	8.9

Table 12.1 - *continued*

Age of woman at conception and year of conception	Number of conceptions (thousands)			Percentage of all conceptions				Conception rates per 1,000 women in age-group		
	Total con-ceptions	Conceptions leading to maternities	Conceptions terminated by abortion	Outcome		Occurrence		Total con-ceptions	Conceptions leading to maternities	Conceptions terminated by abortion
				Leading to maternities	Terminated by abortion	Within marriage	Outside marriage			
40 and over*										
1989	**11.8**	6.7	5.1	56.6	43.4	70.2	29.8	**6.5**	3.7	2.8
1990	**12.0**	6.8	5.2	56.8	43.2	70.1	29.9	**6.6**	3.7	2.8
1991	**12.1**	7.1	5.0	58.4	41.6	68.9	31.1	**6.6**	3.8	2.7
1992	**12.2**	7.1	5.0	58.5	41.5	67.6	32.4	**6.9**	4.1	2.9
1993	**12.5**	7.5	5.0	59.8	40.2	66.2	33.8	**7.4**	4.4	3.0
1994	**12.9**	7.6	5.3	59.1	40.9	66.4	33.6	**7.6**	4.5	3.1
1995	**13.2**	8.2	5.0	62.0	38.0	64.4	35.6	**7.9**	4.9	3.0
1996	**14.1**	8.8	5.3	62.4	37.6	63.2	36.8	**8.4**	5.3	3.2
1997	**14.7**	9.1	5.6	62.0	38.0	62.8	37.2	**8.7**	5.4	3.3
1998	**15.4**	9.6	5.8	62.1	37.9	61.8	38.2	**8.9**	5.5	3.4
1999	**16.0**	10.1	5.9	63.0	37.0	60.5	39.5	**9.1**	5.7	3.4

* Rates per 1,000 women aged 40-44

Table 12.2 Teenage conceptions (numbers and rates): outcome and age of woman (single years) at conception, 1989-1999

England and Wales
Residents

Age of woman at conception and year of conception	Number of conceptions			Conception rates per 1,000 women in age-group			Age of woman at conception and year of conception	Number of conceptions			Conception rates per 1,000 women in age-group		
	Total conceptions	Conceptions leading to maternities	Conceptions terminated by abortion	Total conceptions	Conceptions leading to maternities	Conceptions terminated by abortion		Total conceptions	Conceptions leading to maternities	Conceptions terminated by abortion	Total conceptions	Conceptions leading to maternities	Conceptions terminated by abortion
Under 16*							**16**						
1989	**7,950**	3,814	4,136	**8.9**	4.3	4.6	1989	**14,703**	8,396	6,307	**44.6**	25.5	19.1
1990	**8,139**	4,006	4,133	**9.5**	4.7	4.8	1990	**13,923**	8,051	5,872	**45.1**	26.1	19.0
1991	**7,480**	3,655	3,825	**8.9**	4.3	4.6	1991	**12,623**	7,505	5,118	**42.1**	25.0	17.1
1992	**7,217**	3,707	3,510	**8.4**	4.3	4.1	1992	**11,932**	7,202	4,730	**41.5**	25.1	16.5
1993	**7,267**	3,643	3,623	**8.1**	4.1	4.0	1993	**11,031**	6,708	4,323	**40.1**	24.4	15.7
1994	**7,795**	3,875	3,920	**8.3**	4.1	4.2	1994	**11,336**	6,833	4,503	**40.5**	24.4	16.1
1995	**8,051**	4,218	3,833	**8.6**	4.5	4.1	1995	**12,382**	7,668	4,714	**40.6**	25.2	15.5
1996	**8,857**	4,498	4,359	**9.5**	4.8	4.7	1996	**14,284**	8,606	5,678	**45.0**	27.1	17.9
1997	**8,271**	4,164	4,107	**8.9**	4.5	4.4	1997	**14,058**	8,364	5,694	**44.5**	26.5	18.0
1998	**8,452**	4,023	4,429	**9.0**	4.3	4.7	1998	**13,802**	8,078	5,724	**44.5**	26.0	18.4
1999	**7,945**	3,762	4,183	**8.3**	3.9	4.4	1999	**13,334**	7,489	5,845	**42.8**	24.0	18.8
Under 14†							**17**						
1989	**223**	110	113	**0.8**	0.4	0.4	1989	**23,817**	14,941	8,876	**67.6**	42.4	25.2
1990	**316**	133	183	**1.2**	0.5	0.7	1990	**22,694**	14,316	8,378	**68.4**	43.2	25.3
1991	**318**	126	192	**1.1**	0.5	0.7	1991	**19,985**	12,913	7,072	**64.2**	41.5	22.7
1992	**363**	147	216	**1.2**	0.5	0.7	1992	**18,403**	11,965	6,438	**61.4**	39.9	21.5
1993	**368**	165	203	**1.2**	0.5	0.6	1993	**17,504**	11,426	6,078	**60.9**	39.8	21.1
1994	**397**	167	230	**1.3**	0.5	0.7	1994	**16,960**	11,036	5,924	**61.6**	40.1	21.5
1995	**382**	150	232	**1.2**	0.5	0.8	1995	**17,447**	11,321	6,126	**62.1**	40.3	21.8
1996	**451**	192	259	**1.5**	0.6	0.8	1996	**20,349**	12,975	7,374	**66.6**	42.5	24.1
1997	**365**	149	216	**1.2**	0.5	0.7	1997	**21,029**	13,242	7,787	**66.1**	41.6	24.5
1998	**423**	170	253	**1.3**	0.5	0.8	1998	**21,865**	13,503	8,362	**69.1**	42.7	26.4
1999	**406**	174	232	**1.2**	0.5	0.7	1999	**20,749**	12,686	8,063	**66.7**	40.8	25.9
14							**18**						
1989	**1,650**	722	928	**5.5**	2.4	3.1	1989	**32,414**	21,641	10,773	**86.8**	57.9	28.8
1990	**1,754**	760	994	**6.1**	2.7	3.5	1990	**31,183**	20,676	10,507	**88.4**	58.6	29.8
1991	**1,686**	717	969	**6.1**	2.6	3.5	1991	**27,851**	18,984	8,867	**83.6**	57.0	26.6
1992	**1,632**	730	902	**5.8**	2.6	3.2	1992	**25,218**	17,373	7,845	**80.9**	55.7	25.2
1993	**1,774**	761	1,013	**5.8**	2.5	3.3	1993	**23,422**	15,910	7,512	**78.0**	53.0	25.0
1994	**1,938**	804	1,134	**6.1**	2.5	3.6	1994	**22,614**	15,389	7,225	**78.5**	53.4	25.1
1995	**1,834**	878	956	**5.8**	2.8	3.0	1995	**22,402**	15,073	7,329	**81.0**	54.5	26.5
1996	**1,961**	838	1,123	**6.3**	2.7	3.6	1996	**24,150**	15,912	8,238	**85.7**	56.5	29.2
1997	**1,964**	866	1,098	**6.3**	2.8	3.5	1997	**25,618**	16,828	8,790	**83.6**	54.9	28.7
1998	**1,988**	821	1,167	**6.4**	2.6	3.8	1998	**27,939**	17,969	9,970	**87.5**	56.3	31.2
1999	**1,866**	785	1,081	**5.8**	2.4	3.3	1999	**26,627**	16,990	9,637	**83.8**	53.5	30.3
15							**19**						
1989	**6,077**	2,982	3,095	**19.7**	9.7	10.0	1989	**36,843**	25,710	11,133	**99.6**	69.5	30.1
1990	**6,069**	3,113	2,956	**20.3**	10.4	9.9	1990	**37,391**	25,776	11,615	**99.9**	68.9	31.0
1991	**5,476**	2,812	2,664	**19.1**	9.8	9.3	1991	**33,686**	23,519	10,167	**94.9**	66.2	28.6
1992	**5,222**	2,830	2,392	**19.0**	10.3	8.7	1992	**30,648**	21,523	9,125	**91.7**	64.4	27.3
1993	**5,125**	2,717	2,408	**18.3**	9.7	8.6	1993	**27,949**	19,616	8,333	**89.4**	62.8	26.7
1994	**5,460**	2,904	2,556	**17.9**	9.5	8.4	1994	**26,647**	18,590	8,057	**88.4**	61.7	26.7
1995	**5,835**	3,190	2,645	**18.4**	10.1	8.3	1995	**26,305**	18,359	7,946	**90.8**	63.4	27.4
1996	**6,445**	3,468	2,977	**20.4**	11.0	9.4	1996	**27,233**	18,494	8,739	**97.9**	66.5	31.4
1997	**5,942**	3,149	2,793	**19.2**	10.2	9.0	1997	**27,031**	18,110	8,921	**95.4**	63.9	31.5
1998	**6,041**	3,032	3,009	**19.4**	9.7	9.7	1998	**29,569**	19,643	9,926	**96.0**	63.8	32.2
1999	**5,673**	2,803	2,870	**18.3**	9.0	9.2	1999	**30,132**	19,734	10,398	**94.0**	61.6	32.4

* Rates per 1,000 women aged 13-15
† Rates per 1,000 women aged 13

Table 12.3 Conceptions within marriage (numbers and percentages): outcome and marriage order, and age of woman at conception, 1989-1999

England and Wales
Residents

Age of woman at conception and year of conception	Total number of conceptions within marriage (000s)	Percentage of conceptions within marriage				Age of woman at conception and year of conception	Total number of conceptions within marriage (000s)	Percentage of conceptions within marriage			
		Leading to maternities			Terminated by abortion			Leading to maternities			Terminated by abortion
		All marriages	First marriage	Second or later marriage				All marriages	First marriage	Second or later marriage	
All ages						**25-29**					
1989	**499.2**	92.4	85.7	6.7	7.6	1989	**201.4**	94.6	89.4	5.2	5.4
1990	**494.4**	92.2	85.6	6.6	7.8	1990	**200.6**	94.6	89.6	5.0	5.4
1991	**480.2**	92.2	85.6	6.6	7.8	1991	**194.4**	94.6	89.8	4.8	5.4
1992	**460.5**	92.1	85.6	6.5	7.9	1992	**185.0**	94.4	90.0	4.4	5.6
1993	**454.7**	92.3	85.8	6.5	7.7	1993	**180.2**	94.6	90.3	4.2	5.4
1994	**435.9**	92.1	85.8	6.4	7.9	1994	**169.2**	94.6	90.5	4.1	5.4
1995	**417.7**	92.1	85.7	6.4	7.9	1995	**156.8**	94.5	90.6	3.9	5.5
1996	**416.3**	91.7	85.4	6.4	8.3	1996	**152.6**	94.3	90.5	3.8	5.7
1997	**401.5**	91.5	85.2	6.3	8.5	1997	**142.9**	94.1	90.6	3.5	5.9
1998	**388.8**	91.2	85.1	6.1	8.8	1998	**133.2**	94.0	90.7	3.3	6.0
1999	**373.5**	91.2	85.4	5.9	8.8	1999	**123.5**	94.0	90.9	3.1	6.0
Under 18						**30-34**					
1989	**1.4**	94.6	94.3	0.3	5.4	1989	**119.2**	91.5	80.4	11.1	8.5
1990	**1.3**	93.6	93.5	0.1	6.4	1990	**123.6**	91.5	80.9	10.6	8.5
1991	**1.2**	93.3	93.3	0.0	6.7	1991	**126.3**	91.6	81.5	10.2	8.4
1992	**1.1**	94.7	94.5	0.2	5.3	1992	**127.6**	91.7	81.9	9.8	8.3
1993	**1.1**	93.9	93.8	0.1	6.1	1993	**132.7**	92.2	82.8	9.5	7.8
1994	**1.1**	93.9	93.9	0.1	6.1	1994	**133.5**	92.1	83.3	8.8	7.9
1995	**1.0**	93.7	93.7	0.0	6.3	1995	**134.9**	92.3	83.6	8.8	7.7
1996	**1.0**	94.1	94.1	0.0	5.9	1996	**139.2**	92.2	83.9	8.2	7.8
1997	**1.0**	93.0	93.0	0.0	7.0	1997	**138.4**	92.3	84.3	7.9	7.7
1998	**1.0**	91.1	91.1	-	8.9	1998	**136.3**	91.9	84.5	7.4	8.1
1999	**0.9**	92.0	91.9	0.1	8.0	1999	**132.4**	92.3	85.2	7.1	7.7
Under 20						**35-39**					
1989	**12.0**	95.4	95.2	0.2	4.6	1989	**40.0**	81.9	65.3	16.6	18.1
1990	**10.9**	94.8	94.6	0.2	5.2	1990	**40.7**	82.0	65.3	16.7	18.0
1991	**9.6**	94.5	94.3	0.2	5.5	1991	**41.5**	82.7	66.5	16.2	17.3
1992	**8.5**	95.4	95.2	0.2	4.6	1992	**42.4**	82.6	66.8	15.8	17.4
1993	**7.8**	95.1	94.9	0.1	4.9	1993	**44.5**	83.5	68.4	15.1	16.5
1994	**7.0**	94.8	94.6	0.3	5.2	1994	**46.0**	84.1	69.2	14.9	15.9
1995	**6.6**	94.8	94.6	0.2	5.2	1995	**46.9**	84.5	70.0	14.5	15.5
1996	**6.5**	94.3	94.2	0.1	5.7	1996	**50.8**	84.0	69.9	14.1	16.0
1997	**6.4**	94.0	93.8	0.1	6.0	1997	**52.3**	84.6	70.8	13.8	15.4
1998	**6.7**	93.2	93.1	0.1	6.8	1998	**54.1**	84.7	71.5	13.1	15.3
1999	**6.4**	93.0	92.8	0.1	7.0	1999	**55.8**	85.2	72.9	12.3	14.8
20-24						**40 and over**					
1989	**118.3**	95.0	93.4	1.6	5.0	1989	**8.3**	60.4	44.1	16.3	39.6
1990	**110.2**	94.8	93.2	1.5	5.2	1990	**8.4**	60.8	45.9	15.0	39.2
1991	**100.0**	94.6	93.2	1.4	5.4	1991	**8.4**	62.4	45.8	16.6	37.6
1992	**88.7**	94.7	93.3	1.3	5.3	1992	**8.2**	62.4	46.4	16.0	37.6
1993	**81.2**	94.7	93.4	1.3	5.3	1993	**8.3**	63.6	47.2	16.4	36.4
1994	**71.8**	94.6	93.4	1.2	5.4	1994	**8.5**	63.1	47.9	15.2	36.9
1995	**64.0**	94.4	93.3	1.1	5.6	1995	**8.5**	66.3	50.1	16.2	33.7
1996	**58.4**	94.0	92.8	1.2	6.0	1996	**8.9**	66.8	51.1	15.7	33.2
1997	**52.3**	93.8	92.7	1.1	6.2	1997	**9.2**	66.2	50.1	16.1	33.8
1998	**48.9**	93.4	92.5	0.9	6.6	1998	**9.5**	66.3	50.3	15.9	33.7
1999	**45.6**	93.1	92.2	0.9	6.9	1999	**9.7**	67.5	52.7	14.8	32.5

Table 12.4 Conceptions outside marriage (numbers and percentages): outcome and whether sole or joint registration, and age of woman at conception, 1989-1999

England and Wales
Residents

Age of woman at conception and year of conception	Total number of conceptions outside marriage (000s)	Percentage of conceptions outside marriage				
		Leading to maternities				Terminated by abortion
		Outside marriage			Within marriage	
		Total	Sole*	Joint†		
All ages						
1989	365.6	53.2	14.9	38.3	10.4	36.4
1990	377.1	55.2	14.4	40.7	8.9	35.9
1991	373.5	57.2	13.9	43.3	8.5	34.3
1992	367.5	58.3	13.4	44.9	8.1	33.6
1993	364.3	58.7	13.4	45.3	7.8	33.4
1994	365.6	59.5	13.1	46.4	7.2	33.3
1995	372.5	60.2	13.3	46.9	6.9	32.9
1996	400.6	59.8	12.9	46.9	6.4	33.8
1997	398.9	59.5	12.4	47.1	6.3	34.2
1998	408.2	59.1	11.9	47.1	5.9	35.1
1999	400.4	59.1	11.5	47.6	5.5	35.4
Under 16						
1989	7.9	46.7	24.3	22.4	1.1	52.2
1990	8.1	48.3	24.8	23.5	0.8	50.9
1991	7.5	48.1	24.0	24.1	0.6	51.3
1992	7.2	50.2	22.3	27.9	0.9	48.9
1993	7.2	49.4	23.0	26.4	0.5	50.1
1994	7.8	49.2	23.5	25.7	0.4	50.5
1995	8.0	51.6	23.5	28.1	0.7	47.8
1996	8.8	50.1	22.8	27.2	0.6	49.3
1997	8.2	49.8	22.8	27.0	0.4	49.8
1998	8.4	47.1	20.9	26.1	0.4	52.5
1999	7.9	46.8	21.2	25.6	0.4	52.9
Under 18						
1989	45.1	52.8	21.1	31.7	4.5	42.7
1990	43.5	54.5	21.4	33.1	3.4	42.1
1991	38.9	55.8	20.8	35.0	3.2	41.0
1992	36.5	57.2	19.9	37.4	2.7	40.1
1993	34.7	57.2	21.0	36.2	2.6	40.2
1994	35.0	57.1	20.6	36.6	2.1	40.8
1995	36.9	58.5	21.2	37.4	1.9	39.6
1996	42.5	57.5	20.3	37.1	1.7	40.8
1997	42.3	57.0	19.9	37.1	1.6	41.4
1998	43.1	55.7	19.3	36.5	1.5	42.7
1999	41.1	54.8	18.7	36.2	1.3	43.8
Under 20						
1989	103.7	53.7	18.9	34.7	7.1	39.2
1990	102.5	55.4	18.9	36.5	5.7	39.0
1991	92.0	57.2	18.6	38.6	5.3	37.5
1992	84.9	58.6	18.0	40.7	4.6	36.8
1993	79.4	58.6	18.6	39.9	4.3	37.1
1994	78.3	59.0	18.6	40.5	3.6	37.4
1995	80.0	59.8	19.0	40.8	3.2	37.0
1996	88.4	58.5	18.3	40.2	3.0	38.5
1997	89.6	58.4	18.0	40.3	2.7	39.0
1998	94.9	57.4	17.2	40.2	2.6	40.0
1999	92.4	56.8	16.4	40.4	2.4	40.8
20-24						
1989	132.5	52.4	14.1	38.3	10.8	36.8
1990	134.3	54.4	13.6	40.9	9.3	36.3
1991	133.3	56.6	13.1	43.5	8.6	34.8
1992	127.2	57.7	13.0	44.7	8.2	34.1
1993	122.4	57.9	12.8	45.1	7.7	34.4
1994	118.6	58.6	12.7	45.9	7.1	34.3
1995	117.1	59.0	12.9	46.1	6.7	34.3
1996	121.4	58.7	12.6	46.0	6.1	35.2
1997	115.0	58.1	12.2	45.9	5.9	36.0
1998	114.4	57.6	11.8	45.8	5.5	36.9
1999	112.0	57.6	11.5	46.1	5.0	37.3
25-29						
1989	77.2	54.1	12.6	41.4	12.7	33.2
1990	83.6	56.1	12.4	43.7	11.0	32.9
1991	87.1	58.2	11.9	46.2	10.5	31.4
1992	89.8	58.8	11.4	47.4	10.0	31.1
1993	91.5	59.8	11.5	48.3	9.6	30.5
1994	92.6	60.6	11.1	49.6	8.7	30.7
1995	93.5	61.1	11.1	50.1	8.5	30.4
1996	100.0	61.2	10.7	50.5	7.9	30.9
1997	99.6	60.6	10.2	50.4	8.0	31.5
1998	99.2	60.3	9.6	50.8	7.6	32.1
1999	94.9	60.4	9.3	51.1	7.1	32.4
30-34						
1989	34.5	55.3	12.3	43.0	13.1	31.6
1990	37.8	57.4	11.8	45.6	11.4	31.1
1991	41.2	59.3	11.9	47.4	10.9	29.8
1992	44.4	60.0	11.1	48.9	10.3	29.7
1993	48.3	60.7	11.2	49.6	10.1	29.2
1994	51.5	62.2	11.0	51.2	9.5	28.3
1995	55.4	63.1	11.0	52.1	9.0	27.9
1996	60.8	62.8	10.7	52.2	8.7	28.5
1997	62.6	62.7	9.7	53.0	8.7	28.5
1998	65.1	62.8	9.4	53.5	7.9	29.2
1999	64.7	63.1	8.8	54.3	7.7	29.2
35-39						
1989	14.1	50.4	11.6	38.9	11.7	37.9
1990	15.3	52.9	10.8	42.1	10.3	36.8
1991	16.0	55.1	11.0	44.1	10.8	34.1
1992	17.2	56.1	10.9	45.2	9.9	34.0
1993	18.5	57.4	10.8	46.6	9.0	33.6
1994	20.2	58.3	10.5	47.8	8.7	33.0
1995	21.8	59.6	10.4	49.2	8.7	31.7
1996	24.7	59.9	10.5	49.4	8.1	32.0
1997	26.6	59.8	10.0	49.8	8.0	32.2
1998	28.7	59.2	9.5	49.7	7.6	33.3
1999	30.2	60.0	9.5	50.6	7.0	33.0
40 and over						
1989	3.5	39.9	8.8	31.1	7.8	52.3
1990	3.6	38.9	8.2	30.7	8.5	52.6
1991	3.8	43.1	8.9	34.3	6.5	50.3
1992	3.9	42.8	8.9	33.9	7.8	49.5
1993	4.2	45.0	9.3	35.7	7.4	47.6
1994	4.3	44.8	8.2	36.5	6.6	48.7
1995	4.7	47.4	9.1	38.3	7.0	45.7
1996	5.2	48.1	8.9	39.2	6.6	45.3
1997	5.5	48.7	8.9	39.8	6.2	45.0
1998	5.9	49.2	9.1	40.2	6.0	44.7
1999	6.3	50.5	8.1	42.4	5.6	43.9

* Conceptions leading to births outside marriage registered by the mother alone
† Conceptions leading to births outside marriage registered by both parents

Table 12.5 Conceptions within marriage (numbers and rates) : outcome and age of woman at conception, 1989-1999

England and Wales
Residents

Age of woman at conception and year of conception	Numbers of conceptions (thousands)			Conception rates per 1,000 married women in age-group		
	Total conceptions within marriage	Conceptions leading to maternities within marriage	Conceptions terminated by abortion	Total conceptions within marriage	Conceptions leading to maternities within marriage	Conceptions terminated by abortion
All ages* 1989	**499.2**	461.1	38.0	**84.6**	78.1	6.4
1990	**494.4**	456.0	38.4	**84.7**	78.1	6.6
1991	**480.2**	442.9	37.3	**83.2**	76.8	6.5
1992	**460.5**	424.0	36.5	**82.6**	76.0	6.6
1993	**454.7**	419.6	35.2	**84.0**	77.5	6.5
1994	**435.9**	401.6	34.3	**82.5**	76.0	6.5
1995	**417.7**	384.7	33.1	**81.2**	74.8	6.4
1996	**416.3**	381.8	34.5	**82.8**	75.9	6.9
1997	**401.5**	367.6	34.0	**81.7**	74.8	6.9
1998	**388.8**	354.6	34.2	**81.0**	73.9	7.1
1999	**373.5**	340.8	32.7	**79.5**	72.5	7.0
Under 16 1989	**0.0**	0.0	0.0	:	:	:
1990	**0.0**	0.0	0.0	:	:	:
1991	**0.0**	0.0	0.0	:	:	:
1992	**0.0**	0.0	0.0	:	:	:
1993	**0.0**	0.0	0.0	:	:	:
1994	**0.0**	0.0	0.0	:	:	:
1995	**0.0**	0.0	0.0	:	:	:
1996	**0.0**	0.0	0.0	:	:	:
1997	**0.0**	0.0	-	:	:	:
1998	**0.0**	0.0	0.0	:	:	:
1999	**0.0**	0.0	0.0	:	:	:
16 1989	**0.3**	0.3	0.0	:	:	:
1990	**0.3**	0.3	0.0	:	:	:
1991	**0.2**	0.2	0.0	:	:	:
1992	**0.3**	0.2	0.0	:	:	:
1993	**0.3**	0.2	0.0	:	:	:
1994	**0.2**	0.2	0.0	:	:	:
1995	**0.2**	0.2	0.0	:	:	:
1996	**0.3**	0.2	0.0	:	:	:
1997	**0.3**	0.2	0.0	:	:	:
1998	**0.2**	0.2	0.0	:	:	:
1999	**0.2**	0.2	0.0	:	:	:
17 1989	**1.1**	1.0	0.1	:	:	:
1990	**0.9**	0.9	0.1	:	:	:
1991	**0.9**	0.9	0.1	:	:	:
1992	**0.8**	0.7	0.0	:	:	:
1993	**0.8**	0.7	0.0	:	:	:
1994	**0.8**	0.8	0.1	:	:	:
1995	**0.7**	0.7	0.0	:	:	:
1996	**0.7**	0.7	0.0	:	:	:
1997	**0.8**	0.7	0.1	:	:	:
1998	**0.8**	0.7	0.1	:	:	:
1999	**0.7**	0.6	0.1	:	:	:
18 1989	**3.4**	3.3	0.2	282.3	270.0	12.3
1990	**3.1**	2.9	0.2	293.0	278.2	14.8
1991	**2.7**	2.6	0.1	318.4	302.3	16.1
1992	**2.5**	2.4	0.1	395.4	377.8	17.6
1993	**2.2**	2.1	0.1	471.0	449.4	21.6
1994	**2.0**	1.9	0.1	547.2	522.0	25.2
1995	**2.0**	1.9	0.1	602.4	571.7	30.7
1996	**1.8**	1.7	0.1	582.1	549.7	32.4
1997	**1.9**	1.8	0.1	620.2	585.4	34.8
1998	**2.0**	1.9	0.1	642.7	600.2	42.5
1999	**1.9**	1.8	0.1	675.8	626.4	49.4
19 1989	**7.2**	6.8	0.3	251.6	240.2	11.4
1990	**6.5**	6.2	0.3	256.6	243.6	13.0
1991	**5.7**	5.4	0.3	284.0	268.4	15.6
1992	**5.0**	4.7	0.2	321.8	307.0	14.8
1993	**4.5**	4.3	0.2	375.4	357.2	18.2
1994	**4.0**	3.8	0.2	415.2	393.7	21.5
1995	**3.7**	3.5	0.2	449.9	427.4	22.5
1996	**3.7**	3.4	0.2	475.9	449.0	27.0
1997	**3.5**	3.2	0.2	480.8	452.0	28.8
1998	**3.7**	3.5	0.2	515.9	483.6	32.3
1999	**3.6**	3.3	0.2	517.1	482.8	34.3

* Rates per 1,000 women aged 15-44
Note: Rates for ages under 16, 16 and 17 have been omitted because of the small number of married women at these ages.

Table 12.5 - *continued*

Age of woman at conception and year of conception	Numbers of conceptions (thousands)			Conception rates per 1,000 married women in age-group		
	Total conceptions within marriage	Conceptions leading to maternities within marriage	Conceptions terminated by abortion	**Total conceptions within marriage**	Conceptions leading to maternities within marriage	Conceptions terminated by abortion
Under 20* 1989	**12.0**	11.5	0.6	**266.7**	254.5	12.2
1990	**10.9**	10.3	0.6	**274.4**	260.1	14.3
1991	**9.6**	9.1	0.5	**296.8**	280.4	16.4
1992	**8.5**	8.1	0.4	**358.0**	341.4	16.6
1993	**7.8**	7.4	0.4	**431.7**	410.3	21.4
1994	**7.0**	6.6	0.4	**487.8**	462.7	25.1
1995	**6.6**	6.3	0.3	**522.3**	495.1	27.2
1996	**6.5**	6.1	0.4	**539.0**	508.4	30.6
1997	**6.4**	6.0	0.4	**559.2**	525.4	33.8
1998	**6.7**	6.3	0.5	**590.8**	550.9	39.9
1999	**6.4**	6.0	0.5	**604.5**	561.9	42.5
20-24 1989	**118.3**	112.3	6.0	**207.8**	197.3	10.5
1990	**110.2**	104.4	5.8	**204.7**	194.0	10.7
1991	**100.0**	94.6	5.4	**204.3**	193.3	11.0
1992	**88.7**	84.0	4.7	**204.5**	193.5	10.9
1993	**81.2**	76.9	4.3	**212.7**	201.5	11.3
1994	**71.8**	67.9	3.9	**217.7**	205.9	11.8
1995	**64.0**	60.4	3.6	**227.2**	214.4	12.7
1996	**58.4**	54.9	3.5	**244.8**	230.1	14.7
1997	**52.3**	49.1	3.2	**256.5**	240.6	15.8
1998	**48.9**	45.7	3.2	**271.4**	253.4	18.0
1999	**45.6**	42.5	3.1	**276.4**	257.4	19.0
25-29 1989	**201.4**	190.5	10.9	**169.4**	160.3	19.1
1990	**200.6**	189.8	10.9	**171.8**	162.5	19.3
1991	**194.4**	184.0	10.4	**167.9**	158.9	19.0
1992	**185.0**	174.8	10.3	**166.3**	157.1	19.2
1993	**180.2**	170.5	9.7	**169.7**	160.5	19.2
1994	**169.2**	160.1	9.1	**167.3**	158.3	19.0
1995	**156.8**	148.1	8.7	**165.5**	156.3	19.2
1996	**152.6**	143.9	8.7	**172.0**	162.3	19.8
1997	**142.9**	134.5	8.5	**174.7**	164.3	10.3
1998	**133.2**	125.2	8.0	**177.6**	166.9	10.7
1999	**123.5**	116.1	7.5	**180.1**	169.3	10.9
30-34 1989	**119.2**	109.0	10.1	**92.0**	84.2	7.8
1990	**123.6**	113.1	10.5	**94.4**	86.3	8.0
1991	**126.3**	115.7	10.6	**94.9**	87.0	8.0
1992	**127.6**	117.0	10.7	**95.5**	87.5	8.0
1993	**132.7**	122.4	10.3	**99.2**	91.5	7.7
1994	**133.5**	122.9	10.5	**99.6**	91.7	7.8
1995	**134.9**	124.6	10.3	**101.2**	93.5	7.8
1996	**139.2**	128.3	10.9	**105.7**	97.5	8.3
1997	**138.4**	127.6	10.7	**107.5**	99.2	8.3
1998	**136.3**	125.3	11.0	**109.3**	100.5	8.8
1999	**132.4**	122.2	10.2	**109.9**	101.5	8.5
35-39 1989	**40.0**	32.8	7.2	**30.1**	24.6	5.4
1990	**40.7**	33.4	7.3	**31.3**	25.6	5.6
1991	**41.5**	34.4	7.2	**32.2**	26.6	5.6
1992	**42.4**	35.0	7.4	**32.9**	27.2	5.7
1993	**44.5**	37.2	7.4	**34.5**	28.8	5.7
1994	**46.0**	38.7	7.3	**35.4**	29.8	5.6
1995	**46.9**	39.6	7.3	**35.8**	30.2	5.5
1996	**50.8**	42.7	8.1	**38.2**	32.1	6.1
1997	**52.3**	44.2	8.0	**38.9**	33.0	6.0
1998	**54.1**	45.8	8.3	**40.0**	33.8	6.1
1999	**55.8**	47.5	8.3	**40.9**	34.8	6.1
40 and over† 1989	**8.3**	5.0	3.3	**5.6**	3.4	2.2
1990	**8.4**	5.1	3.3	**5.7**	3.5	2.2
1991	**8.4**	5.2	3.1	**5.7**	3.5	2.1
1992	**8.2**	5.1	3.1	**6.0**	3.7	2.2
1993	**8.3**	5.3	3.0	**6.3**	4.0	2.3
1994	**8.5**	5.4	3.2	**6.6**	4.2	2.4
1995	**8.5**	5.7	2.9	**6.8**	4.5	2.3
1996	**8.9**	6.0	3.0	**7.2**	4.8	2.4
1997	**9.2**	6.1	3.1	**7.4**	4.9	2.5
1998	**9.5**	6.3	3.2	**7.6**	5.0	2.6
1999	**9.7**	6.6	3.2	**7.7**	5.2	2.5

* Rates per 1,000 women aged 15-19
† Rates per 1,000 women aged 40-44

Table 12.6 Conceptions outside marriage (numbers and rates) : outcome and age of woman at conception, 1989-1999

England and Wales *Residents*

Age of woman at conception and year of conception	Numbers of conceptions (thousands)					Conception rates per 1,000 unmarried women in age-group				
	Total con-ceptions outside marriage	Conceptions leading to maternities			Conceptions terminated by abortion	Total con-ceptions outside marriage	Conceptions leading to maternities			Conceptions terminated by abortion
		Total	Outside marriage	Within marriage following marriage after conception			Total	Outside marriage	Within marriage following marriage after conception	
All ages* 1989	365.6	232.4	194.4	38.0	133.2	71.7	45.6	38.1	7.4	26.1
1990	377.1	241.6	208.0	33.7	135.4	73.3	47.0	40.4	6.5	26.3
1991	373.5	245.5	213.7	31.9	127.9	71.6	47.1	40.9	6.1	24.5
1992	367.5	243.9	214.1	29.8	123.6	69.6	46.2	40.6	5.6	23.4
1993	364.3	242.5	214.0	28.5	121.8	68.1	45.3	40.0	5.3	22.8
1994	365.6	244.0	217.7	26.3	121.7	67.1	44.7	39.9	4.8	22.3
1995	372.5	249.8	224.2	25.6	122.7	66.7	44.7	40.1	4.6	22.0
1996	400.6	265.4	239.7	25.6	135.3	70.1	46.5	42.0	4.5	23.7
1997	398.9	262.3	237.3	25.0	136.6	68.3	44.9	40.6	4.3	23.4
1998	408.2	265.0	241.0	24.0	143.2	68.4	44.4	40.4	4.0	24.0
1999	400.4	258.5	236.5	22.0	141.9	65.7	42.4	38.8	3.6	23.3
Under 16† 1989	7.9	3.8	3.7	0.1	4.1	8.9	4.3	4.2	0.1	4.6
1990	8.1	4.0	3.9	0.1	4.1	9.5	4.6	4.6	0.1	4.8
1991	7.5	3.6	3.6	0.0	3.8	8.9	4.3	4.3	0.1	4.5
1992	7.2	3.7	3.6	0.1	3.5	8.4	4.3	4.2	0.1	4.1
1993	7.2	3.6	3.6	0.0	3.6	8.0	4.0	4.0	0.0	4.0
1994	7.8	3.8	3.8	0.0	3.9	8.3	4.1	4.1	0.0	4.2
1995	8.0	4.2	4.1	0.1	3.8	8.5	4.5	4.4	0.1	4.1
1996	8.8	4.5	4.4	0.1	4.4	9.5	4.8	4.7	0.1	4.7
1997	8.2	4.1	4.1	0.0	4.1	8.9	4.5	4.4	0.0	4.4
1998	8.4	4.0	4.0	0.0	4.4	8.9	4.2	4.2	0.0	4.7
1999	7.9	3.7	3.7	0.0	4.2	8.2	3.9	3.9	0.0	4.4
16 1989	14.4	8.1	7.6	0.5	6.3	43.8	24.7	23.1	1.6	19.1
1990	13.6	7.8	7.4	0.4	5.9	44.3	25.3	24.1	1.2	19.0
1991	12.4	7.3	6.9	0.4	5.1	41.4	24.4	23.2	1.2	17.1
1992	11.7	7.0	6.7	0.2	4.7	40.7	24.3	23.4	0.8	16.4
1993	10.8	6.5	6.3	0.2	4.3	39.2	23.6	22.8	0.8	15.7
1994	11.1	6.6	6.4	0.2	4.5	39.6	23.6	22.9	0.7	16.0
1995	12.1	7.4	7.3	0.2	4.7	39.8	24.4	23.8	0.6	15.4
1996	14.0	8.4	8.2	0.2	5.7	44.2	26.4	25.8	0.5	17.9
1997	13.8	8.1	8.0	0.2	5.7	43.7	25.7	25.2	0.5	18.0
1998	13.6	7.9	7.7	0.1	5.7	43.8	25.4	24.9	0.5	18.4
1999	13.1	7.3	7.2	0.1	5.8	42.2	23.5	23.0	0.4	18.7
17 1989	22.7	13.9	12.5	1.4	8.8	65.1	39.8	35.8	4.1	25.3
1990	21.8	13.4	12.4	1.1	8.3	66.2	40.9	37.7	3.2	25.3
1991	19.1	12.1	11.2	0.9	7.0	61.8	39.1	36.3	2.8	22.7
1992	17.6	11.2	10.6	0.7	6.4	59.2	37.7	35.4	2.3	21.5
1993	16.7	10.7	10.0	0.6	6.0	58.4	37.3	35.1	2.3	21.1
1994	16.1	10.3	9.8	0.5	5.9	58.8	37.4	35.6	1.9	21.4
1995	16.7	10.7	10.2	0.5	6.1	59.9	38.1	36.5	1.7	21.7
1996	19.6	12.3	11.8	0.5	7.3	64.5	40.4	38.8	1.6	24.1
1997	20.3	12.5	12.1	0.5	7.7	63.9	39.5	38.0	1.5	24.4
1998	21.1	12.8	12.3	0.5	8.3	66.9	40.6	39.1	1.5	26.3
1999	20.0	12.0	11.7	0.4	8.0	64.6	38.8	37.6	1.2	25.8
18 1989	29.0	18.3	15.9	2.5	10.6	79.4	50.3	43.5	6.8	29.1
1990	28.1	17.8	15.8	1.9	10.4	82.1	51.8	46.2	5.6	30.2
1991	25.1	16.4	14.9	1.5	8.7	77.4	50.5	45.9	4.7	26.9
1992	22.7	15.0	13.7	1.2	7.7	74.4	49.1	45.0	4.1	25.3
1993	21.3	13.9	12.8	1.1	7.4	71.9	46.8	43.3	3.6	25.1
1994	20.7	13.5	12.6	0.9	7.1	72.6	47.5	44.4	3.2	25.1
1995	20.4	13.2	12.4	0.8	7.2	74.8	48.3	45.4	2.9	26.5
1996	22.3	14.2	13.3	0.9	8.1	80.1	50.8	47.8	3.1	29.2
1997	23.7	15.0	14.2	0.8	8.7	78.1	49.5	46.9	2.6	28.6
1998	25.9	16.1	15.3	0.8	9.8	81.9	50.8	48.3	2.5	31.1
1999	24.7	15.2	14.5	0.7	9.5	78.5	48.3	46.0	2.3	30.2
19 1989	29.7	18.9	16.0	2.9	10.8	86.4	54.9	46.5	8.4	31.5
1990	30.9	19.6	17.2	2.4	11.3	87.6	55.6	48.8	6.8	32.0
1991	28.0	18.1	16.1	2.1	9.9	83.5	54.1	47.9	6.2	29.4
1992	25.7	16.8	15.1	1.6	8.9	80.6	52.7	47.5	5.2	27.9
1993	23.4	15.3	13.9	1.4	8.1	77.9	50.9	46.1	4.8	27.0
1994	22.7	14.8	13.6	1.2	7.9	77.7	50.8	46.7	4.1	26.9
1995	22.6	14.9	13.8	1.1	7.8	80.3	52.8	48.9	3.8	27.6
1996	23.6	15.1	14.0	1.1	8.5	87.2	55.7	51.7	3.9	31.6
1997	23.6	14.9	13.9	0.9	8.7	85.3	53.8	50.4	3.4	31.5
1998	25.9	16.2	15.2	1.0	9.7	86.0	53.8	50.5	3.3	32.2
1999	26.5	16.4	15.5	0.9	10.2	84.6	52.2	49.3	2.9	32.4

* Rates per 1,000 aged 15-44
† Rates per 1,000 aged 13-15

Table 12.6 - *continued*

Age of woman at conception and year of conception		Numbers of conceptions (thousands)					Conception rates per 1,000 unmarried women in age-group				
		Total conceptions outside marriage	Conceptions leading to maternities			Conceptions terminated by abortion	Total conceptions outside marriage	Conceptions leading to maternities			Conceptions terminated by abortion
			Total	Outside marriage	Within marriage following marriage after conception			Total	Outside marriage	Within marriage following marriage after conception	
Under 20*	1989	**103.7**	63.0	55.7	7.4	40.7	**61.2**	37.2	32.9	4.4	24.0
	1990	**102.5**	62.5	56.7	5.8	39.9	**62.9**	38.4	34.8	3.6	24.5
	1991	**92.0**	57.5	52.7	4.8	34.5	**59.2**	37.0	33.9	3.1	22.2
	1992	**84.9**	53.6	49.8	3.9	31.3	**57.2**	36.1	33.5	2.6	21.1
	1993	**79.4**	49.9	46.5	3.4	29.5	**55.2**	34.7	32.4	2.4	20.5
	1994	**78.3**	49.1	46.2	2.8	29.3	**54.6**	34.2	32.2	2.0	20.4
	1995	**80.0**	50.4	47.8	2.6	29.6	**54.9**	34.6	32.8	1.8	20.3
	1996	**88.4**	54.4	51.7	2.6	34.0	**59.5**	36.6	34.8	1.8	22.9
	1997	**89.6**	54.7	52.3	2.4	34.9	**58.9**	35.9	34.4	1.6	22.9
	1998	**94.9**	56.9	54.5	2.5	38.0	**61.1**	36.6	35.1	1.6	24.4
	1999	**92.4**	54.7	52.5	2.2	37.7	**59.2**	35.0	33.6	1.4	24.1
20-24	1989	**132.5**	83.8	69.4	14.3	48.7	**91.9**	58.1	48.2	10.0	33.8
	1990	**134.3**	85.6	73.1	12.5	48.7	**94.2**	60.0	51.3	8.8	34.1
	1991	**133.3**	86.9	75.4	11.5	46.4	**91.9**	59.9	52.0	7.9	32.0
	1992	**127.2**	83.8	73.4	10.4	43.4	**87.1**	57.4	50.3	7.1	29.7
	1993	**122.4**	80.3	70.9	9.4	42.1	**84.1**	55.2	48.7	6.5	28.9
	1994	**118.6**	77.9	69.5	8.4	40.7	**82.5**	54.2	48.4	5.9	28.3
	1995	**117.1**	76.9	69.1	7.9	40.2	**82.4**	54.1	48.6	5.5	28.3
	1996	**121.4**	78.7	71.2	7.4	42.8	**87.8**	56.9	51.5	5.4	30.9
	1997	**115.0**	73.6	66.8	6.7	41.4	**85.5**	54.7	49.7	5.0	30.8
	1998	**114.4**	72.2	65.9	6.3	42.2	**86.4**	54.5	49.7	4.7	31.9
	1999	**112.0**	70.2	64.5	5.7	41.8	**83.7**	52.5	48.2	4.2	31.3
25-29	1989	**77.2**	51.5	41.7	9.8	25.7	**92.5**	61.8	50.0	11.8	30.7
	1990	**83.6**	56.1	46.9	9.2	27.5	**93.4**	62.7	52.4	10.3	30.7
	1991	**87.1**	59.8	50.7	9.1	27.3	**94.2**	64.6	54.8	9.8	29.5
	1992	**89.8**	61.9	52.9	9.0	28.0	**92.2**	63.5	54.3	9.2	28.7
	1993	**91.5**	63.5	54.7	8.8	27.9	**90.9**	63.1	54.4	8.8	27.7
	1994	**92.6**	64.2	56.2	8.1	28.4	**89.8**	62.2	54.4	7.8	27.5
	1995	**93.5**	65.1	57.1	8.0	28.4	**88.7**	61.7	54.2	7.5	26.9
	1996	**100.0**	69.2	61.2	7.9	30.9	**92.0**	63.6	56.3	7.3	28.4
	1997	**99.6**	68.3	60.3	7.9	31.3	**89.2**	61.2	54.0	7.1	28.1
	1998	**99.2**	67.4	59.9	7.5	31.8	**87.1**	59.2	52.5	6.6	27.9
	1999	**94.9**	64.1	57.4	6.8	30.8	**82.7**	55.9	50.0	5.9	26.8
30-34	1989	**34.5**	23.6	19.1	4.5	10.9	**78.3**	53.5	43.3	10.2	24.8
	1990	**37.8**	26.0	21.7	4.3	11.8	**78.9**	54.3	45.3	9.0	24.6
	1991	**41.2**	28.9	24.5	4.5	12.3	**77.8**	54.6	46.2	8.5	23.2
	1992	**44.4**	31.2	26.7	4.6	13.2	**77.0**	54.1	46.2	7.9	22.8
	1993	**48.3**	34.2	29.3	4.9	14.1	**76.7**	54.3	46.6	7.7	22.4
	1994	**51.5**	37.0	32.1	4.9	14.6	**75.2**	53.9	46.8	7.2	21.3
	1995	**55.4**	39.9	34.9	5.0	15.5	**74.7**	53.9	47.1	6.7	20.8
	1996	**60.8**	43.5	38.2	5.3	17.3	**77.3**	55.3	48.6	6.7	22.0
	1997	**62.6**	44.7	39.2	5.5	17.9	**75.9**	54.2	47.6	6.6	21.7
	1998	**65.1**	46.1	40.9	5.2	19.0	**76.5**	54.1	48.1	6.1	22.4
	1999	**64.7**	45.8	40.8	5.0	18.9	**74.1**	52.5	46.8	5.7	21.6
35-39	1989	**14.1**	8.8	7.1	1.7	5.4	**40.2**	25.0	20.3	4.7	15.2
	1990	**15.3**	9.7	8.1	1.6	5.6	**42.2**	26.7	22.3	4.4	15.5
	1991	**16.0**	10.6	8.8	1.7	5.5	**41.8**	27.6	23.0	4.5	14.2
	1992	**17.2**	11.4	9.6	1.7	5.8	**42.3**	28.0	23.8	4.2	14.4
	1993	**18.5**	12.3	10.6	1.7	6.2	**42.7**	28.4	24.5	3.8	14.4
	1994	**20.2**	13.5	11.8	1.8	6.7	**43.5**	29.1	25.3	3.8	14.3
	1995	**21.8**	14.9	13.0	1.9	6.9	**43.6**	29.8	26.0	3.8	13.8
	1996	**24.7**	16.8	14.8	2.0	7.9	**45.8**	31.1	27.4	3.7	14.6
	1997	**26.6**	18.0	15.9	2.1	8.6	**45.6**	30.9	27.3	3.7	14.7
	1998	**28.7**	19.2	17.0	2.2	9.6	**45.8**	30.5	27.1	3.5	15.2
	1999	**30.2**	20.2	18.1	2.1	10.0	**44.6**	29.9	26.8	3.1	14.7
40 and over†	1989	**3.5**	1.7	1.4	0.3	1.8	**10.4**	5.0	4.1	0.8	5.4
	1990	**3.6**	1.7	1.4	0.3	1.9	**10.1**	4.8	3.9	0.9	5.3
	1991	**3.8**	1.9	1.6	0.2	1.9	**10.1**	5.0	4.3	0.7	5.1
	1992	**3.9**	2.0	1.7	0.3	2.0	**10.5**	5.3	4.5	0.8	5.2
	1993	**4.2**	2.2	1.9	0.3	2.0	**11.0**	5.8	4.9	0.8	5.2
	1994	**4.3**	2.2	1.9	0.3	2.1	**10.9**	5.6	4.9	0.7	5.3
	1995	**4.7**	2.6	2.2	0.3	2.2	**11.5**	6.2	5.4	0.8	5.2
	1996	**5.2**	2.8	2.5	0.3	2.4	**12.1**	6.6	5.8	0.8	5.5
	1997	**5.5**	3.0	2.7	0.3	2.5	**12.2**	6.7	6.0	0.8	5.5
	1998	**5.9**	3.2	2.9	0.4	2.6	**12.4**	6.9	6.1	0.7	5.6
	1999	**6.3**	3.6	3.2	0.4	2.8	**12.7**	7.1	6.4	0.7	5.6

*   Rates per 1,000 women aged 15-19
†   Rates per 1,000 women aged 40-44

Table 12.7 Conceptions (numbers and percentages): occurrence within/outside marriage and outcome, area of usual residence, and age of woman at conception, 1999

England and Wales, England, Wales,
government office regions,
metropolitan counties,
health regional office areas
Residents

Area of usual residence	Total number of conceptions (000s)	Percentage of all conceptions		Percentage of all conceptions		Total number of conceptions outside marriage (000s)	Percentage of conceptions outside marriage				
		Within marriage	Outside marriage	Leading to maternities	Terminated by abortion		Leading to maternities				Terminated by abortion
							Outside marriage			Within marriage following marriage after conception	
							Total	Sole*	Joint†		
All women											
England and Wales	**774.0**	**48.3**	**51.7**	**77.4**	**22.6**	**400.4**	**59.1**	**11.5**	**47.6**	**5.5**	**35.4**
England	735.5	48.6	51.4	77.3	22.7	378.4	58.7	11.4	47.3	5.5	35.8
Wales	38.5	42.6	57.4	80.3	19.7	22.1	65.8	13.4	52.4	5.6	28.5
Government Office Regions											
North East	33.2	40.0	60.0	79.6	20.4	19.9	66.6	13.9	52.7	4.3	29.1
North West	96.6	43.4	56.6	78.8	21.2	54.7	64.0	14.7	49.4	4.4	31.6
Yorkshire and the Humber	69.5	46.7	53.3	80.2	19.8	37.1	64.3	11.9	52.4	5.1	30.6
East Midlands	56.1	48.5	51.5	80.8	19.2	28.9	64.7	11.4	53.4	5.7	29.5
West Midlands	78.0	48.7	51.3	78.6	21.4	40.0	61.0	12.6	48.3	5.0	34.0
East	75.0	53.4	46.6	80.5	19.5	34.9	60.8	9.3	51.4	6.7	32.6
London	152.5	47.6	52.4	68.1	31.9	79.9	45.2	10.8	34.4	5.2	49.6
South East	112.8	53.6	46.4	79.4	20.6	52.3	58.5	8.8	49.6	6.6	35.0
South West	61.9	50.6	49.4	80.6	19.4	30.6	61.6	9.6	52.0	6.5	31.9
Metropolitan Counties											
Greater London	152.5	47.6	52.4	68.1	31.9	79.9	45.2	10.8	34.4	5.2	49.6
Greater Manchester	38.4	43.0	57.0	78.7	21.3	21.9	64.6	14.3	50.2	4.0	31.5
Merseyside	19.7	35.2	64.8	76.0	24.0	12.8	63.9	19.0	44.9	3.4	32.7
South Yorkshire	17.8	41.9	58.1	79.0	21.0	10.3	65.2	11.0	54.2	4.7	30.2
Tyne And Wear	14.6	38.4	61.6	77.6	22.4	9.0	64.5	13.9	50.5	4.1	31.4
West Midlands	42.7	47.9	52.1	77.3	22.7	22.3	60.6	14.3	46.3	4.0	35.3
West Yorkshire	31.3	49.8	50.2	81.1	18.9	15.7	64.2	12.9	51.3	5.0	30.7
Health Regional Office Areas											
Northern and Yorkshire	84.5	45.5	54.5	80.3	19.7	46.0	65.1	12.9	52.2	4.9	30.0
Trent	68.5	46.2	53.8	80.2	19.8	36.8	64.8	11.3	53.5	5.4	29.8
Eastern	75.0	53.4	46.6	80.5	19.5	34.9	60.8	9.3	51.4	6.7	32.6
London	152.5	47.6	52.4	68.1	31.9	79.9	45.2	10.8	34.4	5.2	49.6
South East	122.0	53.3	46.7	79.5	20.5	57.0	59.0	9.0	50.0	6.5	34.5
South West	61.9	50.6	49.4	80.6	19.4	30.6	61.6	9.6	52.0	6.5	31.9
West Midlands	78.0	48.7	51.3	78.6	21.4	40.0	61.0	12.6	48.3	5.0	34.0
North West	93.1	43.2	56.8	78.6	21.4	52.9	64.0	14.8	49.2	4.3	31.7

* Conceptions leading to births outside marriage registered by the mother alone
† Conceptions leading to births outside marriage registered by both parents

Table 12.7 - *continued*

Area of usual residence	Total number of conceptions (000s)	Percentage of all conceptions		Percentage of all conceptions		Total number of conceptions outside marriage (000s)	Percentage of conceptions outside marriage				
							Leading to maternities				Terminated by abortion
		Within marriage	Outside marriage	Leading to maternities	Terminated by abortion		Outside marriage			Within marriage following marriage after conception	
							Total	Sole*	Joint†		
Women aged under 18											
England and Wales	**42.0**	2.2	97.8	**57.0**	**43.0**	**41.1**	54.8	18.7	36.2	1.3	43.8
England	**39.2**	2.3	97.7	56.5	43.5	**38.3**	54.3	18.5	35.8	1.3	44.4
Wales	**2.8**	1.0	99.0	63.9	36.1	**2.8**	62.3	21.0	41.4	1.3	36.3
Government Office Regions											
North East	**2.7**	0.6	99.4	63.1	36.9	**2.6**	61.9	21.7	40.2	1.0	37.1
North West	**6.3**	1.9	98.1	60.1	39.9	**6.2**	58.6	22.7	35.8	0.9	40.5
Yorkshire and the Humber	**4.6**	2.7	97.3	60.9	39.1	**4.5**	58.7	18.7	40.0	1.4	40.0
East Midlands	**3.2**	1.4	98.6	59.8	40.2	**3.2**	58.2	18.2	40.1	1.2	40.6
West Midlands	**4.8**	3.5	96.5	59.4	40.6	**4.7**	56.9	19.8	37.1	1.1	41.9
East	**3.4**	1.5	98.5	54.0	46.0	**3.4**	52.1	15.0	37.0	1.4	46.6
London	**6.0**	4.6	95.4	46.7	53.3	**5.7**	42.7	17.7	25.0	1.9	55.4
South East	**5.1**	1.6	98.4	54.4	45.6	**5.0**	52.2	15.8	36.5	1.5	46.2
South West	**3.2**	0.8	99.2	53.9	46.1	**3.1**	52.1	15.3	36.8	1.4	46.5
Metropolitan Counties											
Greater London	**6.0**	4.6	95.4	46.7	53.3	**5.7**	42.7	17.7	25.0	1.9	55.4
Greater Manchester	**2.6**	2.8	97.2	64.1	35.9	**2.5**	62.2	23.5	38.7	1.1	36.7
Merseyside	**1.3**	0.5	99.5	56.6	43.4	**1.3**	56.3	25.9	30.5	0.1	43.6
South Yorkshire	**1.3**	1.3	98.7	60.5	39.5	**1.3**	58.5	16.9	41.6	1.5	40.0
Tyne And Wear	**1.2**	0.8	99.2	62.2	37.8	**1.2**	61.6	21.9	39.7	0.4	38.0
West Midlands	**2.8**	4.9	95.1	61.5	38.5	**2.7**	58.7	21.9	36.8	1.1	40.2
West Yorkshire	**2.0**	4.8	95.2	63.6	36.4	**1.9**	60.5	19.6	40.8	1.7	37.9
Health Regional Office Areas											
Northern and Yorkshire	**5.8**	2.1	97.9	62.3	37.7	**5.7**	60.4	20.5	39.9	1.2	38.4
Trent	**4.4**	1.4	98.6	59.9	40.1	**4.3**	58.3	17.7	40.6	1.2	40.5
Eastern	**3.4**	1.5	98.5	54.0	46.0	**3.4**	52.1	15.0	37.0	1.4	46.6
London	**6.0**	4.6	95.4	46.7	53.3	**5.7**	42.7	17.7	25.0	1.9	55.4
South East	**5.6**	1.5	98.5	54.8	45.2	**5.5**	52.7	16.0	36.7	1.5	45.8
South West	**3.2**	0.8	99.2	53.9	46.1	**3.1**	52.1	15.3	36.8	1.4	46.5
West Midlands	**4.8**	3.5	96.5	59.4	40.6	**4.7**	56.9	19.8	37.1	1.1	41.9
North West	**6.1**	2.0	98.0	60.0	40.0	**6.0**	58.5	23.0	35.5	0.9	40.6

* Conceptions leading to births outside marriage registered by the mother alone
† Conceptions leading to births outside marriage registered by both parents

Table 12.8 Conceptions (numbers and rates): age of woman at conception, outcome, and area of usual residence, 1999

England and Wales, England, Wales, government office regions, metropolitan counties, health regional office areas
Residents

Area of usual residence	All conceptions				Conceptions at ages under 18				Conceptions at ages under 16			
	Number (000s)	Rates per 1,000 women aged 15-44			Number (000s)	Rates per 1,000 women aged 15-17			Number	Rates per 1,000 women aged 13-15		
		Total	Maternities	Abortions		Total	Maternities	Abortions		Total	Maternities	Abortions
England and Wales	**774.0**	**71.7**	**55.5**	**16.2**	**42.0**	**45.0**	**25.7**	**19.4**	**7,945**	**8.3**	**3.9**	**4.4**
England	735.5	71.9	55.6	16.3	39.2	44.7	25.2	19.5	7,408	8.2	3.9	4.4
Wales	38.5	67.8	54.5	13.4	2.8	50.8	32.5	18.4	537	9.5	5.0	4.5
Government Office Regions												
North East	33.2	63.0	50.1	12.9	2.7	55.0	34.7	20.3	499	10.0	5.2	4.8
North West	96.6	69.2	54.5	14.7	6.3	48.6	29.2	19.4	1,178	8.8	4.4	4.5
Yorkshire and the Humber	69.5	68.2	54.7	13.5	4.6	50.9	31.0	19.9	919	9.8	4.7	5.1
East Midlands	56.1	66.3	53.6	12.7	3.2	43.3	25.9	17.4	616	8.0	3.8	4.2
West Midlands	78.0	73.0	57.3	15.6	4.8	49.2	29.2	20.0	890	8.8	4.4	4.4
East	75.0	68.7	55.3	13.4	3.4	36.4	19.7	16.7	627	6.5	2.9	3.6
London	152.5	89.9	61.2	28.7	6.0	51.2	23.9	27.3	1,058	8.9	3.8	5.1
South East	112.8	68.8	54.7	14.2	5.1	35.8	19.5	16.3	963	6.7	3.0	3.7
South West	61.9	65.5	52.8	12.7	3.2	37.2	20.0	17.1	658	7.5	3.4	4.1
Metropolitan Counties												
Greater London	152.5	89.9	61.2	28.7	6.0	51.2	23.9	27.3	1,058	8.9	3.8	5.1
Greater Manchester	38.4	71.3	56.1	15.2	2.6	52.4	33.6	18.8	498	9.8	5.5	4.4
Merseyside	19.7	68.1	51.7	16.4	1.3	49.4	28.0	21.4	225	8.1	4.1	4.0
South Yorkshire	17.8	67.4	53.2	14.1	1.3	57.7	35.0	22.8	275	11.7	5.4	6.4
Tyne And Wear	14.6	63.3	49.1	14.2	1.2	56.9	35.4	21.5	210	10.1	5.0	5.1
West Midlands	42.7	78.9	61.0	17.9	2.8	56.1	34.5	21.6	530	10.3	5.4	4.9
West Yorkshire	31.3	70.9	57.5	13.4	2.0	50.6	32.2	18.4	390	9.7	4.9	4.8
Health Regional Office Areas												
Northern and Yorkshire	84.5	65.9	52.9	12.9	5.8	50.0	31.1	18.9	1,119	9.3	4.6	4.7
Trent	68.5	66.2	53.1	13.1	4.4	48.2	28.9	19.3	866	9.2	4.4	4.8
Eastern	75.0	68.7	55.3	13.4	3.4	36.4	19.7	16.7	627	6.5	2.9	3.6
London	152.5	89.9	61.2	28.7	6.0	51.2	23.9	27.3	1,058	8.9	3.8	5.1
South East	122.0	69.1	54.9	14.2	5.6	36.5	20.0	16.5	1,056	6.8	3.0	3.8
South West	61.9	65.5	52.8	12.7	3.2	37.2	20.0	17.1	658	7.5	3.4	4.1
West Midlands	78.0	73.0	57.3	15.6	4.8	49.2	29.2	20.0	890	8.8	4.4	4.4
North West	93.1	69.4	54.6	14.8	6.1	48.9	29.3	19.6	1,134	8.8	4.4	4.4

Appendix Table 1 Estimated resident population: sex and age, 1990-2000 **England and Wales**

thousands

	Age	Year										
		1990	1991	1992	1993	1994	1995	1996	1997	1998	1999	2000
Persons	**All ages**	**50,869.5**	**51,099.5**	**51,276.9**	**51,439.2**	**51,620.5**	**51,820.2**	**52,010.2**	**52,211.2**	**52,427.9**	**52,689.9**	**52,943.3**
Males	**All ages**	**24,871.7**	**24,995.1**	**25,098.6**	**25,198.4**	**25,303.6**	**25,433.1**	**25,557.4**	**25,684.5**	**25,816.7**	**25,984.6**	**26,142.3**
Females	**All ages**	**25,997.8**	**26,104.4**	**26,178.2**	**26,240.8**	**26,316.9**	**26,387.1**	**26,452.8**	**26,526.7**	**26,611.2**	**26,705.3**	**26,801.0**
	15-44	10,999.1	10,987.0	10,854.7	10,759.4	10,734.3	10,728.6	10,741.2	10,754.2	10,769.3	10,795.8	10,851.3
	15-19	1,666.1	1,586.5	1,508.0	1,454.9	1,449.4	1,469.0	1,498.1	1,533.8	1,565.1	1,571.4	1,568.8
	20-24	1,971.5	1,940.6	1,894.5	1,837.8	1,766.6	1,703.4	1,622.0	1,549.0	1,504.7	1,502.8	1,525.4
	25-29	2,059.7	2,083.3	2,086.8	2,068.5	2,043.6	2,001.9	1,974.6	1,935.1	1,889.5	1,833.3	1,789.7
	30-34	1,798.9	1,859.3	1,913.8	1,966.8	2,025.3	2,074.6	2,102.8	2,111.2	2,097.9	2,077.7	2,047.1
	35-39	1,666.9	1,672.8	1,695.6	1,724.6	1,763.6	1,810.6	1,868.4	1,925.2	1,982.1	2,041.9	2,098.0
	40-44	1,835.9	1,844.5	1,756.1	1,706.7	1,685.8	1,669.1	1,675.3	1,699.8	1,730.0	1,768.8	1,822.3
	45-49	1,493.1	1,559.2	1,694.9	1,770.5	1,804.9	1,828.2	1,836.6	1,749.0	1,700.7	1,681.0	1,669.1

Appendix Table 2 Estimated resident female population*: age and marital condition, 1990-2000 **England and Wales**

thousands

	Age	Year										
		1990	1991	1992	1993	1994	1995	1996	1997	1998	1999	2000
Married	15-44	5,837.9	5,769.4	5,575.5	5,411.8	5,282.3	5,143.0	5,028.8	4,913.3	4,800.6	4,700.2	4,616.1
	15-19	39.6	32.3	23.8	18.3	14.4	12.7	12.1	11.5	11.4	10.6	9.2
	20-24	538.3	489.5	434.0	381.5	329.6	281.8	238.4	203.9	180.2	165.0	154.2
	25-29	1,167.9	1,158.0	1,112.5	1,061.9	1,011.4	947.5	886.9	818.5	750.1	685.7	632.8
	30-34	1,309.7	1,329.8	1,336.5	1,338.0	1,340.0	1,332.8	1,316.2	1,286.7	1,247.2	1,204.9	1,158.9
	35-39	1,302.3	1,289.7	1,289.7	1,291.4	1,299.5	1,310.6	1,327.6	1,341.8	1,354.2	1,364.7	1,370.6
	40-44	1,480.1	1,470.0	1,379.0	1,321.0	1,287.4	1,257.8	1,247.6	1,251.0	1,257.5	1,269.3	1,290.4
	45-49	1,208.1	1,248.6	1,351.4	1,400.8	1,415.3	1,419.4	1,411.4	1,324.5	1,271.5	1,241.5	1,220.7
Single, widowed and divorced	15-44	5,146.5	5,217.6	5,279.2	5,347.6	5,452.0	5,585.6	5,712.4	5,840.9	5,968.7	6,095.7	6,235.3
	15-19	1,628.0	1,554.2	1,484.2	1,436.9	1,435.1	1,456.3	1,486.0	1,522.4	1,553.7	1,560.7	1,559.6
	20-24	1,425.8	1,451.0	1,460.6	1,456.3	1,436.9	1,421.6	1,383.6	1,345.2	1,324.5	1,337.9	1,371.2
	25-29	895.3	925.3	974.3	1,006.6	1,032.2	1,054.4	1,087.7	1,116.7	1,139.4	1,147.7	1,156.9
	30-34	479.4	529.5	577.3	628.9	685.3	741.8	786.6	824.5	850.6	872.9	888.2
	35-39	362.0	383.1	405.9	433.2	464.1	500.0	540.7	583.4	627.9	677.1	727.4
	40-44	356.0	374.5	377.0	385.7	398.4	411.4	427.8	448.7	472.6	499.5	531.9
	45-49	288.6	310.6	343.5	369.7	389.6	408.8	425.3	424.5	429.2	439.4	448.4

* See Section 2.1

Appendix Table 3	Estimated standard errors for numbers in analyses by social class	England and Wales

Estimated number* (thousands)	Standard error (thousands)	Standard error as a percentage of estimated number
0.5	0.07	14.0
1.0	0.09	9.0
5.0	0.21	4.2
10.0	0.30	3.0
20.0	0.42	2.1
30.0	0.50	1.7
40.0	0.58	1.4
50.0	0.64	1.3
60.0	0.69	1.2
70.0	0.74	1.1
80.0	0.78	1.0
90.0	0.82	0.9
100.0	0.86	0.9
150.0	0.99	0.7
200.0	1.07	0.5
250.0	1.10	0.4
300.0	1.10	0.4

* Numbers relate to those estimated in section 11 (social class) of this volume from a ten per cent sample.

Appendix Table 4	Estimated standard errors for percentages in analyses by social class	England and Wale

Estimated number* on which percentage is based (thousands)	Percentages					
	5 or 95	10 or 90	20 or 80	30 or 70	40 or 60	50
0.5	2.9	4.0	5.4	6.1	6.6	6.7
1.0	2.1	2.8	3.8	4.3	4.6	4.7
5.0	0.9	1.3	1.7	1.9	2.1	2.1
10.0	0.7	0.9	1.2	1.4	1.5	1.5
20.0	0.5	0.6	0.8	1.0	1.0	1.1
30.0	0.4	0.5	0.7	0.8	0.8	0.9
40.0	0.3	0.4	0.6	0.7	0.7	0.8
50.0	0.3	0.4	0.5	0.6	0.7	0.7
60.0	0.3	0.4	0.5	0.6	0.6	0.6
70.0	0.2	0.3	0.5	0.5	0.6	0.6
80.0	0.2	0.3	0.4	0.5	0.5	0.5
90.0	0.2	0.3	0.4	0.5	0.5	0.5
100.0	0.2	0.3	0.4	0.4	0.5	0.5
150.0	0.2	0.2	0.3	0.4	0.4	0.4
200.0	0.1	0.2	0.3	0.3	0.3	0.3
250.0	0.1	0.2	0.2	0.3	0.3	0.3
300.0	0.1	0.2	0.2	0.3	0.3	0.3

* Numbers relate to those estimated in section 11 (social class) of this volume from a ten per cent sample.

Annex A   Draft entry form used currently for registering live births (Form 309(Rev))

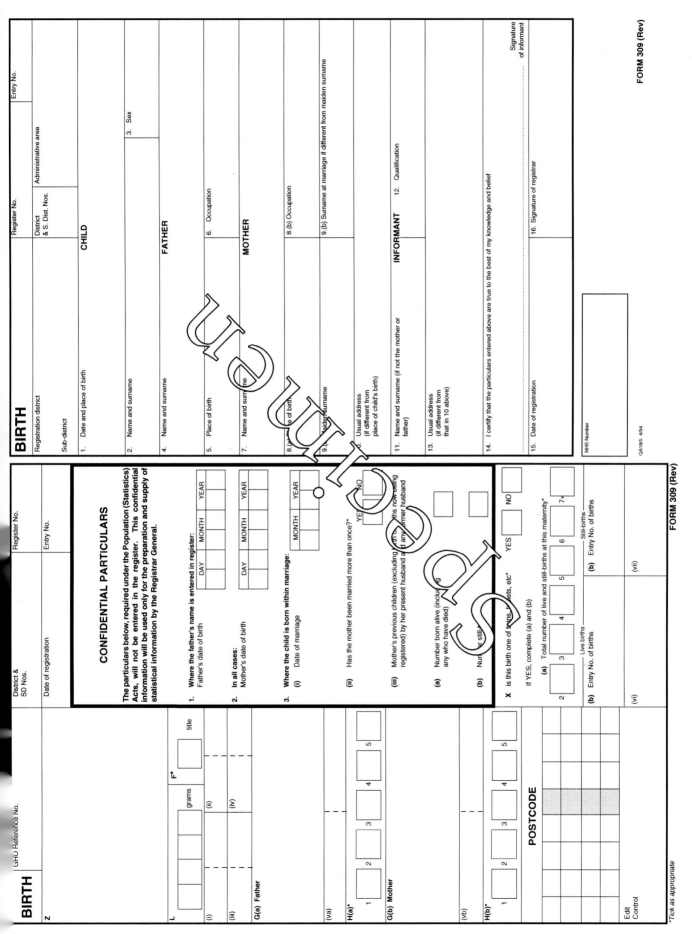

Draft entry form used currently for registering still-births (Form 308(Rev))

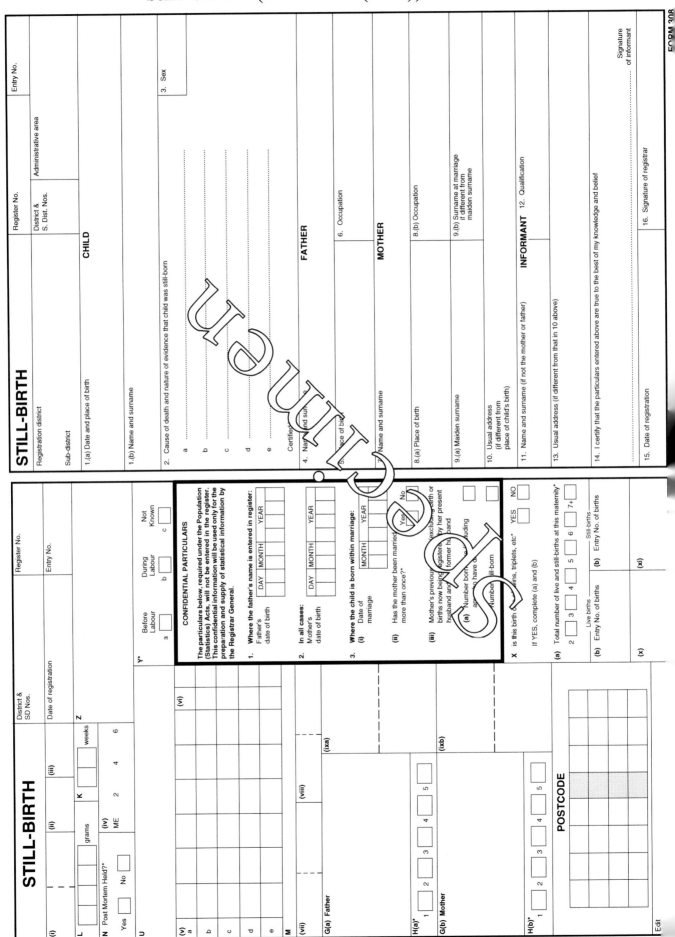

ISBN 0-11-705584-0

9 780117 055841

www.tso.co.uk